DISCARD

T. S. Eliot's *The Waste Land* is often considered the most important poem written in English in the twentieth century. The poem dramatically shattered old patterns of form and style, proposed a new paradigm for poetry and poetic thought, demanded recognition from all literary quarters, and changed the ways in which it was possible to approach, read, and write poetry. *The Waste Land* helped define the literary and artistic period known as modernism. This *Companion* is the first dedicated to the work as a whole, offering thirteen new essays by an impressive group of international scholars on an extensive range of topics. Written in a style that is at once sophisticated and accessible, these fresh critical perspectives will serve as an invaluable guide for scholars, students, and general readers alike.

Gabrielle McIntire is Associate Professor in the Department of English at Queen's University, Canada. She is the author of *Modernism, Memory, and Desire: T. S. Eliot and Virginia Woolf* (Cambridge University Press, 2008) and has published articles on T. S. Eliot, Virginia Woolf, Joseph Conrad, Nella Larsen, and James Joyce in journals and collections including *Modern Fiction Studies*, *Modernism/modernity*, *Narrative*, and *Callaloo*. Her poetry has also appeared internationally, and she sits on the editorial boards of *Twentieth-Century Literature* and *T. S. Eliot Studies Annual*.

A complete list of books in the series is at the back of this book.

THE CAMBRIDGE
COMPANION TO
THE WASTE LAND

THE CAMBRIDGE
COMPANION TO
THE WASTE LAND

EDITED BY
GABRIELLE MCINTIRE
Queen's University, Canada

CAMBRIDGE
UNIVERSITY PRESS

32 Avenue of the Americas, New York, NY 10013-2473, USA

Cambridge University Press is part of the University of Cambridge.

It furthers the University's mission by disseminating knowledge in the pursuit of education, learning, and research at the highest international levels of excellence.

www.cambridge.org
Information on this title: www.cambridge.org/9781107672574

© Cambridge University Press 2015

First published 2015

Printed in the United States of America

A catalog record for this publication is available from the British Library.

Library of Congress Cataloging in Publication Data
The Cambridge Companion to the Waste Land / [edited by] Gabrielle McIntire,
Queen's University, Canada.
pages cm. – (Cambridge companions to literature)
Includes bibliographical references.
ISBN 978-1-107-05067-9 (hardback) – ISBN 978-1-107-67257-4 (paperback)
1. Eliot, T. S. (Thomas Stearns), 1888–1965. *The Waste Land.*
I. McIntire, Gabrielle, editor.
PS3509.L43W3635   2015
821'.912–dc23   2014047360

ISBN 978-1-107-05067-9 Hardback
ISBN 978-1-107-67257-4 Paperback

for Clara Sophia

CONTENTS

CONTENTS

CONTRIBUTORS

RICHARD BADENHAUSEN is Professor and Kim T. Adamson Chair at Westminster College in Salt Lake City, where he also directs the honors program. He is the author of *T. S. Eliot and the Art of Collaboration* (2009) and is working on a book-length study entitled *T. S. Eliot's Traumatic Texts*.

JEWEL SPEARS BROOKER, Professor Emerita, Eckerd College, has had visiting positions at Yale, Harvard, Hebrew University of Jerusalem, and Merton College, Oxford. She has published nine books, including *Mastery and Escape: T. S. Eliot and the Dialectic of Modernism* (1994), and is the coeditor of two volumes of Eliot's *Complete Prose* (2014 and forthcoming).

DAVID E. CHINITZ, Professor of English at Loyola University Chicago, is the author of *T. S. Eliot and the Cultural Divide* (2003) and *Which Sin to Bear? Authenticity and Compromise in Langston Hughes* (2013). He is the editor of *A Companion to T. S. Eliot* (2009) and coeditor, with Gail McDonald, of *A Companion to Modernist Poetry* (2014). Currently he is coediting, with Ronald Schuchard, *The Complete Prose of T. S. Eliot, Volume 6: 1940–1946*.

MICHAEL COYLE is Professor of English at Colgate University. He is the founding President of the Modernist Studies Association and currently serves as President of the T. S. Eliot Society. His edited collections include *Ezra Pound and African American Modernism* (2001); *Broadcasting Modernism*, with Debra Rae Cohen (2009); and, with Steven Yao, *Ezra Pound and Education* (2012). He is also the author of *Ezra Pound, Popular Genres, and the Discourse of Culture* (1995), and he writes broadly on modernist literature and jazz.

ANTHONY CUDA is Associate Professor of English at the University of North Carolina, Greensboro. He is the author of *The Passions of Modernism: Eliot, Yeats, Woolf, and Mann* (2010) and the coeditor, with Ronald Schuchard, of *The Complete Prose of T. S. Eliot: The Critical Edition, Volume 2: The Perfect Critic, 1919–1926* (2014).

JULIA E. DANIEL is Assistant Professor of Modern American Poetry at West Virginia University. Her current book project, *Building Nature: City Planning, Landscape Architecture, and Modern American Poetry*, combines her interests in ecocriticism and urban studies. Her work has appeared in *A Companion to Modernist Poetry*, *Modern Drama*, and the *Journal of the Midwest Modern Language Association*.

LYNDALL GORDON studied American literature at Columbia University and is a Fellow of St. Hilda's College, Oxford. She is the author of two memoirs and six biographies, including *The Imperfect Life of T. S. Eliot* (1999, 2015) and *Lives Like Loaded Guns: Emily Dickinson and Her Family's Feuds* (2010).

MICHAEL LEVENSON is William B. Christian Professor of English at the University of Virginia and author of *A Genealogy of Modernism* (1984), *Modernism and the Fate of Individuality* (1990), *The Spectacle of Intimacy* (coauthored with Karen Chase, 2000), and *Modernism* (2011). He has also edited *The Cambridge Companion to Modernism* (2000, 2011).

GABRIELLE MCINTIRE is Associate Professor in the Department of English at Queen's University, Canada. She is the author of *Modernism, Memory, and Desire: T. S. Eliot and Virginia Woolf* (2008), and she has published articles or chapters on T. S. Eliot, Virginia Woolf, Joseph Conrad, James Joyce, and Nella Larsen. Her poetry has also appeared internationally.

SPENCER MORRISON, a Killam Postdoctoral Fellow at the University of Alberta, researches urban representation in late modernism. His work is published or forthcoming in *ELH*, *American Literature*, and *Fueling Culture: Energy, History, Politics* (2016).

RACHEL POTTER is Professor of Modern Literature at the University of East Anglia. She is the author of *Modernism and Democracy: Literary Culture, 1900–1930* (2006); *The Edinburgh Guide to Modernist Literature* (2012); and *Obscene Modernism: Literary Censorship and Experiment, 1900–1940* (2013). She has also coedited *The Salt Companion to Mina Loy* (2010) and *Prudes on the Prowl: Fiction and Obscenity in England, 1850–Present Day* (2013). She is currently starting a project on International P.E.N., writers, and free speech.

JEAN-MICHEL RABATÉ, Professor of English and Comparative Literature at the University of Pennsylvania, is a cofounder and curator of Slought Foundation, an editor of the *Journal of Modern Literature*, and a Fellow of the American Academy of Arts and Sciences. He has authored more than thirty books and collections on modernism, psychoanalysis, and philosophy – most recently *Crimes of the Future* (2014), *An Introduction to Literature and Psychoanalysis* (2014), and *1922: Literature, Culture, Politics* (2014).

EVE SORUM is Associate Professor of English at the University of Massachusetts, Boston. She is the recipient of a 2013–14 Fulbright Fellowship and has published articles on World War I poetry and prose, T. S. Eliot, Thomas Hardy, W. H. Auden, Virginia Woolf, and Ford Madox Ford.

BARRY SPURR was appointed as Australia's first Professor of Poetry at the University of Sydney in 2011. His published research is focused on early modern poetry and on the Modernists. His recent study, *Anglo-Catholic in Religion: T. S. Eliot and Christianity* (2010), written at the request of Valerie Eliot, is the first full account of the subject.

ACKNOWLEDGMENTS

I want to thank first of all my contributors, whose careful work and deep commitment to ongoing explorations of *The Waste Land* have been inspiring throughout the process of making this book. Each contributor has been a marvelous interlocutor, and I will always be grateful for their patience, good humor, exciting new perspectives, and meticulous attention to the details. Special thanks, too, to the contributors who went beyond the call of duty and provided important feedback on overall concepts or on other individual chapters – I appreciate your collegiality immensely. Great thanks, too, go to the anonymous readers of the proposal for this project whose insights helped shape and nuance the aims of the *Companion* long before the volume had come into existence. This *Companion* also owes an enormous debt to Ray Ryan at Cambridge University Press, whose wisdom, acumen, and sheer common sense are unfailing. Thank you, Ray – we could not have done any of this without you. Both Louis Gulino and Caitlin Gallagher at the Press have also been delightful in every exchange, and I am grateful for their good spirit and care with the manuscript. Patrick Moran gave a thorough final read-through of my own chapter on ecocritique in *The Waste Land*, and I want to acknowledge the extraordinary helpfulness of his commentary. A number of colleagues and friends also encouraged me through the incarnation of this *Companion*, either directly or indirectly. For their thoughtfulness, insights, and friendship, I want to mention especially Hortense Spillers, Molly Hite, Linda Hutcheon, Benjamin Hagen, Eduardo Cadava, Dominick LaCapra, John Whittier-Ferguson, Daniel Schwarz, Frances Dickey, Vincent Sherry, Patricia Rae, Edward Lobb, Marta Straznicky, Andrew Bingham, Adriana Hetram, Jodie Medd, Daniel Brayton, Antonia Losano, Greg Stork, Brian Bitar, Kelly Drukker, Claire Boudet, Craig Walker, Farah Cimafranca, Rahul Sapra, John Sutton, and Lee Zimmerman. Each of you gave your time, energy, wisdom, and support at important moments in the book's evolution, and I want to express much gratitude for your presence in my life personally as well as professionally.

My thanks, too, go to the Department of English at Queen's University for continuing to provide me with a place to feel at home intellectually and collegially. During the making of this *Companion* I had the good fortune of teaching a graduate and an undergraduate seminar devoted in large part to T. S. Eliot. Both groups were exceptional and I was touched by the passion and dedication among those students, some of whom were coming to Eliot for very nearly the first time. The poet and actor John Farrell recited Eliot's entire *Four Quartets* from memory at Queen's during the final stages of editing, and the event infused a new kind of visionary stimulus into the project of always learning how to reread Eliot. During the summer of 2014, my colleagues and students at the T. S. Eliot International Summer School at the University of London, who came from all over the world just for the love of Eliot, gave a final boost of energy and excitement. In London I want especially to thank Gail McDonald, Wim Van-Mierlo, and Christopher Adams for their gracious hospitality and for fostering such a rich intellectual environment. Jeffrey Dzogola helped me prepare the manuscript for submission, and I greatly appreciate his willingness to be another pair of eyes on the material. And through the project I had generous support from the Social Sciences and Humanities Research Council of Canada (SSHRC), for which I am profoundly grateful. Finally, I could not have done any of this without the care and love of my family: Olivia, Matthias, Eliot, Céline, Madeleine, Isabelle, Thomas, Rebekah, Harley, Mary Carolyn, and little Clara, I thank you from the bottom of my heart – you mean the world to me.

1888   On September 26 Thomas Stearns Eliot is born to Henry Ware Eliot and Charlotte Champe Stearns Eliot in St. Louis, Missouri. He is the youngest by nine years of seven children, one of whom had died in infancy. In his adult years Eliot was especially close to his brother Henry, born in 1879.

1898   Eliot enrolls at Smith Academy, St. Louis. His grandfather, William Greenleaf Eliot, had founded the academy in 1854 and was its first chancellor.

1905   Eliot publishes several poems in the *Smith Academy Record* and graduates from high school. Moves to Massachusetts to attend Milton Academy, a prestigious preparatory school founded in 1798.

1906   Begins his first year at Harvard College, though does not initially excel academically. He studies broadly in the humanities, languages, and literatures, taking courses in the history of ancient art, philosophy, French, German, Greek, Latin, and English literatures.

1907   His poem, "Song," appears in the *Harvard Advocate*. He continues to publish in the *Advocate* through his college years and takes up a position on the editorial board in 1909.

1909   Graduates from Harvard with an A.B. and begins his M.A., again taking a wide range of courses, especially in English literature, philosophy, and art history. He studies with Irving Babbitt and George Santayana.

1910   Creates a poetry notebook titled *Inventions of the March Hare*. Drafts portions of "Portrait of a Lady." In the fall he leaves for Paris to study at the Sorbonne, where he attends lectures by Henri Bergson at the Collège de France and lives at 151 bis rue St. Jacques, near the Pantheon and the Sorbonne. He receives private language tutoring with Alain-Fournier and befriends Jean Verdenal.

1911   Graduates from Harvard with his M.A. after another trip to Europe where he visits London, Munich, and Northern Italy. Eliot returns to Boston, commencing the doctoral program in philosophy at Harvard where he studies Indian philosophy and Sanskrit. He finishes his first major poems, including "The Love Song of J. Alfred Prufrock," "Portrait of a Lady," "Prelude" [sic], and "Rhapsody on a Windy Night."

1912   Meets and begins a romantic relationship with Emily Hale. He is appointed assistant in philosophy at Harvard.

1913   Reads F. H. Bradley's *Appearance and Reality*, which becomes the subject of his doctoral dissertation.

1914   Meets Bertrand Russell, a visiting professor at Harvard. Travels to London, England, and then Marburg, Germany, en route to taking up a one-year fellowship at Merton College, Oxford. Germany declares war on Russia and invades Luxembourg and Belgium while Eliot is in Marburg; he only manages to reach England several weeks later. Within a week of his arrival in London, he meets Ezra Pound, who is deeply impressed with "Prufrock" and sends it to *Poetry* magazine.

1915   Meets Vivien Haigh-Wood in April. Jean Verdenal is killed in the Dardanelles in May. *Poetry* publishes "Prufrock" in June, and in October "The Boston Evening Transcript," "Aunt Helen," and "Cousin Nancy" are also printed in *Poetry*. Eliot marries Vivien Haigh-Wood at the Hampstead Registry Office, London, on June 26. His father stops all financial support. Wyndham Lewis's *Blast* publishes "Preludes," and "Portrait of a Lady" appears in *Others*. Eliot travels to Massachusetts to visit his family and decides not to move back to Boston. Upon his return to England he takes up a teaching post at the High Wycombe Grammar School, established in 1550.

1916   Takes up a teaching position at Highgate Junior School in London, founded in 1565. Completes his doctoral thesis, which is accepted by Harvard, but with ocean passage delayed for several days he decides not to return to Boston for his oral defense. Moves with Vivien to Crawford Mansions, London. Starts publishing reviews in *The Monist* and begins lecturing on French and English literature.

1917   Gives up teaching at the preparatory school level, though he continues lecturing. Takes up a position with the Colonial and Foreign Department of Lloyd's Bank, London. In April the United States enters the war; Eliot tries to enlist but is declined due to a congenital hernia. The Egoist Limited publishes his first volume of poetry, *Prufrock and Other Observations*. Eliot becomes assistant editor of *The Egoist* magazine.

1918   Eliot is still trying to enlist with the U.S. Navy against Vivien Eliot and Ezra Pound's wishes; despite Eliot's ill health the U.S. Military Service sends him an Order of Induction in November but he never sees service. He continues to lecture on Elizabethan literature in London.

1919   Eliot's father, Henry Ware Eliot, dies on January 7. Eliot is offered an assistant editorship at the *Athenaeum* but declines. Virginia and Leonard Woolf's Hogarth Press issues *Poems*, his second volume of poetry. Eliot reads and is impressed by James Joyce's *Ulysses* in its serial publication. He lectures on "Poetry" in London, and publishes "Tradition and the Individual Talent" in *The Egoist*.

1920   Publishes *Ara Vos Prec* in England, and Knopf issues *Poems* – including the addition of "Gerontion" – in the United States. In August Eliot meets James Joyce in Paris and takes a cycling tour in northern France with Wyndham Lewis. *The Sacred Wood*, Eliot's first collection of essays, is published by Methuen.

1921   Begins to draft *The Waste Land*. From June to August Eliot's mother, his sister Marian, and his brother Henry visit from the United States. In the fall Eliot suffers a breakdown, seeks medical help, and receives a leave from Lloyd's Bank. He goes to Margate, Kent, by the sea to recuperate, and then to Lausanne, Switzerland, where he is treated by Dr. Roger Vittoz. In November, Eliot shows Ezra Pound drafts of *The Waste Land*.

1922   Eliot's health is still unstable, but he decides to found and edit a new journal, the *Criterion*, which he edits until he closes it down in 1939. He finishes *The Waste Land* and publishes it in the first issue of the *Criterion* in October. The *Dial* publishes *The Waste Land* in the United States, and Eliot receives the *Dial* prize. Boni and Liverwright publish *The Waste Land* in book form.

1923   Virginia and Leonard Woolf publish *The Waste Land* in book form with their Hogarth Press; the poem has already sold 1,250 copies in the United States through the Boni and Liverwright publication. Vivien's health is very poor. Eliot is emotionally and physically taxed by full-time work at Lloyd's Bank, running the *Criterion*, and various personal struggles. The "Bel Esprit" (the "Eliot Fellowship Fund") is launched in an effort by friends and admirers to allow Eliot to leave his job at the bank.

1925   Leaves Lloyd's Bank to work with Faber and Gwyer (later Faber and Faber). Publishes *Poems 1909–1925*, which includes "The Hollow Men."

1926   Gives Clark lectures at Cambridge University. Publishes *Sweeney Agonistes*. Falls to his knees while visiting Michelangelo's *Pietà* in Rome.

1927   Baptized into the Church of England by W. Force Stead at Holy Trinity Church, Bishop's Palace Cuddesdon, near Oxford. He also takes British citizenship.

1929   Eliot's mother dies.

1930   Publishes *Ash-Wednesday* with Faber and Faber, with print runs in the United States and Britain.

1932   Delivers Charles Eliot Norton lectures at Harvard University for several months (through March 1933). Publishes *Selected Essays: 1917–1932*.

1933   Separates from his wife, Vivien Eliot. Publishes *After Strange Gods*. Lectures at Johns Hopkins University and at the University of Virginia.

1934   Visits Burnt Norton manor in the Cotswolds with Emily Hale.

1935   *Murder in the Cathedral* is first performed at Canterbury Cathedral.

1936   Publishes *Collected Poems 1909–1935*; the volume includes the first publication of *Burnt Norton*.

1938   With her brother, Maurice Haigh-Wood, Eliot commits Vivien Eliot to a mental hospital, Northumberland House, Finsbury Park, London. She will remain there until her death in 1947. Eliot meets Mary Trevelyan.

1939   Publishes *Old Possum's Book of Practical Cats* and *The Family Reunion*. Ceases publication of the *Criterion*, in part due to his growing disillusionment about the possibility for genuine pan-European exchanges of ideas and literatures. The Second World War breaks out. Eliot volunteers as a firewatcher and air-raid warden in London.

1940   Publishes *The Idea of a Christian Society*.

1943   Publishes all of *Four Quartets*, which had each already appeared in individual pamphlet form. *Notes Towards the Definition of Culture* appears serially.

1945   Visits Ezra Pound at St. Elizabeth's Hospital in Washington, DC. The war ends.

1946   Moves in with the critic, John Davy Hayward, with whom he lives until Eliot marries Valerie Fletcher Eliot in 1957.

1948   Eliot is awarded the Order of Merit and the Nobel Prize in Literature. *Selected Poems* is published by Penguin, with a run of 50,000 copies. *Notes Towards the Definition of Culture* is published in book form. He lectures at Princeton University and travels to Andover, Massachusetts, to see Emily Hale.

1950   Publishes *The Cocktail Party*, and it is performed at the Edinburgh Festival.

1952   *The Complete Poems and Plays* is published by Harcourt in New York. Sees Emily Hale again in Andover, Massachusetts.

1953   Travels with Emily Hale and his sister Marian to St. Louis.

1957   Eliot marries Valerie Fletcher, his secretary at Faber and Faber since 1949, in secret at St. Barnabus Church, London. Their years together were ones he described as his happiest. Breaks off contact with Emily Hale.

1961 Delivers his last public lecture, "To Criticize the Critic."

1963 After collapsing in December 1962 he spends five weeks in hospital in London in an oxygen tent. *Collected Poems 1909–1962* published by Harcourt in New York.

1965 Eliot dies on January 4 in London. Following his wishes, his ashes are later interred in St. Michael and All Angels Anglican Church, East Coker.

GABRIELLE MCINTIRE

Introduction

Many have called T. S. Eliot's *The Waste Land* the greatest poem in English
of the twentieth century. In its particular historical moment of 1922
the poem articulated and helped to define both an epistemology and an
ontology – a new way of thinking and being during an era that W. H. Auden
in 1947 would retrospectively call "The age of anxiety."[1] The poem dramatically shattered old patterns of form and style, proposed a new paradigm
for poetry and poetic thought, demanded recognition from all literary quarters, and changed the ways in which it was possible to approach, read, and
write poetry. *The Waste Land* also insisted unequivocally on the fractured
nature of modern subjectivities by exerting pains to expose the complex and
sometimes disordered nature of the human mind. If Stéphane Mallarmé had
declared a crisis in verse during his lecture tour in England in 1895 – "They
have done violence to verse"[2] – then Eliot was one of his most important
modernist inheritors, mingling free verse with old formal patterns to generate a poetic rupture with past practices that nevertheless remained profoundly self-conscious about its debts to literary tradition.

  The Waste Land became monumental nearly as soon as it was published,
ensconcing T. S. Eliot as arguably *the* major poet of his generation. The piece
still stands as a key culmination point within British and Anglo-American
literature, published in that dramatic Rubicon year of modernism in which
James Joyce gave the world *Ulysses*, Virginia Woolf published her first
experimental novel, *Jacob's Room*, and Marcel Proust's *A la recherche du
temps perdu* was translated into English as *In Search of Lost Time*. Among
other epochal shifts, Benito Mussolini, leader of the National Fascist Party,
became prime minister of Italy; and, closer to Eliot's adopted home, the
Irish Free State was formed. The immediate postwar period of 1918–22
had seen astonishing changes to the face of Europe, its allies, and colonies –
politically, culturally, sociologically, and psychologically – and by the time
of *The Waste Land*'s composition in 1921, the horrors of the First World
War were still barely receding. As Michael North points out, "1922 was for

England the first real postwar year," when, as the *Daily Mail* noted at the time, "'signs of, and restrictions connected with, the Great War were finally abolished.'"[3] If many, like Paul Fussell, in his influential *The Great War and Modern Memory*, have convincingly argued that the First World War helped to inaugurate the "modern" age,[4] we might consider *The Waste Land* as *the* exemplary ur-modernist poem: completely original and unforgettable, the poem reflects some of the deepest concerns of its era while also asking its readers to see the world from radically new, "modern" perspectives. It has cast a long shadow of influence over subsequent generations of writers and thinkers, and even today Eliot continues to be one of the most-cited poets in popular media, appearing with striking frequency in newspapers, blogs, magazines, and online discussions. Despite the difficulty and sometimes seeming impenetrability of his work, Eliot continues to compel and enthrall an extensive body of readers around the world.

What is *The Waste Land* about? The essays assembled here suggest that the only brief answer to this question is *many things*. Certainly it concerns the year, 1922, in its march through temporality and history, and the poem is replete with reflections and fragments from Eliot's time and milieu, including snippets from the popular cultures, technologies, and arts of the period that were very alive to Eliot – from emerging musical genres like jazz, to the rise of film, popular interests in horoscopes and tarot cards, the nascent technologies of the gramophone, and newly motorized cars and taxis. And, in a poem entitled *The Waste Land*, Eliot offers us a sustained meditation on the very meaning of locale, spatiality, and topography, juxtaposing the recently bombed London cityscape with mythic desertscapes, a bleak seascape, and named sites throughout Europe, Canada, South Asia, and North Africa. Place in the poem becomes a subject in and of itself, existing as both a theme and a ground. Eliot also shows an ecological awareness about the polluting effects of modern, industrialized society on the natural environment, pointing to such indicators of degradation as "the brown fog of a winter noon" (208), and the river that "sweats/ Oil and tar" (266–7), while elegiacally longing for the pure simplicities of a clean and soothing "Sweet Thames" (176 and ff.).[5] Yet even while the poem recognizes crisis and devastation as (almost) normalized states of being in the modern world as its speakers struggle to discover strategies for survival – "these fragments I have shored against my ruins" (430) – *The Waste Land* never gives up striving for transcendent meaning that would help resolve the catastrophes of the present.

The Waste Land also relentlessly experiments with form, style, and poetics. Through self-conscious intertextual borrowing, mimicry, and pastiche, Eliot engages with a host of literary, religious, artistic, and mythical antecedents ranging from Ovid and Homer to the Bible, Dante, Chaucer,

Shakespeare, Donne, and Wagner, among others. His textual juxtapositions of past and current literary history sought to revise and remake as part of the new avant-garde, following his own maxim to the letter from a recent essay of 1920 that "Immature poets imitate; mature poets steal."[6] Importing lines, tropes, and motifs from other people's work into the fold of *The Waste Land* as if they were his own, he implicitly and metacritically commented on the hermeneutics of such dialogic exchanges. *The Waste Land* thus tells us about the processes of writing itself, including what it means to compose and revise literature with the collaborative help of both his wife, Vivien Eliot, and his friend and mentor, the poet Ezra Pound. The poem was not completed in isolation, and each of Eliot's interlocutors left a significant stamp on the final poem. In terms of form and aesthetics, Eliot made it so "new" in *The Waste Land* that there could be no looking back. There could be no imitations of the singularity he struck to the page with the advice of Pound especially, to whom he dedicates the poem with the enigmatic epigraph: "*il miglior fabbro*" – the better maker – as if Pound were the master and Eliot the apprentice.

This *Companion* also wants to make the point that contrary to Eliot's fascinating claims in his 1919 essay, "Tradition and the Individual Talent," where he insists on the poet's radical "impersonality,"[7] *The Waste Land* is surprisingly personal, too. It concerns, for instance, Eliot's attempts to come to terms with his ongoing and sometimes disabling personal, familial, medical, and marital crises. At the same time, the poem explores and critiques the loosening up of early twentieth-century gender roles and sexual identities, particularly by making the transgendered figure of Tiresias, Ovid's blind seer who haunts the work, "the most important personage in the poem." [8] Tiresias presides over the poem's central scene of sexual violation between "The typist home at teatime" and "the young man carbuncular" (222; 231), and, in witnessing this traumatic encounter, he suffers too. Yet this is only one of several tableaux about failures of intimacy and the dysfunctional and even violent character of contemporary de-romanticized sexual relations that Eliot presents. Indeed, these renditions of the personal punctuate the poem in ways that indicate Eliot's own interests in emerging perspectives on early twentieth-century psychology and Freudian and post-Freudian psychoanalysis – as if he is seeking both to grasp and deploy new mappings of the psyche.

The Waste Land continues to move us and change our worlds. It remains one of those rarest species of literature that feels almost *world-generating*, as the philosopher Martin Heidegger might propose. One of Eliot's early eminent interpreters, William Empson, writes in 1958 – more than thirty-five years after the poem's publication – "I do not know for certain how much of my own mind [Eliot] invented, let alone how much of it is a reaction against him or indeed a consequence of misreading him. He has a very penetrating influence, not unlike an east wind."[9] This is a poem that invites itself into the very fabric of our being. It addresses so much of what is difficult and important about human experience, while presenting what is tragic in a light that dignifies it and gestures toward redemption. For tragedy in the poem is simultaneously the pathos of the ordinariness of modern everyday life – infused as it is with a proto-existentialist sense of emptiness and banality – and the pathos expressed in the great Eastern and Western myths and religions that Eliot weaves into his poem. Ovid's reflections in the *Metamorphoses*, the mysteries of Christ on the journey to Emmaus, and the thunder of the Hindu *Upanishads* are as present to the poem as the "crowd" that "flowed over London Bridge" (62) or the noisy clamor of modern city life with "The sound of horns and motors" (197) in the street.

The Waste Land, then, frames the tensions between different temporalities – and between the ordinary and the transcendent – as participating in dynamic exchanges where each is ever-present. In a poem that is haunted by countless spectral figures ("so many/ I had not thought death had undone so many," 62–3), the shifting narrative voice asks in part V, "Who is the third who walks always beside you?" (359), as if insisting that there is "always" a case for a missing third, "always" an Other realm that shadows the everyday. Yet, the transcendence that the poem leans toward remains elusive: just as Madame Sosostris, the "famous clairvoyante" (43) does not "find/ The Hanged Man" (54–5), neither does the poem find God. Still, Eliot asks us to consider our own brokenness and personal ruins as inviting the wisdom of three great world religions – Hinduism, Buddhism, and Christianity – even as he challenges us to experience this through a radical experiment in poetic form. The tentative redemption the poem presents is never didactic, and *The Waste Land* ends by uttering a prayer for peace ("Shantih shantih shantih," 433): a repetitive chant with no final punctuation, as if these words might carry us to a redemptive elsewhere beyond the page and beyond the poem's end.

The essays collected here reflect an exciting range of styles, approaches, generations, and modes of reading that attest to the vibrancy of ongoing critique and debates about the complexities and inspirations of *The Waste Land*. The collage of perspectives brings to bear some of the most current lenses of critical thinking about *The Waste Land* while always keeping the poem at the forefront, and each essay complements the others by conveying an underlying sense of the poem's continued originality and urgent ways of speaking to us. The book is divided into three parts, with thirteen independent essays, although turns to favorite passages recur: the strained dialogue where communication fails between what seems to be a husband and wife in part II, "A Game of Chess," and the colloquial chitter-chatter about abortion, modern medication, and war veterancy in the pub scene catch the imagination of several critics here, as do the figures of Tiresias and his modern-day counterpart, Madame Sosostris. Biographical and literary historical criticism also undergird many of the chapters.

No new *Cambridge Companion* to T. S. Eliot or to any of his works has been published since A. David Moody's wonderful 1994 *Cambridge Companion to T. S. Eliot*. Much has, of course, changed in these more than two decades of criticism. Perhaps most importantly Eliot is being understood through broader and more diverse lenses than ever, including perspectives from gender, queer, ecocritical, new historical, trauma, psychoanalytic, religious, and cultural studies. Readers have also had access, for the past several years, to Eliot's published letters beyond the talismanic end date of 1922, which had been the finite horizon of most of our glimpses into his private life ever since Eliot's widow, Valerie Eliot, published *The Letters of T. S. Eliot: Volume One, 1898–1922* in 1988. We waited a long time, but beginning in 2009, under the editorship of Valerie Eliot and Hugh Haughton, five new volumes of Eliot's letters have been published, covering the period from 1922–1931. More are on the way. This opening up of the Eliot archive has allowed the contributors here to write with greater knowledge about who the Eliot of 1921 – composing *The Waste Land* – would become as a man and poet through the 1920s. Further, the first two volumes of *The Complete Prose of T. S. Eliot: The Critical Edition – The Apprentice Years (1905–1918)*, and *The Perfect Critic (1919–1926)* – have recently gone live online, with more soon to come. The *Complete Prose* volumes will include essays that have hitherto been uncollected, inaccessible, or available only to those able to undertake archival research. We are thus on the cusp of yet more revelations about T. S. Eliot and his oeuvre, even as we find ourselves at the centenary of Eliot's publishing career – "The Love Song of J. Alfred Prufrock," "Preludes," "Rhapsody on a Windy Night," and "Portrait of a Lady" all appeared in 1915. We are still yet beginning again, and always learning to read *The Waste Land* afresh, "renewed, transfigured, in another pattern" (*Little Gidding*, 166).

NOTES

1 W. H. Auden, *The Age of Anxiety: A Baroque Eclogue* (1947; Princeton: Princeton University Press, 2011).

2 Stéphane Mallarmé, "Crise de vers," "Variations sur un sujet," *Ouevres complètes*, ed. Henri Mondor and G. Jean-Aubry (Paris: Gallimard, 1945), 643–4.

3 Michael North, *Reading 1922: A Return to the Scene of the Modern* (New York: Oxford University Press, 1999), 5. G. A. Leask, "Changing London," in David Williamson, ed., *The Daily Mail Year Book for 1923* (London: Associated Newspapers Ltd., 1923), 77, qtd. in North, 5.

4 This is a thesis that runs through the book. See Paul Fussell, *The Great War and Modern Memory* (Oxford: Oxford University Press, 1975).

5 T. S. Eliot, *The Complete Poems and Plays* (London: Faber and Faber, 1969). Subsequent references to *The Waste Land* and *Little Gidding* will be cited parenthetically by line number.

6 Eliot, "Philip Massinger," *The Sacred Wood* (1920; London: Methuen, 1969), 125.

7 Eliot, "Tradition and the Individual Talent," *Selected Essays* (1932; London: Faber and Faber, 1999), 22.

8 Eliot, note to line 218 of *The Waste Land*.

9 William Empson, "The Style of the Master," in *T. S. Eliot: A Symposium*, ed. Tambimuttu and Richard March (1948; London: Frank Cass and Co., 1965), 35.

PART I

Historical, Cultural, and Personal Contexts

I

JEAN-MICHEL RABATÉ

"The World Has Seen Strange Revolutions Since I Died"[1]: *The Waste Land* and the Great War

The devastation brought by the First World War to Europe had incalculable consequences that still shape our world; there were also calculable costs, whether financial or moral. T. S. Eliot took on the task to reckon with these, first as a clerk working on German debts and reparations at Lloyds Bank in London, then as a poet who tried to rethink the foundations of the world order emerging after 1918. A war first imagined as a Napoleonic campaign, with swift defeats and victories, had turned into a general stalemate, a mechanized mass slaughter in a bitter tussle of attrition in which most industrialized nations were forced to participate. Never a "war to end all wars," World War I would soon herald worse times to come, partly because the map of the world changed radically after the collapse of the Austro-Hungarian Empire and the Ottoman Empire. Europeans had discovered that, indeed, "civilizations were mortal," as Paul Valéry wrote in 1919, when he analyzed the current "crisis of the spirit."[2] The European "spirit" was a Hegelian *Geist* that was turning into ghosts, into too many ghosts, whereas the geography of Europe revealed itself to be just the tip of a "peninsula," an excrescence from a continent redefined by the new awakenings of Russia and Asia. A similar ontological crisis was condensed in Eliot's lines from *The Waste Land*:

> Falling towers
> Jerusalem Athens Alexandria
> Vienna London
> Unreal[3]

I. Places

Like Valéry, Eliot included Smyrna (in Turkey) and Alexandria (in Egypt) in his map of Europe, while he, too, perceived that Europe had "exhausted its modernism."[4] In its symbolic geography, *The Waste Land* is thus more a modernist postwar poem than a modernist war poem. This holds true of its themes and its gestation, much as *Ulysses* and *In Search of Lost Time* would not be the same texts they are today without the delays in publication brought about by the war. The difference between the authors' processes is that Joyce and Proust used the extra time they gained to expand and revise their novels. Eliot, collecting and rearranging previous texts, writing in the aftermath, attempted to make sense of the collective and personal traumas by condensing and refining (with the help of Ezra Pound) a sprawling mass of manuscripts and typescripts until he reached just 433 lines. Its incantatory and exhortatory affirmation of "Peace" – "Shantih" in Sanskrit – from the *Upanishads* at the end of the poem looks to a dim European future with a mystical assertion of hope while the poem attempts to give a diagnosis of the causes of the Great War.

If Joyce analyzed a prewar society in Dublin, Eliot looked to the future, as did Franz Kafka. In the end, from two different sides in the conflict, Eliot and Kafka had made similar career choices, both positing a strong link between the raging military conflict and "war" in the sentimental and sexual domains. This link can be exemplified for Eliot by a short story of which he was fond. In December 1917, when the war was raging, *The Egoist*, of which Eliot had become assistant editor, published "War," a story by his friend Mary Hutchinson.[5] Mary had passed it first to Vivien, who then made sure her husband would get it published.[6] Readers must have expected a war story, whereas it mostly deals with love. It begins with a conversation between Jane, a rich, married, and fashionable young lady of twenty-five, and her new would-be lover, Mr. Giniver, a writer, traveler, and self-declared cynic. Their talk is interrupted by drums and a brass band. They see soldiers at drill, marching through a London street. A little later, Jane confides to her friend Sabine that she feels drawn to Giniver. Sabine asserts skeptically that Jane will be a mere diversion for him. Jane grows "hysterical" (171) and convinces herself that she is in love. At night, Giniver reappears for a night visit that proves decisive. He has brought a manuscript but decides not to read it to her. They are both nervous, irritable, embarrassed; their conversation trails off and they keep nagging each other. Finally, silence reigns. Giniver, sensing the chill, cannot seize her hand; Jane makes the break-up final, saying: "I don't suppose we shall meet again for some time" (172). Giniver takes leave abruptly and Jane remains alone, inert. She falls asleep, to be woken up by a bugle sounding the reveille in the nearby barracks. The reminder of a war outside brings relief. The text ends on these words: "Afterwards she slept as though she knew the earth to be a spherical and comfortable place" (172). This is one of the meanings of "war," a meaning to which Eliot was attuned, a delicate blend of the war of sexes, with its tangled strategies of seduction, hysteria, and rejection, alongside military campaigns, which end up offering a unity of the self with the universe.

It is likely that Mary Hutchinson, who was then very close to both Eliots, was slyly referring to the ups and downs of the affair her friend Vivien Haigh-Wood, Eliot's wife, was having with Bertrand Russell. As with Kafka's particular situation in Prague – Kafka, like Eliot, was not drafted for medical reasons – the war provided these Londoners the opportunity for an ongoing discussion about love, the compatibility of married life with literary creation, and the possibility of torturing one's partner in a couple. The difference was that Kafka would not marry Felice, his eternal bride-to-be. He tortured her (and himself) via an abundant and frantic correspondence.[7] Sensing the need to put as much distance between his family and himself as he could, Eliot had taken the war as a pretext for a situation of exception that allowed him to get married quickly to a seductive and brilliant English woman. He would torture her (and himself) in words and deeds, in action and in inaction, erecting the temple of eternal love on the murky foundations of sexual impotence and gender indecision.

The war made Eliot aware that he had chosen a place to settle. We can imagine him, had there been no war, moving back and forth between Boston and Marburg, St. Louis and Oxford, New York and Paris. His 1910–11 stay in Paris had given him a taste of cosmopolitan culture and put him in contact with a cultivated French milieu. He was close to Alain-Fournier, who died in combat as a lieutenant near Verdun in September 1914, one of the first literary victims of the war. Another victim of the war was Eliot's close friend from Paris, Jean Verdenal. The echo between Verdun and Verdenal is not a coincidence: the family name "Verdenal" is linked to a village in the Meurthe and Moselle region. It was exactly on the border separating Alsace-Lorraine, the contested German possession after the 1871 war and the treaty of Frankfurt, from the rest of France. That region was the site of many battles in 1914 and 1915, and the inhabitants of Verdenal are called the "Verdunois."

While in Paris in 1910 and 1911, Eliot had shared with Verdenal and Alain-Fournier a love of Wagner and Jules Laforgue, and he had discovered the works of Dostoevsky thanks to Alain-Fournier. Before 1914, these young French intellectuals were more Germanophile than Anglophile, which was a common tendency among later Symbolist poets. Mallarmé's wife was German; Jules Laforgue had spent five happy years in Berlin when he was a reader for the German Empress Augusta. Similarly, as an American living in England, Eliot bore no grudge to Germany and refused to associate himself with the shrill patriotism that was dominant then and later.

Despite the numerous signals that an international storm was brewing – signs that observant American writers like Morton Fullerton had been able to decipher[8] – Eliot himself had no inkling that a world war was in the making. On July 26, 1914, he wrote to his friend Eleanor Hinkley: "I shan't have anything very exciting to narrate this summer; this is as peaceful a life as one could well find" (Eliot 2011, 54). Ironically, just two days later, Archduke Ferdinand was murdered in Sarajevo, and the assassination triggered the successive declarations of war. I survey the timeline of the war's many theaters in order to parallel them with Eliot's experiences.

II. Parallel Wars

July 2, 1914. Publication of *Blast*.

August 4, 1914. England declares war on Germany after the latter invades Belgium.

August 22, 1914. Coming back from a trip to Marburg, Germany, Eliot settles in London and explains to his mother that it was fine to be a citizen of the United States because the Germans did their best to be friendly to the Americans (58).

September 5, 1914. The Battle of the Marne.

September 7, 1914. Eliot tells his brother that it is "more interesting to be in London now than it was to be in Germany" (59). He meets Ezra Pound, who is enthusiastic about Eliot's poems and who agrees to print "Prufrock." Eliot sends a "war poem" to Conrad Aiken that ends with:

> What ho! they cry'd, we'll sink your ship!
> And so they up and sink'd her.
> But the cabin boy was sav'd alive
> And bugger'd, in the sphincter. (64)

Eliot adds that the poem had to be rejected because "it paid too great a tribute to the charms of German youth to be acceptable to the English public" (64). On October 5, Eliot, still at Merton College, Oxford, entertains hopes of returning to a German university as a "neutral[]" in the spring (65).

October 19, 1914. First Battle of Ypres. The resulting stalemate leads to a defensive war.

November and December 1914. Eliot finds that "Oxford even at this time is peaceful, always elegiac" (75). Yet he feels "more alive" in London as he "hate[s] university towns"; "Oxford is very pretty, but I don't like to be dead" (81).

February 1915. Beginning of the Dardanelles campaign when an Anglo-French army attacks Gallipoli (in present-day Turkey). A corps made up of "Anzac" soldiers from Australia and New Zealand, wearing large Stetson hats instead of helmets, establishes a beachhead, the "Anzac cove." Allied forces attempt to combine ground forces and amphibious naval attacks fail, unlike during the Roman triumph over Carthage at Mylae, in 260 BCE, during the first Punic war, when the Roman boats, equipped with bridges, linked themselves to enemy ships, allowing legionnaires to fight as if they were on solid ground. Echoes of these historical details find their way into The Waste Land.

February 25, 1915. Eliot complains of Oxford and the war: "the War suffocates me," and he adds that he cannot stand the British weather and food (95). London remains the place for excitement and artistic innovation, especially because of the work occurring in the group around Ezra Pound and Wyndham Lewis. In March, Eliot meets Vivien Haigh-Wood at a party organized by Scofield Thayer in Oxford. A powerful, innovative participant, Henri Gaudier-Brzeska, is killed in action on June 5, 1915.

May 2, 1915. Jean Verdenal, a French army medical officer, is killed during the Gallipoli campaign, just before he would have turned twenty-five. According to reports, he had spent a night in water up to his waist, helping evacuate wounded soldiers by sea, when he was shot by enemy fire.

June 26, 1915. After three months of courtship, Eliot marries Vivien Haigh-Wood almost secretly, not having mentioned his decision to his parents. Ezra Pound and Bertrand Russell defend Eliot's position in the face of his family's incomprehension.

May and July 2015. Despite the sinking of the *Lusitania* on May 7, 1915, Eliot travels to America alone on July 24 to give news of his marriage. He returns to England on September 4, 1915. Bertrand Russell, a sort of symbolic father, has helped the couple, and soon becomes Vivien's lover when he understands the sexual incompatibility between his two friends.

July 15, 1915. The second and last issue of *Blast* is published. This *War Number* includes Eliot's "Preludes" I to IV and "Rhapsody on a Windy Night."

January 1916. Eliot mentions the death of Jean Verdenal in a letter to Conrad Aiken that also carries the news of his teaching position in a high school, and news of the recurrent illnesses of his wife (137). Despite the strain, his spirits are high: "I am having a wonderful life nevertheless. I have *lived* through material for a score of long poems, in the last six months" (138).

February 21, 1916. Beginning of the battle of Verdun.

March and June 1916. Eliot sends his dissertation on Bradley's philosophy to Harvard but is prevented from sailing back to defend it. The thesis is accepted in June 1916. Eliot never comes for the examination.

July 1, 1916. Beginning of the battle of the Somme.

August 1916. Eliot explains to Aiken that his wife is mostly suffering from "nerves, complicated by physical ailments" (157). He justifies his decision to stay in England to his father in that "setting the war aside, I have succeeded in what I have undertaken." Yet, he later cannot hide the fact that "When [Vivien] worries she bleeds internally, in a metaphorical sense" (176–7).

March 15, 1917. Tsar Nicholas II abdicates.

March 1917. Eliot begins working at Lloyds Bank as a clerk in the foreign department, earning £2 10 s. a week, preferring this to teaching schoolchildren. He works on international accounts, which forces him to brush up on his French and Italian, and to study Danish, Swedish, Norwegian, and Spanish. He gives lectures on English literature on Mondays.

April 6, 1917. The United States declares war on Germany.

April and June 1917. Vivien states that she dreads the American declaration of war, fearing that her husband "might have, some day, to fight" (192). Eliot becomes a contributing editor to *The Egoist*. Eliot explains that he cannot understand "war *enthusiasm*," and that, from the testimony of those who have returned, like Vivien's brother Maurice, the war is "something very sordid and disagreeable which must be put through" (203). His first book, *Prufrock and Other Observations* is published, with a dedication to Jean Verdenal, "mort aux Dardanelles."

April 16–17, 1917. The Nivelle offensive is so costly in human lives that rebellions and desertions in the French army begin. These are severely punished by summary executions. On June 7, 1917, the Battle of Messines begins with the biggest and loudest mine explosions ever: nineteen mines explode almost at once, the noise being audible in London and Dublin, killing thousands of German men. Just before, the second army chief of staff, Harington, had declared to the press: "Gentlemen, we may not make history tomorrow, but we shall certainly change the geography."[9]

June 23, 1917. Eliot publishes a letter by his brother-in-law, Maurice Haigh-Wood, which describes the horrors of trench warfare. He quotes Maurice, who mentions "swollen and blackening corpses of hundreds of young men. The appalling stench of rotting carrion," and "Mud like porridge, trenches like shallow and sloping cracks in the porridge – porridge that stinks in the sun" (205). Maurice adds: "Wounded men lying in the shell holes among the decaying corpses: helpless under the scorching sun and bitter nights, under repeated shelling. Men with bowels dropping out, lungs shot away, with blinded, smashed faces, or limbs blown into space. Men screaming and gibbering." He points out that some people just "shudder" and forget, including "regular" army officers, "jolly good fellows – who have never stopped to think in their lives" (205). Eliot will not follow Bertrand Russell's militant pacifism. Russell is helped and accompanied in his courageous activism by Vivien.

November 7, 1917. The Bolsheviks overthrow the Russian government.

July 1917. Eliot had suspected that things might "go to pieces in Russia" (211). In April 1918, he writes that one cannot believe in a "fight for civilisation" because the term has lost most of its meaning (262).

February 16, 1918. Lithuania's Act of Independence, recognizing it as free state.

Later, in *The Waste Land* Eliot renders a version of Marie Larisch's narration of parts of her life to him in 1911, writing "Bin gar keine Russin, stamm' aus Litauen, echt deutsch" ("I am not Russian, I come from Lithuania, I am a pure German" (12, my translation). Countess Marie Louise Larisch von Moennich (1858–1940) was the niece and confidante of Empress Elisabeth of Austria. She had acted as a go-between for her cousin, Crown Prince Rudolf, during his affair with Mary Vetsera, a friend of hers. When the scandal broke in 1889 after their death, Marie was shunned by the imperial court. She published her memoir, *My Life*, in 1913.

July 15, 1918. Second Battle of the Marne.

August to October 1918. Eliot attempts to be enlisted in the U.S. Navy as an intelligence officer or a noncombatant interpreter. The plans fail, and he returns to the bank. In July 1918, Bertrand Russell is sentenced to six months in prison for libel and for being a pacifist.

November 11, 1918. The armistice is signed at Compiègne.

In December, Eliot announces that he is exhausted by his dealings with the army and by bouts of influenza. He needs complete mental rest. His father dies on January 7, 1919. Eliot speaks of having experienced a "collapse" in February 1919. *Poems* is published by the Hogarth Press on May 12, 1919. In May 1919, Vivien makes a firm decision to stop seeing Bertrand Russell.

February 14, 1919. Beginning of the Polish-Soviet War, which lasts until March 1921. Soviet Russia and Soviet Ukraine fight against the Second

Polish Republic and the Ukrainian People's Republic. This is widely seen as an attempt by the Soviet regime to spread the revolution westward.

The first draft of *The Waste Land* mentions "hooded hordes swarming / ... Over Polish plains," which is crossed out and changed to "endless plains" (Eliot 1971, 73–5, lines 48–9).

June 28, 1919. The Treaty of Versailles is signed and is never ratified by the United States.

On July 2, 1919, Eliot explains to his brother why he will stay in London: he finds it hard to blend in, but on the whole agrees that life there is more civilized, exciting, and also dangerous: "London is something one has to fight very hard in, in order to survive" (Eliot 2011, 370). In August, Eliot takes a walking tour in the south of France with Pound and his health is much better. The last issue of *The Egoist* is published in December 1919, with the second installment of "Tradition and the Individual Talent." On December 18, 1919, Eliot criticizes the American delays to a global peace, pointing out the starvation of the Viennese population: "I suppose Americans realise now what a fiasco the reorganisation of nationalities has been: the 'Balkanisation' of Europe" (425). He then sorts out prewar debts between the bank and Germany, which gives him an opportunity to study the effects of the Peace Treaty, with the knotty issue of war reparations to be paid by the German state.

January 20, 1920. According to the Treaty of Versailles, the Danzig (or Polish) corridor is established, giving Poland access to the Baltic Sea, dissolving the former German province of West Prussia.

1920. "Gerontion" presents "History" as having "many cunning passages, contrived corridors" (34), which alludes to the new map of Europe, and to the complicated "schemes" of the victorious Allies.

III. Demobilization as Demoralization

I have focused on the war years because we know a lot about the series of mental collapses and psychosomatic depressions that Eliot experienced in 1921 – leading to his stay at Margate and to the cure in Lausanne with Dr. Vittoz – and not enough about the war years, even though it seems obvious that *The Waste Land* is a response to this dramatic period. In the same way Eliot had been told that the demobilization process had been a failure in the United States, which accounted for the American public opinion's swing against Wilson's generous but misguided international politics, his poem dramatizes the difficulty of returning to a "normal" life after the immense sacrifices made in the name of "saving civilization." We see this in the dialogue of "A Game of Chess" when Lil is reproached for not knowing how to keep her looks – her recently "demobbed" husband will want to enjoy himself and will be excused for having a roving eye:

> and think of poor Albert,
> He's been in the army four years, he wants a good time,
> And if you don't give it him, there's others will, I said. (147–9)

However, we soon learn via Tiresias that the postwar, newly found sexual freedom leads to mechanical and meaningless lovemaking. The typist is only glad that sexual congress can be dispatched quickly; the young man carbuncular does not even notice her indifference. Given this landscape of barrenness (Lil's problems come from her having aborted with dubious pills) and sexual apathy, it may come as a surprise that, according to the classical tradition synthesized by Ovid's *Metamorphoses*, Tiresias's main teachings to the gods were to ascertain that female orgasms are stronger than men's. It is as if the demobilization has triggered a general demoralization, which would be marked by a loss of sensual appetite and a vanishing of desire.

Such a moral and sexual detumescence cannot be blamed on the fact that Eliot felt guilty for not having seen combat. Eliot may partly be identified with Gerontion, who readily admits his absence from the battlefield:

> I was neither at the hot gates
> Nor fought in the warm rain
> Nor knee deep in the salt marsh, heaving a cutlass,
> Bitten by flies, fought. (3–6)

This passage is often read as an echo of Jean Verdenal's death near Gallipoli. Although Eliot's friendship with Verdenal may have been asexual, Eliot's French friend conveyed a sense of delight and enjoyment of life's simple pleasures. These pleasures seem to have vanished after the Great War. "Gerontion," the poem that was to serve as an introduction to *The Waste Land*, lists other possible sources of enjoyment, although they appear sterile. The "chilled delirium" (62) of "Gerontion" is related to a "wilderness of *mirrors*" (65, emphasis added), a startling image that conceals an allusion to the *Galerie des Glaces* at Versailles, the huge hall where the international treaty was signed on June 28, 1919. Hence, the loss of enjoyment and the *aphanisis* (the term coined by Ernest Jones in 1927 to denote the disappearance of sexual desire), marking a new sexual morality, seem predicated on the demoralization of the peace period rather than on war itself.

This might be confirmed by a letter to Eleanor Hinkley from 1917 in which Eliot rehearses his absence from combat while stressing that he waged his *other war* – his sexual tug of war with Bertrand Russell and Vivien. Eleanor speaks of America as if life went on as usual, which was not the case for Eliot, who writes:

> Life moves so rapidly over here that one never hears twice of the same person as being in the same place or doing quite the same thing. It is either killed or wounded, or fever, or going to gaol, or being let out of gaol, or being tried, or summoned before a tribunal of some kind. I have been living in one of Dostoevsky's novels, you see, not in one of Jane Austen's. If I have not seen the battlefield, I have seen other strange things, and I have signed a cheque for £200,000 while bombs fell about me. I have dined with a princess and with a man who expected two years hard labour; and it all seems like a dream. The most real thing was a little dance we went to a few days ago, something like yours used to be, in a studio with a gramophone. (210)

This reveals a curious loss of reality that the poet seems to have experienced because of the war. The small pleasures like listening to the gramophone and dancing to its tunes can ward off for a moment the sexual and psychic upheavals caused by a disastrous marriage. Eliot is alluding here to Bertrand Russell, who had avoided imprisonment in 1917 but would not be so lucky in 1918. The Great War thus generated a double unreality: the unreality of the unspeakably traumatic scenes described by Maurice Haigh-Wood in the trenches and the unreality of everyday life in London. Such a feeling of unreality affected many people, especially shell-shocked soldiers sheltered from an unbelievable massacre by self-induced hysteria or psychosis.

At the same time, it seems that Eliot experienced life more deeply and felt more alive than before. He had gauged life in all its horror because he experienced pain, excess, and ecstasy fully. In fact, he was granted what he was asking for before the war, as we see in a letter to Conrad Aiken from July 1914, in which he complains that he "lack[s] inspiration" and "feel[s] very constipated intellectually" (47). He adds: "Some people say that pain is necessary ('they learn in suffering' *etc*).... what is necessary is a *certain kind* (could one but catch it!) of *tranquility*, and *sometimes* pain does bring it. A kind of tranquility which Dostoievsky [*sic*] must <on second thoughts I delete the line> have known when he was writing his masterpieces at top-speed to keep from starving" (47). Six days later, as in guise of an illustration, Eliot appends to another letter several poems, including "The Love Song of St Sebastian" in which he dwells on sadomasochistic fantasies: the speaker flogs himself till he bleeds, then he strangles a woman (51). The trope of *pathos mathos* (suffering brings knowledge) thus applies to a prewar poet who dimly senses that he has not experienced life: he feels that he is a virgin not only in sexual matters but also in his apprehension of reality.

In the letter to Eleanor Hinkley from July of 1917, Eliot refers to novels, not to poetry or tragedy, in order to get a grip on the unthinkable reality of the war. The Great War imposes a paradigm shift in the choice of literary examples – if before the war, life was like a Jane Austen novel, during the war it has turned into a Dostoevsky novel. He is alluding to the fact that he had acted in "An Afternoon with Mr. Woodhouse," a sketch based on Jane Austen's life that Eleanor had organized at Cambridge, Massachusetts, in 1913, but the reference to Austen is apt: it captures the prewar world of young men and women who aim at making a good marriage. Dostoevsky's novels bring in a different mode of being, with excesses of hysteria well summarized by Bertrand Russell, who knew that Vivien Eliot loved reading the Russian novelist. Russell confides to Ottoline Morrell that Vivien can be cruel facing her husband: "It is a Dostoevsky type of cruelty.... She is a person who lives on a knife edge, & will end as a criminal or a saint – I don't know which yet."[10] Russell's cliché of a "Russian" personality seems to characterize Vivien, whom he saw as a bipolar seducer, capable of murdering either her husband or her lover, in the hope of being punished or killed herself.

The "Russian" psychology Russell understood to be exemplified by Dostoevsky's characters, presenting a combination of hysteria and sadomasochism, also appears in the first draft of the "Fresca" section in the first draft of The Waste Land:

> The Scandinavians bemused her wits,
> The Russians thrilled her to hysteric fits. (Eliot 1971, 27, lines 58–9)

Sigmund Freud, who wrote a psychobiography of Dostoevsky in 1928, mentions in "The Economic Problem of Masochism" people who are prone to "sinful acts" because these actions will unleash reproaches from their sadistic conscience – which he claims "is exemplified in so many Russian character-types."[11] Eliot provides a similar diagnosis in his "London Letter" published in The Dial in September 1922. He mentions that "Dostoevsky had the gift, a sign of genius in itself, for utilizing his weaknesses; so that epilepsy and hysteria cease to be the defects of an individual and become – as a fundamental weakness can, given the ability to face it and study it – the entrance to a genuine and personal universe."[12] He had just read Hermann Hesse's perceptive analysis in the essay "The Brothers Karamazov or The Downfall of Europe," whose ending is quoted in German in the Notes to The Waste Land: "Schon ist halb Europa, schon ist zumindest der halbe Osten Europas auf dem Wege zum Chaos, fährt betrunken im heiligen Wahn am Abgrund entlang und singt dazu, singt betrunken und hymnisch wie

Dmitri Karamasoff sang. Ueber diese Lieder lacht der Bürger beleidigt, der Heilige und Seher hört sie mit Tränen" (Note 366–76).

In this impassioned meditation written in 1919, Hesse links Friedrich Nietzsche and Dostoevsky, noting that both were able to use their diseases creatively. The convulsions of the Karamazov family, leading to the murder of a demented father, allegorize the downfall of Europe. The fate of Dmitri, the immoralist with an artist's sensitivity, who acts according to the promptings of his inner voice, points to a possible renewal. This renewal would entail leaving behind the old Christian morality and engaging with a wisdom from Asia.[13] According to Hesse, Dostoevsky calls for an "Asian ideal" of mystical sainthood that would avoid the dichotomies of "good" and "evil" (126) since Asia is the true mother of Europe, and the only way one can avoid a return to the catastrophic conditions that precipitated a world war is to bypass ethics and understand the need for a new sainthood. Yet Hesse's essay has too often been reduced to a condemnation of the Soviet Revolution. Indeed, the essay ends with the passage that is quoted by Eliot: "Soon half of Europe, at least half of Eastern Europe, is on the road to chaos, reeling into the abyss in a state of drunken delirium, singing drunken hymns as Dmitri Karamazov did. These songs are heard with wounded laughter by the bourgeois, and with tears by the saint and the seer" (139–40, my translation). In fact, Hesse is not so much damning the Russian Revolution as he is condemning the bourgeois complacency shown by Western Europeans. Both Dostoevsky and the Russian revolutionaries suffer from "hysteria," he argues (139), but such hysteria can be productive, since it is linked with artistic creation and mystical visions. On the other hand, an innocent Dmitri Karamazov will be convicted for a murder he has not committed. Here, as Hesse argues, Dostoevsky accuses the enraged and prejudiced bourgeois, who take Dmitri's drunken singing for a confession, as we see in book 12 of *The Brothers Karamazov* (138).

Hesse's reading of Dostoevsky agrees with Eliot's, in that they see the Russian novelist as a prophet of doom and also a renovator of values. The general upheaval of all values, to use Nietzsche's famous phrase of *Umwertung aller Werte*, can also lead to a paradoxical reawakening of spirituality. Like Nietzsche and Dostoevsky, Hesse and Eliot want to bypass the binary logics opposing reason and feeling that have plagued European rationalism since the Enlightenment. This attempt to go beyond the duality of "normal" and "pathological" has political implications. Thus Hesse's thinking follows the model provided by a Catholic thinker of politics, Carl Schmitt, who was at the time rethinking the religious or mystical foundation of politics. Schmitt attempted to make sense of a situation of "exception" caused by war. We can note that *The Waste Land* is contemporary to the publication of Carl Schmitt's *Political Theology*, a book beginning with the famous definition "Sovereign is he who decides on the exception."[14] Like Valéry, in "La crise de l'esprit," which I have already quoted, Schmitt thinks beyond the facile dichotomy of order and chaos. Here is Schmitt: "What characterizes an exception is principally unlimited authority, which means the suspension of the entire existing order. In such a situation it is clear that the state remains, whereas law recedes. Because the exception is different from anarchy and chaos, order in the juristic sense still prevails even if it is not of the ordinary kind" (12). Here is Valéry, comparing the European man of 1919 to Hamlet, but having too many skulls to meditate on: "Our European Hamlet looks at millions of specters.... He thinks of the tedium of rehearsing the past, and of the madness of always innovating. He staggers between two abysses, for two dangers constantly threaten the world: order and disorder" (993). Eliot's thought should not be oversimplified into an opposition between order and chaos.

A last binary that Eliot was trying to overcome – both in *The Waste Land* and in his general thinking – was that of the strict couple of defeat and victory, which explains why his depression came to him not during the war, but after. By a relatively common paradox, the victory of the Allies was also a new debacle. The war had provided the "exception," but without the exception, one would fall back to the impossible choice of either order or chaos. It is such a choice that led to Eliot's moral collapse. This moral collapse was something he had felt in his old role model, Jules Laforgue, and to which he confessed in 1921, in "The Metaphysical Poets," when Eliot quotes one of Laforgue's *Last Verses* to illustrate the way Laforgue can be obscure, difficult, allusive, indirect, all this "in order to force, to dislocate if necessary, language into his meaning."[15] Then Eliot quotes the first stanza from poem X of *Last Verses*, beginning "*O geraniums diaphanes*" in which the key statement is the reiteration of "*débâcles nuptiales!*" Mysterious geraniums have been at war ("*guerroyeurs*") while people have waited in vain for the "*grands soirs*" of a social revolution, and now are stuck in the miserable litany of "transfusions, reprisals, churchings, compresses and the eternal potion" (7–8). The dismal view of sexuality frames the speaker's revulsion at the thought of "Nuptial debacles! Nuptial debacles!" (10). The sexual fiasco of a bad marriage would be intolerable in times of peace, a peace called up by the ending of Laforgue's poem that Eliot does not quote. There, Laforgue includes one exception to the rule of disastrous sexual encounters when he mentions the possibility of sexual bliss. Laforgue was not to enjoy this bliss long, since he died one year after his marriage. But Eliot did not die, not visibly, at least.

The apparent victory of the Allies also allowed Eliot to probe further *débâcles* that lay in store. The term was used regularly for the French defeat of 1870–1. Emile Zola used it in *La débâcle*, a historical novel about the

Franco-Prussian war of 1870–1, which somehow explained the Great War, just as 1919 would explain 1939. The serious task was to inch toward redemption, as Franz Rosenzweig argues in *The Star of Redemption*. The war's aftermath had left too many loaded nationalisms or tricky Danzig corridors ready to explode, all the while contributing baffling instances of Hegel's "cunning of reason."

> After such knowledge, what forgiveness? Think now
> History has many cunning passages, contrived corridors
> And issues, deceives with whispering ambitions,
> Guides us by vanities....
> These tears are shaken from the wrath-bearing tree. ("Gerontion" 33–47)

These urgent admonitions sound less a "*rappel à l'ordre*" (as Ezra Pound, Jean Cocteau, and Andre Gide implied at a time when they wanted to return to a new classicism) than a "reveille," although not from a military bugle, but with words. The new focus is on awakening, as Walter Benjamin argues in his *Arcades Project*. We can no longer sleep, we have to wake up from the four-year trance of "sleepwalkers" going unscathed through mined terrain.[16] Then, even if we have learned that the earth is a small sphere, and that it has become a comfortable place to inhabit, we should try to redeem the times.

As we have seen, the task of redeeming the times entails overcoming the simple dualism opposing order and chaos. This accounts for the ambiguity of an often-quoted line from the end of *The Waste Land*: "These fragments I have shored against my ruins" (430). We know from the drafts that Eliot had initially written "These fragments I have spelt into my ruins" and then, without even crossing out the verb, added above the line: "shored against" (Eliot 1971, 81, line 114). The two verbs are not identical; the meaning of the first version can be construed as: "My poem made up of fragments, *The Waste Land*, is spelling, naming, or writing words into my ruins." The revision adds the meaning of propping up, supporting, as if the poetic fragments were called upon to defend the poet against an impending ruin. In the first concept, the poet's task is to write with a didactic intention so as to mobilize and make new "other withered stumps of time" (104), with the poem itself as another beautiful ruin, capable of surviving by itself among all the other ruins left by the war. In the second concept, the poem is a rampart of words, a tentative construction with prosthetic props which will help the poet survive after having witnessed the destruction, material and moral, brought about by European madness. However, whether these ruins are construed as positive or negative, what stands out is the strong syntax balancing the deictic "these" – which testifies to the objective existence of the poem – and the possessive "my": even if there are ruins, they have become my own ruins.

NOTES

1 First draft version of a black-ink manuscript used near the end of *The Waste Land*. T. S. Eliot, *The Waste Land: A Facsimile and Transcript of the Original Drafts Including the Annotations of Ezra Pound*, ed. Valerie Eliot (New York: Harcourt, 1971), 112–13.

2 Paul Valéry, "La crise de l'esprit," *Oeuvres* I (Paris: Pléiade, 1965), 988.

3 Eliot, *The Waste Land*, in *Collected Poems: 1909–1962* (London: Faber and Faber, 1963), 373–6. Subsequent references to *The Waste Land* will be cited parenthetically by line number.

4 Valéry, "La crise de l'esprit," 992, 996.

5 Mary Hutchinson, "War," *The Egoist* 4, no. 11 (1917): 169–72.

6 See Vivien Eliot's letter to Mary Hutchinson, [September 8?, 1917], in Eliot, *The Letters of T. S. Eliot, Volume 1: 1898–1922*, ed. Valerie Eliot and Hugh Haughton, rev. ed. (New Haven, CT: Yale University Press, 2011), 215. Subsequent letters will be cited parenthetically.

7 The best account of Kafka's war of attrition against marriage is in Frederick Karl's *Franz Kafka, Representative Man: Prague, Germans, Jews and the Crisis of Modernism* (New York: Fromm International Publishing Corporation, 1993), 308–419.

8 See Morton Fullerton, *Problems of Power* (New York: Scribner's Sons, 1913). I have analyzed this book in *1913: The Cradle of Modernism* (Oxford: Blackwell, 2007), 11–12.

9 For a detailed account of the entire military operation, see Alexander Turner, *Messines 1917: The Zenith of Siege Warfare* (Oxford: Osprey, 2010).

10 Bertrand Russell's *Autobiography*, as quoted in Seymour-Jones, 129.

11 Sigmund Freud, "The Economic Problem of Masochism," *General Psychological Theory*, ed. Philip Rieff (1924; New York: Macmillan, 1963), 200.

12 Eliot, "London Letter: The Novel," *The Dial* 73 no. 3 (1922): 331.

13 I am summarizing the essay in Hermann Hesse, *Sämtliche Werke, Band 18, Die Welt im Buch, III, Rezensionen und Aufsätze 1917–1925*, trans. Stephen Hudson (Frankfurt: Suhrkamp Presse: 2002), 125–40. The essay was published, in condensed form, in *The Dial* 72 no. 6 (1922): 607–18.

14 Carl Schmitt, *Political Theology*, trans. George Schwab (Chicago: University of Chicago Press, 2005), 5.

15 Eliot, *The Annotated Waste Land with Eliot's Contemporary Prose*, ed. Lawrence Rainey (New Haven, CT: Yale University Press, 2005), 199.

16 I am alluding to two books that, whether they work via fiction or as historical documentation, imply that when Europe let itself be engulfed in total war it was a sort of collective trance or "sleepwalking": Christopher Clark, *The Sleepwalkers: How Europe Went to War in 1914* (London: Penguin, 2013); Hermann Broch, *The Sleepwalkers*, trans. Willa and Edwin Muir (1947; New York: Random House, 1996).

2

SPENCER MORRISON

Geographies of Space: Mapping and Reading the Cityscape

T. S. Eliot first toured London with the help of a Baedeker travel guide (*London and Its Environs*, published in 1908); in a letter of April 26, 1911 he describes "produc[ing] a map" (likely his Baedeker's) before "an austere Englishman" while charting his route.[1] A decade later, ensconced in London as an (arguably) austere resident, and in the process of composing *The Waste Land*, Eliot voices in *The Dial* his exhilaration at taking in Igor Stravinsky's *Sacre du Printemps*: "[the music] did seem to transform the rhythm of the steppes into the scream of the motor horn, the rattle of machinery, the grind of wheels, the beating of iron and steel, the roar of the underground railway, and the other barbaric cries of modern life."[2] Evoking a putative primitivism ("the rhythm of the steppes," "barbaric") in the clangor of urban modernity, Stravinsky's music acts for Eliot as an alternative Baedeker, indexing urban experience in a form more textured than tourist guides or city maps that present abstract networks of streets and buildings.[3] Such an awareness of mapping's pliability as a representational mode – an awareness that mapping can be carried out not only by government administrators but also by citizens who conjure their own personal orderings of city space – infuses *The Waste Land*, where, near the poem's end, the speaker asks, "Shall I at least set my lands in order?"[4] This question announces the possibility of a future spatial order that repairs the present's fragmentation, with the phrase "set ... in order" enunciating an impulse not just cartographic but governmental.

Yet the interrogative form in which this possibility arises also subtly undercuts governmental mapping: the word "Shall" casts doubt upon the ethics and viability of the project of spatial ordering. *The Waste Land*, often read as "the text of urban disaffection in modernist poetry par excellence," both embodies and questions new ways of ordering, mapping, and artistically governing urban experience, meditating on the prospects for new spatial orders commensurate to the material upheavals of modern city life.[5] Just as Ezra Pound, revising Shelley, claimed that poets should be considered *acknowledged* legislators, *The Waste Land* casts attention on the very processes of urban ordering and governing that it artistically enacts, grounding its reflections on modernity in London's built form, material infrastructure, and urban administration. That is to say, *The Waste Land*'s poetic ordering of city life accentuates and illuminates facets of urban experience inflected by *governmental* processes. It does so by presenting a pervasive sense of unreality engendered in part by the dynamics of imperialism and mass capitalism that elide distances between disparate geographic spaces and historical periods, though also by psychic and ontological fragmentation that are aligned in the poem with cycles of material ruin and reconstruction and catalyzed by municipally endorsed urban renewal. Beyond such a sense of unreality, we can see *The Waste Land*'s governmental inflections in the poem's representation of new forms of collective psychology produced by the unprecedented crowding of modern city life; we also see a heightened awareness of systems of energy generation and waste removal, congruent with massive upheavals in urban infrastructure in Eliot's time. Above all, *The Waste Land*'s rendering of urban modernity both depicts and performs what economist Joseph Schumpeter terms "creative destruction" – the unceasing cycles of development, destruction, and redevelopment that fuel wealth creation in capitalist societies. Eliot's poem bears the traces of an urban order beholden to and materialized by such cycles, even as it rehearses and represents such cycles itself, endowing its poetic form with distinctly governmental, legislative drives.

The poem's cartographic imagination orders city space so as to anchor its presentation of urban experience within specific London sites while nevertheless rendering those sites "Unreal" (376). As many readers have noted, sites and streets familiar to Eliot populate *The Waste Land*: the poem's description of an anonymous crowd crossing London Bridge into the financial district "To where Saint Mary Woolnoth kept the hours" (67) mirrors Eliot's own commute to his position at Lloyds Bank, located behind Saint Mary Woolnoth Church, on Lombard Street. Indeed, the London streets mentioned in *The Waste Land* all emanate from Lombard Street, while locatable neighborhoods like Highbury, and Thames-side locales like Richmond and Kew, and the tube station of Moorgate (the closest stop to Lloyds Bank) disclose a finely grained sense of place. However, as any reader of *The Waste Land* can attest, these place names, evocative of official city maps, unmoor themselves from a sense of stable emplacement, engulfed by a phantasmagoric unreality that suffuses not just London but modern urban experience as such:

Falling towers
Jerusalem Athens Alexandria
Vienna London
Unreal (373-6)

Perhaps the central question for any reader of the poem's engagement with city life thus becomes: in what does *The Waste Land*'s urban unreality and its expression of alternative modes of urban mapping and experience inhere? Whatever our answers, what seems inescapable is a recognition that *The Waste Land*'s urban unreality manifests itself in and through psychological, social, economic, and cultural aspects of urban modernity tied intimately not only to built city space but to the poem's own formal strategies. That is to say, "unreality" embraces not just the poem's representations of urbanity but also its very representational strategies, its poetic form.

The Waste Land's technique of figuring Eliot's London through the frames of desert and jungle geographies, Eastern and Western spiritual traditions, and historical and literary allusions, renders the process of reading city space also one of archaeology. On the one hand, superimposed upon the poem's chartable London place-names, these strata situate the city within more expansive senses of time and place than simply the London of 1922. On the other, they incorporate *The Waste Land*'s named city sites within a sweeping vision of spiritual and cultural decay, thereby acting as vehicles for what critical geographer Henri Lefebvre calls "representational space" – "space which the imagination seeks to change and appropriate."[6] Thus, for instance, pervasive allusions to ancient mythology and ritual, as well as what Eleanor Cook has identified as *The Waste Land*'s invocation of ancient Roman imperial geography, immerse the poem's urban form and culture within not just a cyclical vision of history, but a cyclical vision that is characterized by the rises and falls conventionally ascribed to empires across time. As Cook notes, "London in 1922 was still the center of an empire," and the poem's positioning of London at the end of a list of failed imperial centers (Jerusalem, Athens, Alexandria, Vienna) allows it to shadow its textual city with the prospect of collapse.[7] Such historical resonances plunge *The Waste Land*'s named places within an apocalyptic vision rooted in cyclical temporality. *The Waste Land* in this way adds granulation to these represented sites by locating them within a globe-spanning imperial apparatus. However, the poem's invocation of cyclical imperial histories simultaneously works against this granulating current, resisting any tendency toward urban particularity by redirecting attention to imperial apparatuses *as such*, abstracted from London's specific material form. The past's unceasing presence in *The Waste Land*'s London in this way creates a tension between materiality and abstraction, rendering the urban "real" not quite so.

However, it is not just techniques of literary-historical superimposition and allusion that generate a sense of unreality in Eliot's London; what Michel de Certeau might call *The Waste Land*'s spatial story – its processes of "travers[ing] and organiz[ing] places,"[8] its sequencing of distinct spaces – constructs implicit comparisons between London and the diverse geographies (desert, alpine, and jungle) juxtaposed against it. Thrusting together spatially distant locales, *The Waste Land* encodes in its poetic form a geographic reach that recalls both London's global imperial system and a heightened sense of mobility in Eliot's time enabled by new modes of travel. These distinct spaces, brought into relations of contiguity by the poem's spatial story, assume also relations of metonymy, their proximity on the page conjuring previously unseen ligatures between them, shared qualities that facilitate comparisons through the prism of metaphor. While processes of literary and historical allusion render London a palimpsest striated by urban cultures across time, *The Waste Land*'s collage-like juxtaposition of spaces that are geographically distinct but temporally simultaneous enacts a subtly different type of superimposition: the first is diachronic, the second synchronic.

Take, for instance, *The Waste Land*'s desert. Across the poem shared words and images bind this space to the city, inviting comparison: the "hooded hordes swarming" (368) across the desert recall in their chilling uniformity the crowd of virtual automatons that flows over London Bridge in "The Burial of the Dead;" the "roots that clutch" (19) in the desert anticipate the leaves that "Clutch" (174) the Thames's bank; above the mantel of the house described in "A Game of Chess" lies an image of a nightingale who "Fill[s] all the desert with inviolable voice" (101). While such figural echoes bind London to a host of other spaces across the poem, *The Waste Land*'s desert forcefully evokes a stoniness – a spiritual and cultural emptiness – within urban modernity, even as it locates the source of pervasive urban stoniness in a severance of city experience from the natural landscape. Containing "stony rubbish" (20), this desert's sheer squalor gives to desert life a sense of urgent material deprivation lacking in London, revealing another source of urban unreality in the very material commodities that fill city life, the littered forms of which clog the Thames. The aridity of *The Waste Land*'s desert thus transmutes itself, by way of the poem's spatial story, into a cultural and spiritual aridity within city life produced by material decadence.

However, more than the desert's aridity is figuratively imputed to *The Waste Land*'s London, a city that itself lacks vivifying water, its river polluted. As implied by their shared images of fearfully heteronomous, deindividualized collective life (crowds and hordes), the desert and the city foster similar psychological states in their respective inhabitants. Just as the poem's urbanites suffer psychological isolation, "We think of the key, each in his prison" (413), so the animalistic desert figures seem unable to overcome psychological isolation: the speaker entreats an imagined interlocutor to perceive something other than "Your shadow at morning striding behind you / Or your shadow at evening rising to meet you" (suggesting that desert dwellers cannot perceive a world beyond the shadow, or prison, of selfhood) (28–9). Indeed, the poem's insinuation of a virtually primordial link between landscapes of stony rubbish and the selfhoods of those who inhabit them – this landscape's "red rock" (25) echoes the "red sullen faces [that] sneer and snarl" (344) in "What the Thunder Said" – suggests a broader relationship between subjectivity and space within *The Waste Land* as a whole, in not only its wilderness zones but its urban ones. For instance, the montage of urban images that open "What the Thunder Said" – such as that of "Prison and palace and reverberation" (326) – includes one of "torchlight red on sweaty faces" (322), situating desert-like redness on faces of urbanites, the sweat on their face representing bodily waste redolent of the desert's strewn waste, its "stony rubbish." Moreover, the unintelligible "snarl[s]" (344) heard in *The Waste Land*'s wilderness regions function as a figurative limit case to the decayed public sphere of its urban zones, this decay signaled by the largely trivial conversations that transpire in the London scenes. Desert, alpine, and jungle geographies in *The Waste Land* thus function as multivalent symbols in the poem's representation of urbanism: these symbols do not simply bind urbanity to wilderness zones by foregrounding shared geographical or material features, nor do they simply link these spaces by reference to common psychological states; rather, these figurative connections rely upon, and elaborate, intricate links between material space and subjectivity itself.

In this vein, the spatial trope most crucial in binding city to wilderness, built form to subjectivity, is that of the ruin, a trope intimately tied in the poem to processes of urban ordering and governance. Throughout *The Waste Land* the figure of the ruin functions as both spatial site and spatial process, as both noun and verb, subtending and reconciling the poem's content and form. In the poem's closing stanza we find the rich ambiguity ruins assume:

> I sat upon the shore
> Fishing, with the arid plain behind me
> Shall I at least set my lands in order?
> London Bridge is falling down falling down falling down ...
> *Le Prince d'Aquitaine à la tour abolie*
> These fragments I have shored against my ruins (423–30)

At the level of built urban form, the singsong London Bridge refrain of line 426 images forth the ruin of the very bridge traversed by city crowds in "The Burial of the Dead," evoking a broader sense of urban ruin echoed in the phrase *"tour abolie"* (429), as well as in the "Falling towers" (373) that introduce the poem's list of failed imperial centers, ending in London. Beyond this passage, earlier references to the destroyed ancient city of Carthage, as well as to the Battle of "Mylae" (70) (part of the Punic Wars that resulted in the sack of Carthage in 146 BC), confer upon *The Waste Land*'s ruin imagery the markings of historical cyclicality discussed in this chapter. However, a different type of cyclicality also infuses *The Waste Land*'s urban ruins: as scholars of modern culture such as Marshall Berman have argued, cycles of rapid spatial annihilation and reconstruction – that is, of Schumpeter's "creative destruction" – uniquely inflect modern experience, with forces of mass capitalism and technological innovation reshaping lived geography as never before. The concerns of "profit and loss" (314) that preoccupy Phlebas the Phoenician, Mr. Eugenides, and modern capitalism more generally produce an economic need for continual material consumption and renewal. This economic need in turn necessitates the unending destruction and rebuilding of the urban fabric – a spectral cyclicality captured by Karl Marx's famous phrase "all that is solid melts into air,"[9] a loss of solidity that bolsters a sense of unreality in the poem's city space. *The Waste Land*'s urban ruins thus lie at the intersection of two types of cycles: first, transhistorical cycles of imperial collapse; and second, cycles of creative destruction historically specific to modern capitalism.

We can think, then, of *The Waste Land* as a poem of modern ruin-gazing, where the act of seeing ruins – characteristically understood as an act that elicits both terror and pleasure in the viewer – transpires in a literary form attentive to the new speed of urban destruction. An awareness of the instantaneity of modern forms of ruination inflects *The Waste Land*'s ruin-gazing: whereas earlier Baroque and Romantic traditions of ruin-gazing saw and prized in ruins "natural … processes of decay over long periods of time," Nick Yablon notes that representations of ruins in modern urban sites typically register an unprecedented suddenness inhering in late-nineteenth and early-twentieth-century processes of destruction.[10] In this new, modern mode of ruin-gazing, ruins most commonly arise from either wartime destruction (evoked by *The Waste Land*'s allusion to Mylae) or "equally violent forces unleashed by the internal contradictions of capitalist urbanization" (Yablon 14). The montage-like catalog of ruined imperial centers (directly preceded by the image of "falling towers") captures a speed unique to forms of ruination in modernity; as such poetic form echoes and conveys how swiftly the buildings of urban modernity can be reduced to rubble. The material forces and modes of urban change in modernity thus shape the aesthetic act of ruin-gazing offered to *The Waste Land*'s readers.

However, the semantic and figural density of ruins exceeds mere images of material annihilation in *The Waste Land*: as the speaker notes, "These fragments I have shored against *my* ruins" (430; my italics). Ruination here becomes a psychic, subjective property, not just a spatial one – the speaker's very selfhood assumes the shape and qualities of ruins, girded by the semantically ambiguous "fragments" (430) shored against it. Fragments, of course, constitute the very disordered form designated by the term *ruins*, allowing us to fuse imaginatively the shored fragments described in this line with the speaker's own subjectivity. In so doing, we connect material ruin with *The Waste Land*'s poetic form, since fragmentation aptly describes a central literary strategy of the poem. In this closing stanza of *The Waste Land*, the term "fragments" designates the disjointed quotations immediately preceding line 430 as well as the broader poem itself, as the speaker, sitting by clean water at poem's end, surveys the geographical and literary landscapes traversed in reaching this final site. The fragmentation that befalls ruined buildings manifests itself poetically in *The Waste Land*'s techniques of disorienting montage, collage, and quotation: if we readers "know only / A heap of broken images" (21–2) when encountering this poem, sensing that we can "connect / Nothing with nothing" (301–2), our very reading of *The Waste Land*'s textual fragments resembles the act of sifting through material shards amid urban ruin. Moreover, any provisional meaning formed in our textual encounter with the poem becomes an act of reconstruction analogous to urban rebuilding. That the speaker *shores* these fragments against his or her own subjective ruins recalls the fact that the speaker sits "upon the shore / Fishing" (423–4) in this verse paragraph; this allows us in turn to imagine the speaker's ruined subjectivity as a fluid river structured (and brought into being) by *The Waste Land*'s textual fragments, which collectively form a shore that banks the riverine, ruinous flow. Indeed, our act of reading *The Waste Land* itself, our provisional ordering of its textual fragments, becomes an act of *shoring* analogous to the speaker's: through our readerly processes of meaning-making, we give tentative shape to *The Waste Land*'s fragments, thereby imparting a frail, imperfect order to the ruinous text.

Conceiving of *The Waste Land* as itself a ruin analogous to the material environment and psychological states of urban modernity illuminates also how the ruinous urbanity it depicts inflects its treatment of time. As Tim Edensor writes, "there is an excess of meaning in the remains [of the ruin]: a plenitude of fragmented stories, elisions, fantasies, inexplicable objects and possible events which present a history that can begin and end anywhere."[11]

30

Such referential excess allows urban ruins to invoke multiple and fragmented pasts while simultaneously gesturing to indeterminate possible futures, leaving the ruin a figure that suggests both a prior (lost) order that has fallen into ruin and a potentially utopian future (an order restored atop the ruin's rubble). And it is just this fraught temporality of the ruin – a site that conjures both past and future amid the decay of the present – that inaugurates *The Waste Land* through its opening geographical image. "The Burial of the Dead" introduces us to a "dead land" (2) that "mix[es] / Memory and desire" (2–3): if we read this landscape as oriented simultaneously toward the past (through memory, which peers backward) and the future (through desire, which strives toward an object yet to be attained), the conflicting temporal drives of the poem's world come to replicate the complex temporalities of ruins themselves. The poem's material cityscape, threatened by destruction, thus figures forth broader temporal tensions in *The Waste Land* as a whole. Situated directly before *The Waste Land*'s first image of urbanity (Munich's Hofgarten of line 10), this "dead land" represents a site of both generation ("breeding / Lilacs," 1–2) and loss ("forgetful snow," 6). In this way, the land instantiates temporal and spatial dynamics of upheaval that structure our readerly introduction to the poem's city space only lines later, as we are ushered into Munich, appropriately enough, by way of disjointed, collage-like quotation in a foreign language ("Bin gar keine Russin, stamm' aus Litauen, echt deutsch," 12).

In understanding *The Waste Land* as a text that concerns – and formally enacts – new ways of ordering, mapping, and governing modern city experience, images of ruin then serve as figurative hinges for potentially utopian restructurings of modern urbanity; the utopian potential of such restructuring discloses once more how the ruinous poem routes its urban imagination through legislative and governmental concerns. Indeed, the ruin's fragments, their disorder rendering ambiguous the shape of any future reconstruction, "resonate with a utopian longing for some kind of apotheosis" for many theorists and viewers of modern ruin.[12] Such an impulse for potentially revolutionary reconstruction – not only spatial reconstruction but cultural, social, and governmental – encrypts itself within *The Waste Land*'s iconic images of urban apocalypse in "What the Thunder Said," producing an awareness of how ruination works not just as textual strategy but also as governmental process. To this end, it is noteworthy that immediately before the image of "Falling towers" (373) that ushers in *The Waste Land*'s montage of collapsed imperial centers, we encounter the lines, "What is the city over the mountains / Cracks and reforms and bursts in the violet air" (371–2). While this indeterminate "city over the mountains" evokes cities of myth and legend, channeling in its lack of specificity *The Waste Land*'s preoccupation with abstract urban form as such, the term "reforms" used to describe its destruction carries administrative, governmental connotations that suggest political upheaval. The potential violence of such upheaval reveals itself in the images of "Cracks" and "bursts in the violet air" that attend the urban "reforms" described, the air's "violet" color sonically evoking a *violent* cataclysm. The political upheaval framed in these lines echoes earlier images of potentially revolutionary violence in "What the Thunder Said" such as "The shouting and the crying / Prison and palace and reverberation" (325–6). Indexing a tumult that swamps central buildings of political power (the palace and prison), these textual fragments install in *The Waste Land*'s ruinous, deadened urban space a latent power of revolutionary renewal.

While "What the Thunder Said" clearly posits a wrathful divinity of thunderous voice as the primary instrument of ruin and possible renewal, the lines cited in the preceding verse paragraph posit a second potential instrument of revolutionary urban destruction and rebuilding: unruly urban crowds. After all, the "shouting and the crying" (325) that accompanies urban "reverberation" (326) recalls the cacophony emitted by crowds; moreover, the "hooded hordes swarming / Over endless plains" (368–9) seem causally linked to the "Cracks and reforms and bursts in the violet air" (372), as well as to the "Falling towers" (373), that we encounter shortly after the hordes' appearance. And, of course, the particular London site singled out for ruin in the poem's final verse paragraph, London Bridge, is precisely the bridge crossed by Eliot's enervated crowds in "The Burial of the Dead."

In fact, in many ways *The Waste Land* is a poem formally and thematically concerned with both ruins and crowds – and, more obliquely, with historically specific links between spatial ruination and crowd psychology within the experience of urban modernity. That the conclusion to the spectral crowd scene in "The Burial of the Dead" is a line from Charles Baudelaire's *Les Fleurs du Mal* (1857) reveals how Eliot's poem incorporates aspects of crowd experience central to Baudelaire's work. Baudelaire famously portrays in *Les Fleurs du Mal* the figure of the *flâneur*, the idle urban wanderer who perceives and participates in (but remains finally detached from) crowd life, and *The Waste Land*'s textual tour through London can be read as an act of literary *flâneurie*. Beyond this, however, the experience of shock that Walter Benjamin discerns in Baudelaire's depictions of urban crowds also tinges Eliot's enterprise: for Benjamin, members of urban crowds erect psychic barriers to parry the excessive sensory and psychological stimulation produced by the modern city's sights and sounds, as well as by the undue proximity and jostling of fellow walkers of crowded city streets. The abrupt shocks of urban crowd experience manifest themselves in *The Waste Land*'s fragmentary literary form: the poem's abrupt cuts, as well as its disjointed assemblage of quotations, endow the reader's experience of Eliot's text with the shocks and disorientation germane to modern crowd experience. What has been described earlier in this chapter as a fragmentation characteristic of ruins thus reveals itself also in the psychological states engendered in urban crowd members by the built form of the modern city; the very metropolitan development (governmentally endorsed and regulated) that generates material ruins through creative destruction also fosters a built city space that produces crowding by constraining human movement. *The Waste Land*, in representing London's material ruination, thus also formally and thematically encodes the ruinous psychic states characteristic of urban crowding necessitated by creatively destructive development.

But if one perceives the hooded, crowd-like hordes who topple towers in "What the Thunder Said" as enabling urban ruin that allows for redemptive rebuilding, how is this sense of crowds as potentially revolutionary squared with the patently docile, deadened collectivity we see in "The Burial of the Dead" – a collectivity gripped by anomie and psychic isolation as "each man fixed his eyes before his feet" (65)? As Jeffrey T. Schnapp argues, representations of crowds (a form of agglomeration unique to urban life) across the late nineteenth and early twentieth centuries illuminate the bivalent qualities of the crowd. On the one hand, modern crowds can be seen as heterogeneous, unstable agglomerations: "modern multitudes were ... the volatile protagonists of a volatile era.... They were the result of the promiscuous intermingling and physical massing of social classes, age groups, races, nationalities, and genders along the great boulevards of the modern metropolis."[13] On the other hand, and in contrast to this instability, crowds can be seen as tending towards chilling deindividualization and uniformity, pliable and ripe for the shaping powers of demagoguery: "individuals ... lose their contours in order to regain them within the confines of a single corporate body" (Schnapp 5).

While the zombie-like crowd that flows over London Bridge in "The Burial of the Dead" represents this latter, fearfully homogeneous crowd formation, *The Waste Land* hints at the latent volatility of all collectives by progressing from this image (in the poem's first section) to that of the "hooded hordes" (in the poem's last section). Posed symmetrically, these twinned collectives evoke in *The Waste Land*'s movement between them the possibility of revolutionary upheaval in the poem's deadened city. After all, while the homogeneous crowd of part I traverses London Bridge and stops at the tower of Saint Mary Woolnoth, the "hooded hordes" of part V arise poetically in proximity to "Falling towers" (373) and the destruction of London Bridge ("London Bridge is falling down falling down falling down," 426). Moreover, if (as Eliot scholars have argued) Madame Sosostris's tarot pack includes all the characters who people *The Waste Land*, it is significant that she describes these figures as "crowds of people" (56): the poem's various subjectivities flow into one another (or, alternatively, as Eliot claims in note 218 to the poem, are united in Tiresias), mimicking the dialectics of volatility and homogeneity, autonomy and heteronomy, and selfhood and anonymity that are proper to urban crowds. We can read the poem's intermingling voices as *crowded*, their literary form arising from the conditions of the city, rendering the poem's dialogism an outgrowth of and reflection upon historically specific conditions of civic life and governance in Eliot's time.

In concert with *The Waste Land*'s depictions (and formal enactment) of ruin, a fascination with architectural preservation also animates the poem; this fascination evinces in the poem's treatment of spatial destruction a concomitant awareness of how built space functions vitally in sustaining urban public spheres and communal imaginaries. Such an awareness charges the poem's depiction of a lavish urban interior at the opening of "A Game of Chess." On the room's walls appear representations of a "carvèd dolphin" (96) and "The change of Philomel" (99), yet the narratives these images convey are seemingly obscured from sight by the smoke that mixes in this scene of urban decadence with the "strange synthetic perfumes" (87) of the room's occupant. Here a waste product of urban decadence (the smoke mixed with perfumes) obscures the tales told on the interior's wall, allowing the poem to present a cultural heritage, etched in built space, from which its urbanites are severed. That these narratives are described shortly afterward as "withered stumps of time / ... told upon the walls" (104–5) suggests that the cultural resonances accrued by London's built spaces no longer anchor daily experience, having been reduced to empty citations that cannot be fully remembered. Moreover, in describing these withered stories as "told" upon the walls, the poem evokes their artisanal inscription upon built space but also connotes – by way of the apocalyptic connotations of its homophone, *tolled* – the wall's erosion or decay, revealing the wall's susceptibility to ruin amid urban modernity's cycles of creative destruction.

Hannah Arendt's claim in *The Human Condition* that built space vitalizes human community – "To live together in the world means essentially that a world of things is between those who have it in common"[14] – illuminates the consequences for public discourse of what *The Waste Land* depicts as an affective chasm separating Londoners from the histories and stories layered upon their material cityscape. The poem's preservationist impulse suggests what is lost amid processes of urban demolition fueled by mass capitalism. Beyond this, it also suggests what form a truly restorative process of ruin and rebuilding must take – that is, it must recalibrate how citizens relate to the material cityscape, reinvigorating a sense of lived history encoded in built form, rendering such form more experientially *real*. Andrea Zemgulys convincingly identifies *The Waste Land*'s various churches as sites of preservationist desire, noting that "churches are orienting landmarks and spectacles [in the poem], refuges exceptional in the city even though essential to its fabric."[15] One example of how churches function as spaces of refuge in the poem arises immediately after the sordid tryst between the typist and the young man carbuncular, where we encounter the church of Saint Magnus Martyr, whose walls display "Inexplicable splendour of Ionian white and gold" (265). Zemgulys notes this church's incongruous (albeit perilously decadent) beauty amid *The Waste Land*'s bleak cityscape; however, the "splendour" of its walls recalls the lavish interiors of "A Game of Chess," walls whose historical resonances have diminished. *The Waste Land* fixedly describes the architectural heritage of both Magnus Martyr and the lavish interior while simultaneously registering urbanites' indifference toward this heritage amid the urban bustle of "the profit and loss" (314).

Indeed, *The Waste Land*'s clearest expression of preservationist desire arises in its reference to Magnus Martyr, since Eliot's note to line 264 entreats readers to consult a pamphlet by the London City Council entitled *The Proposed Demolition of Nineteen City Churches*. More than simply championing architectural preservation, however, this reference indicates a thoroughgoing if largely tacit engagement by *The Waste Land* with systems of city governance, planning, and administration. In large part the poem meditates on modes of urban governance by representing, and reflecting upon, vast *infrastructural* shifts in Euro-American cities from the mid-nineteenth century onward. This engagement, for instance, informs something as foundational to the poem as its foregrounding of water as a means of waste removal: as historian Joshua Goldstein notes, modern "Euro-American cities were in the grips of a veritable water mania, consuming water on a greater scale than ever before,"[16] spurring urban governments to pursue "the most economically efficient, healthful, and uniformly consistent infrastructure to handle urban sewage and waste" (333). In this poem, so preoccupied with the removal and cleansing of waste, water's status as a figure of regeneration reflects historically specific shifts in the relationship between urbanites and their material infrastructure. If, as Richard Lehan claims, *The Waste Land* "suggests that as the city lost touch with the land, with the rhythms and the psychic nourishment of nature, a spiritual meaning was lost,"[17] attending to Eliot's renderings of urban infrastructure and energy systems across the poem reveals such psychic, spiritual loss as in part the outgrowth of specific, changeable programs of urban governance.

The Thames River, accorded a central role in London life by *The Waste Land*'s spatial imagination, serves as an intersection for the poem's concerns with material infrastructure, city governance, waste treatment processes, and urban energy systems. In "The Fire Sermon" we learn of the Thames that "The river sweats / Oil and tar" (266–7), with the verb "sweats" likening oil to a bodily excrescence, insinuating its vital role within an urban body politic. These lines inaugurate a scattershot set of voices that reference – in lines whose brevity instills a sense of rapid movement – a series of spaces within and beyond London (Highbury, Richmond, Kew, Moorgate, Margate Sands) ending in the ruined site of Carthage, whose temporal and geographic distance from the other cataloged spaces renders it a figure for the ruin that threatens them. Itself a fuel source for the rapid movement poetically enacted in this conclusion to "The Fire Sermon," oil (and its fuel derivative, gasoline) subtly undergirds the section's indictment of urban form and culture: beyond the oily face of the young man carbuncular, gasoline appears in the image of the typist "light[ing] / Her stove" (222–3), as well as in the "gashouse" (190) behind which the speaker sits while fishing in the Thames. Oil, the river's pollutant, fuels not only the automobiles whose "sound[s] of horns and motors" (197) the speaker hears, it also fuels *The Waste Land*'s very multivocality. Oil's subtle but vital presence to *The Waste Land*'s poetic form reveals itself in Tiresias's description of himself as "throbbing between two lives" (218) – an image of subjective flux that recalls the lines that immediately precede it, where a human body appears as a "human engine wait[ing] / Like a taxi throbbing" (216–17). Both Tiresias and the gasoline-powered taxi *throb*, yet if we read Tiresias as this poem's organizing consciousness, then Tiresias's "throbbing," taxi-like movements between diverse characters and voices reveal themselves as steeped in an urban infrastructure reliant upon oil. Reflecting new energy systems of urban modernity, *The Waste Land*'s poetic form in this way can be understood as *oil-fueled*.

This oil-soaked infrastructure informs city life across *The Waste Land*: London's persistent "brown fog" (61), as well as the "Sighs ... exhaled" (64) by its crowd members, recall automotive exhaust. Yet the poem offers, even if only provisionally, a model for restorative urban governance through the oil-soaked Thames water it depicts. This model discloses itself through the poem's twinned fishing scenes – the first in "The Fire Sermon," the second in "What the Thunder Said." In the first scene, the speaker, at whose back lies the city's oil-saturated energy and transportation infrastructure (as evoked by sounds of cars, as well as by the gashouse), fishes in the polluted river while reflecting on those who recently populated its shores, such as the "loitering heirs of City directors" (180). While primarily referencing executives in London's financial sector, the phrase "City directors" also connotes those who *direct* London itself – that is, its administrators and governors. (Indeed, the referential richness of "directors" here signals the extent to which the interests of financiers and urban administrators converge in this city of creatively destructive development.) Echoing this first fishing scene, "What the Thunder Said" offers at its conclusion a speaker once more fishing, with the speaker's back turned not to a sordid city but instead to "the arid plain" (424) left after the city's destruction. Once more, too, this representation of fishing coincides with an image of governance; however, this second scene offers a form of governance far removed from that connoted by the phrase "City directors." Rather, fishing resurfaces in *The Waste Land* immediately after the thunder's final injunction:

> *Damyata*: The boat responded
> Gaily, to the hand expert with sail and oar
> The sea was calm, your heart would have responded
> Gaily, when invited, beating obedient
> To controlling hands (418–23)

This passage posits a method of governance (*Damyata* means "control") attuned to water's flows – and, more broadly, to the natural world. In this way, it evinces the sorts of "reforms" that *The Waste Land* envisions as vital to what could become a renewed urban order. It is not surprising, then, that immediately following these images of governance and fishing we encounter the question that serves as this chapter's introduction to urban form in the poem: "Shall I at least set my lands in order?" (425). By this point, having traversed *The Waste Land*'s ruinous geographies, readers can better comprehend the ethical, political, and aesthetic stakes of the speaker's proposal. Ordering, whether administrative or poetic, emerges in *The Waste Land* as inescapably provisional, an imperfect attempt to shore volatile forces against an eroding bank. This is because Eliot's poetic ordering of urban experience charts the unsettling *disorder* occasioned by urban modernity while nevertheless performing and imagining new urban forms.

NOTES

1 T. S. Eliot to Eleanor Hinkley, April 26, 1922, in *The Letters of T. S. Eliot, Volume 1: 1898–1922*, ed. Valerie Eliot and Hugh Haughton, rev. ed., (London: Faber and Faber, 2009), 17.

2 Eliot, "London Letter," *The Dial* (October 1921): 453.

3 For a sweeping treatment of *The Waste Land*'s engagement with notions of primitivism, see Robert Crawford, *The Savage and the City in the Work of T. S. Eliot* (Oxford: Clarendon, 1987).

4 Eliot, *The Complete Poems and Plays* (London: Faber and Faber, 1969), 426. Subsequent references to *The Waste Land* will be cited parenthetically by line number.

5 Eluned Summers-Bremner, "Unreal City and Dream Deferred: Psychogeographies of Modernism in T. S. Eliot and Langston Hughes," *Geomodernisms: Race, Modernism, Modernity*, ed. Laura Doyle and Laura Winkiel (Bloomington: Indiana University Press, 2005), 262.

6 Henri Lefebvre, *The Production of Space*, trans. Donald Nicholson-Smith (1974; Oxford: Blackwell, 1991), 39.

7 Eleanor Cook, "T. S. Eliot and the Carthaginian Peace," *ELH* 46 (1979): 342.

8 Michel de Certeau, *The Practice of Everyday Life*, trans. Steven Rendall (1984; Berkeley: University of California Press, 1988), 115.

9 Karl Marx, *The Marx-Engels Reader*, ed. Robert C. Tucker (New York: Norton, 1978), 476.

10 Nick Yablon, *Untimely Ruins: An Archaeology of American Urban Modernity, 1819–1919* (Chicago: University of Chicago Press, 2009), 7.

11 Tim Edensor, *Industrial Ruins: Space, Aesthetics and Materiality* (London: Berg, 2005), 141.

12 Yablon, *Untimely Ruins*, 5.

13 Jeffrey T. Schnapp, "Mob Porn," *Crowds*, ed. Schnapp and Matthew Tiews (Stanford, CA: Stanford University Press, 2006), 3.

14 Hannah Arendt, *The Human Condition* (1958; Chicago: University of Chicago Press, 1998), 52.

15 Andrea Zemgulys, *Modernism and the Locations of Literary Heritage* (Cambridge: Cambridge University Press, 2008), 144.

16 Joshua Goldstein, "Waste," *The Oxford Handbook of the History of Consumption*, ed. Frank Trentmann (Oxford: Oxford University Press, 2012), 332.

17 Richard Lehan, *The City in Literature: An Intellectual and Cultural History* (Berkeley: University of California Press, 1998), 134.

3

LYNDALL GORDON

"Mixing/Memory and Desire": What Eliot's Biography Can Tell Us

During the Christmas vacation in 1914, T. S. Eliot stayed at 1 Gordon Street, Gordon Square, in the Bloomsbury area of London. At that time it was a pension full of transient Americans. Eliot himself was a Harvard graduate student on a year's traveling fellowship at Merton College, Oxford. He didn't care much for Oxford and was astonished by the license it gave women students – this would be Vera Brittain's generation of spirited feminists[1] – to intrude themselves upon lectures. It disturbed his sense of fitness that they came "right into" a men's college. "No one looks at them," he assured his proper, Boston family.[2]

Yet he could not entirely avert his eyes from urban women in the streets of London. "One walks about the street with one's desires," he confided to his Harvard friend, Conrad Aiken, on New Year's eve. "[N]ervous sexual attacks" came upon him, while his "refinement" rose up "like a wall" – shyness built up by ingrained propriety. It worried him to be still a virgin at the age of "twenty-six."[3] What Eliot does not tell Aiken is that his father looked on extramarital sex as tantamount to consorting with "the Devil." Syphilis was "God's punishment for nastiness," and Mr. Eliot senior hoped that a cure would never be found.[4] His son was to share his father's disgust in a series of loveless scenes in *The Waste Land*: the automatism of the clerk and typist who couple like "crawling bugs" (in Eliot's draft of this scene, toned down by Ezra Pound),[5] followed by the sorry stories of the Thames daughters, one of whom "'raised my knees/ Supine on the floor of a narrow canoe'" (294–5). A merchant invites his prey for a weekend at "the Metropole" (214) – not a very nice hotel – and the far from refined Sweeney is driving along, amidst "horns and motors," on his way to Mrs. Porter's brothel (197–8).

I want to suggest how rooted *The Waste Land* was in personal issues and preoccupations coming to the fore in Eliot's life from 1911 to 1915, many years before the poem, as we know it, came to light in 1922. These were the years just before and after he left America for Europe. One question is the impact of Eliot's migration on the poem that would emerge from a prolonged period of engagement with – or, it may be, disengagement from – a foreign place, intensified by union with an Englishwoman who proved stranger in her ways than he dreamed when they met.

In March 1915, after another dull term in wartime Oxford, a fellow American at Magdalen College introduced Eliot to a flamboyant young woman, Vivienne Haigh-Wood. She was a few months older, nearly twenty-seven, and had fairly recently lost her boyfriend. (This schoolmaster, Charles Buckle, had enlisted on the outbreak of war, but it is evident, from Vivienne's diary, that he was relieved to get away from her.) There was a lunch party, followed by punting and dancing. She danced with verve, caught on to transatlantic steps, smoked, offered daring opinions on the arts, and encouraged Eliot to be what he felt himself to be: a poet. Her outspokenness and emotional extravagance, novel to the formal rectitude of Eliot's New England, seemed to offer rescue from that wall of inhibition.

Six days after Eliot went down from Oxford, he changed the course of his life. Instead of returning, as expected, to America, he married Vivienne in London, at the Hampstead Registry Office, a quick, secret marriage before parents on either side could be told. It may have been the only way that a moral young man could abandon virginity.

Vivienne's father was a successful artist, a Royal Academician, and the family lived in middle-class comfort in Compayne Gardens on the fringe of Hampstead – a respectable address, though not on the literary heights of this north London suburb. The Haigh-Woods' origin, which Vivienne was determined to leave behind, was Lancashire craftsman; that is, not as grand as the Eliots, who belonged to the Boston elite, with a line of divines (as Puritan New England ministers were called) behind them. The spontaneous freedom of Vivienne's voice and actress-manner did not make her the kind of lady a gentleman of that time would wish to introduce to his mother,[6] yet there was the stimulus, for Eliot, of Vivienne's eagerness to push him forward. "I supply the motive power," she informed Eliot's brother, Henry Ware Eliot Jr., "and I *do* shove."[7]

Eliot's impulse was not without a rationale, urged by Pound, who, like Vivienne, at once recognized the modernist revolution of "The Love Song of J. Alfred Prufrock" and Eliot's other early poems. The idea was to remain in London as an international literary center. Like Pound, Eliot despised "provincialism," and though he actually had much in common with Nathaniel Hawthorne, historically and temperamentally, he was resolved not to fall into what he saw as the narrowness of the New England writer. Eliot meant to jolt himself onto a different biographical track: expatriation at any cost – with the advantage to his poetry of inspecting that cost (as he does at once in a prose-poem, "Hysteria," based on the shock of Vivienne's uncontrolled public behavior). His impulsive commitment to her, well below the impersonal surface of *The Waste Land*, is, conceivably, a source for "The awful daring of a moment's surrender" (403).

If "surrender" meant licensed surrender to a woman – a legitimate wife – it was certainly "daring" in the sense of reckless, for Eliot barely knew Vivienne, and his attraction to her did not survive. By July 9, two weeks into the marriage, Vivienne confessed to her husband's one-time teacher, Bertrand Russell,[8] that she had married Eliot to stimulate him, and had found she could not do so. Since Eliot was present, reclining listlessly across the table, it was a measure of Vivienne's disappointment that she spoke so openly. Her need of reassurance was not lost on Russell, who began to fix his lascivious eye on this unhappy bride.

To Eliot this was a "Poe-bride" in a quite different drama to Russell's diverting scene of seduction. In one of the fragments of *The Waste Land* manuscript, Eliot imagines the horror of a man who finds himself joined to a draining creature who will leave him lifeless. Vivienne both acted out this horror tale and upstaged it with the domestic English narrative of her letters.

Vivienne's letters and her satiric fictional sketches in the early twenties dramatize how foreign Americans appear to her, requiring explanations of Englishness (in part, insistent justifications of her conduct). The three-way situation she sets up with Russell, which will lead to a prolonged flirtation and an act of adultery, has the added tension of an Anglo-American drama in which the American is the alien party. In short, a power game was in play, which would persist throughout the marriage. Both husband and wife were given to disillusion – this much, they had in common – and locked together on this shaky basis, they groped toward a measure of sympathy for each other. Marriage in the Eliot family was irrevocable. There was no precedent for divorce.

Yet the line, "By this, and this only, we have existed" (405), which follows "[t]he awful daring" (403), should give us pause. Eliot himself existed as more than lover or husband or even as aspiring poet; his life both before and after his surrender to marriage suggests a desire for surrender to what *The Waste Land* calls "controlling hands" (422).

The earliest source for words voiced in the poem are Sanskrit instructions in a book that Eliot acquired ten years before *The Waste Land* was published. In 1912, when Eliot attended J. R. Lanman's classes in Indic philosophy at Harvard, his teacher gave him a copy of *The Twenty-Eight Upanishads*, and tipped in by Lanman were words of wisdom, "*da datta, dāmyata, dayadhvam.*"[9] These remained lodged in Eliot's memory until he wrote them down in December 1921 as the finale to *The Waste Land*, part V, "the only part that justifies the whole, at all," as Eliot told Bertrand Russell.[10]

The Sanskrit instructions, resonating in thunder, are thrillingly unfamiliar: give, sympathise, control. (Control, "*Damyata*," comes last in the poem.) None of these words means what the translation appears to suggest. Eliot's gloss on "give" is not in the first place moral. There is no sense of charity; more the awful daring of surrender. " Sympathise," again is not exactly moral; rather an openness to "aetherial rumours" (415); and "control" means to beat "obedient / To controlling hands" (421–2). In Eliot's gloss it involves a more complete and momentous surrender, something like conversion. It makes the message of the thunder a divine call, as momentous in its way as the commandments delivered to the Israelites, who had turned their backs on civilization, Egypt, to wander in the wilderness of Sinai.

A desire to beat obedient to divine control is not what we commonly understand by "desire;" and is not, in fact opposed to, sexual desire in the base, exploitative practice exhibited by the poem. We might even say that sexual desire, as showcased in the poem, is limited to lust, a contaminating kind of lust, if we recall that in one of Eliot's drafts he noted the scurf in the clerk's hair and his pause to urinate and spit on his way downstairs. Where the poem is taking us, once we are suitably appalled by the flesh, is into the mountains, along the route of some forgotten pilgrimage, past a broken chapel, toward a sign.[11] Religious or not, we are moved toward some intimation of desire as spiritual thirst – thirst for something we do not know, which lies outside the poem, lost in dead-end worldly narratives throughout the ages, but alive to Eliot as a student raising overwhelming questions in his Harvard classes.

In the course of Eliot's philosophical studies, on October 20, 1912, he heard a lecture about the ancient Greek philosopher, Heraclitus, who (Eliot notes) disowned the city for a life of contemplation in the hills. Much of Eliot's reading during his last years at Harvard confirms his exploration of extreme states of being on the outposts of existence, courting death. This is the biblical landscape of spiritual desire and trial. The earliest fragments of what would become *The Waste Land* take place at these outposts: "I am the Resurrection," "So through the evening" (the earliest version of the climactic part V), and a failed-martyr poem, "The Death of St. Narcissus," which Eliot completed during his stay in Gordon Square during that Oxford vacation of 1914–15.[12]

Like the Desert Fathers of the fourth century, Narcissus goes into a desert to pray and commune with himself; only, his motives are impure. He has a masochistic view to martyrdom. And he is a solitary who cannot bear the crowd, the press of thighs and knees. This looks forward to a comment Eliot made to Lytton Strachey in 1919 two years into his post at Lloyd's Bank in the City: "I am sojourning among the termites."[13] This, in turn, looks forward to one of the opening scenes of *The Waste Land*, caught on camera in a book of *London Views*, which Eliot owned: the crowd flowing to work over London Bridge, "so many,/ I had not thought death had undone so many" (62–3). The workaday crowd on London Bridge, near Lloyd's Bank, turns out to be a scene from Dante's *Inferno*. This is one central strategy: to transform the documentary into the surreal. What he makes of the scene goes back, once again, to 1911–12, for at that time Eliot carried a copy of Dante in his pocket and learned passages by heart on long train journeys between St. Louis and Massachusetts.

Repeatedly in his poetry, Eliot also recalls the sea as he knew it at Cape Ann, Massachusetts. In 1896 his father had built a house at Eastern Point, beyond the fishing town of Gloucester. In the harbor were the tall masts of what was an all-sail fishing fleet; and fishermen, lounging at the corner of Main Street and Duncan Street, told yarns of storms and shipwrecks on the half-hidden rocks offshore. Working in winter gales, the deep-sea fishermen put out from their schooner in tiny dories which often capsized or were lost in fog or snow. As a boy Eliot took in casual acts of heroism, and they are the source for the original part IV in *The Waste Land* manuscript: a long narrative of a fishing expedition that takes men to the edge of mortality, ending with a sailor washed clean and refashioned by the ocean.[14] Not far from where Eliot worked in the City, he encountered the "fishmen" who "lounge at noon" (263) at the Billingsgate fish market in Lower Thames Street. Eliot's enduring memory of the Gloucester fishermen make them precursors to a rare scene in the grim London of *The Waste Land*. For a moment, the fishmen lift the spirit, as does the "Inexplicable splendour of Ionian white and gold" (265) of the high Anglo-Catholic church, St. Magnus the Martyr, on the same street.

In Cambridge, Massachusetts, Eliot frequented the home of his mother's widowed sister, Mrs. Holmes Hinkley, at 1 Berkeley Place. He felt especially at home with his cousin, Eleanor Hinkley, a graduate of Radcliffe College, who enrolled in a playwriting course. Eliot, sharing her taste for drama, delighted in offering her absurd scenarios. Here, at Eleanor's home in about 1912, Eliot met her friend, Emily Hale, another young woman serious about drama. Emily had the gifts to be an actress: a presence, a resonant voice, and an ear for language. She also had beauty: wavy dark brown hair that shone when the light fell on it; a lovely curve to her cheek; and a slim, upright figure. Her manners combined the decorum of old Boston with humor and empathy.

She and Eliot performed together on February 17, 1913 in a comic scene from Jane Austen's *Emma*, dramatized by Eleanor. Eliot, who tended to worry over his health, was cast as the wrapped-up hypochondriac Mr. Woodhouse, and Emily Hale played the vulgar snob, Mrs. Elton, as elegant as pearls could make her, who continually brings talk around to the smartness of her sister's barouche-landau. The scene was part of a Stunt Show,[15] in aid of charity, with an audience of family and friends. Eliot and Emily Hale performed in front of the fireplace in the parlor in the Hinkley home.

Her aplomb as an actress had about it an air of courage which, given her history, was touching. She was born in 1891, three years after Eliot. When her infant brother died, her mother became a permanent mental invalid, and Emily was brought up by her mother's sister, Aunt Edith, and her husband, Uncle John, on Beacon Hill among the leading families of Boston. Uncle John was the Reverend John Carroll Perkins, a pillar of Boston Unitarianism (as were several of Eliot's relatives). Uncle John and Aunt Edith did not approve of the stage for a lady, so Emily, who was devoted to them, had to content herself with amateur performances. Her uncle did not send Emily to college, a handicap to her future career as a speech and drama teacher and director of plays in various schools and colleges from Scripps in California to Smith in Northampton, Massachusetts. It is testimony to how terrific she was at her job that she managed wherever she went to excite schoolgirls and students about drama.

Eliot fell in love with Emily between 1912 and leaving Boston in mid-1914 for his year's traveling fellowship; and though, at the close of that year, he chose to remain in England and cast his lot with Vivienne, he never forgot Emily Hale. He would draw repeatedly on her memory not only in *The Waste Land* but also in his plays and in *Burnt Norton* ("Footfalls echo in the memory"), the first of his *Four Quartets*. In the thirties Eliot sought her advice about his most autobiographical play, *The Family Reunion*, in which the relations of Harry and Mary are derived from Eliot's renewed tie to Emily Hale after he finally left Vivienne.

At the start of their tie, Eliot wrote a poem about a girl of memorable loveliness and pathos, weeping when her lover leaves. What's curious about "La Figlia che Piange" is the date: 1912.[16] It means that Eliot composed this scene immediately on meeting Emily, and two years before he left America. It's prophetic that in this poem love does not stand a chance. The lover and a girl with her arms full of flowers part with artistic grace, her body posed and directed for maximum effect:

Stand on the highest pavement of the stair –
Lean on a garden urn –
Weave, weave the sunlight in your hair –
Clasp your flowers to you with a pained surprise –
Fling them to the ground and turn
With a fugitive resentment in your eyes:
But weave, weave the sunlight in your hair. ("La Figlia Che Piange" 1–7)

The poet does wonder "how they should have been together!" (21) but prefers his fantasy of the beautifully controlled, unmessy parting – "a gesture and a pose" (22) (– which he may enshrine forever in his memory and his art. The lover loses the flesh and blood; the poet yet possesses her. There is more than a hint of triumph amid his regret, like Henry James lamenting Minny Temple's death. (Minny would be "a pure and eloquent vision" locked, incorruptibly, in the crystal walls of the past.)[17] Nine years later Eliot worked a scene like this into *The Waste Land* and, from that distance in mood and time, a regretful voice remembers "when we came back, late, from the hyacinth garden, / Your arms full, and your hair wet" (37–8). This might-have-been has no place in the waste of the present, where there is no longer a fertile love with the power to transform him: "Those are pearls that were his eyes" (48).

We know as yet too little, but my guess is that an ambiguous Jamesian situation lies behind this momentary escape through memory from a life-less existence. Eliot tells posterity (in a late memoir reported briefly by his second wife) that, before he left America, he offered Emily a declaration of love, but (so far) we are not told that he proposed marriage, and if he did not, she had to be cautious. He was leaving to go abroad; if he did not commit himself in so many words, she was not obliged to commit herself to waiting for him. An elderly Eliot presents a forlorn image of a rejected lover when he says that Emily showed no sign whatever of reciprocating his feel-ings, but it is likely that the situation between them was more complex. For one thing, the misogyny in Eliot's obscene Bolo and Columbo verses, which he began circulating as an undergraduate and was still tossing off in 1914, works up a counter to lovelorn reverence. The traditional polarization of the female into innocent "figlia" versus the "whore" of the Bolo verses puts living women at a distance, to dwell instead on the grotesque spectacle of a penis so mighty it can rip up a whore "from my cunt to my navel."[18] This revel in sexual violence, carried by bouncing rhymes, is varied by the antics of King Bolo and his Big Black Kween whose bum is a big as a soup tureen.

On the one hand, there was the Eliot whom Emily Hale would recognize as "a man of extremes."[19] On the other hand, there was his home-loving aspect, which Eliot's second wife, Valerie, saw as definitive. Undoubtedly, Eliot had this domestic side, in play later with Janet Adam Smith, who described the way he fitted into her family life, and with self-effacing Mrs. Tandy, whom he called affectionately, "Pollytandy," a deserted wife, who knitted him a Fair Isle pullover, bought him scarlet slippers, and sent him fresh produce from the country, with eggs tucked in moss, at Easter. During the eight years of his second marriage, from 1957 until the end, he lived entirely in his domestic character with a wife who would protect him for a generation after his death.

Home was all the more precious after what home had been during the "most awful nightmare" of his first marriage.[20] That nightmare of an incompatible couple locked together is an obvious source for the disaffected couple in the second part of *The Waste Land*. Pound thought this scene too close to life: he scrawled "photo" on the typescript next to the wife's stinging challenge, "Are you alive, or not?"[21] Vivienne thought their non-dialogue "WONDERFUL."[22] The couple have irreconcilable narratives in their heads. The questioning, nervous wife is playing a scene from a marriage: legal union should be leading to empathy. She hopes for communication; the husband shuts her out. "'Do you remember / Nothing?'" (122–3), she prods. "I remember / The hyacinth garden" is his silent, inexorable reply in a passage Eliot cut.[23]

The memory the husband preserves is not of Emily Hale as she was, a comic actress performing as Mrs. Elton, nor of the Emily whom Eliot enquired after in polite tones when he wrote to his cousin, Eleanor Hinkley, and to whom he sent "a nice letter" in the summer of 1919.[24] She was not perhaps even the Emily to whom Eliot had sent a sheaf of pink or red roses (through Aiken) late in 1914 (in honor of her Saturday night performance for the Cambridge Dramatic Society), just three months before he met Vivienne. By the time Eliot conceived the memory of the "hyacinth girl" in 1921, Emily the person was stilled as an image of purity, elevated above the dross of daily contacts. This scene, "mixing / Memory and desire" (2–3), sets up a defiant claim to intact, unadulterated desire. Emily Hale, sealed off in memory, has yet a role to play, not necessarily in the flesh but crucially in a creative future[25] in which love must pass beyond its object, "Looking into the heart of light, the silence" (41).

While Vivienne brought a history of illness into the marriage, Eliot brought a revulsion for the body (fueled by fantasies of dirty frenzy) evident in his Bolo verses. During the period of *The Waste Land's* gestation, he was prepared to publish these verses, but Wyndham Lewis, to whom they were offered for his avant-garde magazine, *Blast*, declined to print words "Ending in –Uck, -Unt and -Ugger."[26]

At first, when I came upon the Bolo verses, I assumed these to be a juvenile aberration. The recently published third volume of *Letters* (covering the period of Eliot's conversion to the Anglican faith in June 1927) presents a challenge. For the obscene verse that Eliot continued to write and disseminate as late as the age of forty-four[27] is not in his own post-conversion view an aberration. In an exchange with fellow publisher Geoffrey Faber, in August 1927, he commends obscenity, in the manner of Swift, as an eye for evil.[28]

Here is an elevated justification, and I have tried to accept it.[29] All the same, hesitation has lingered. For one thing, an eye for evil is dangerously godlike, a danger acknowledged by Eliot's Puritan forebear, Andrew Eliott, who condemned innocents to death in the Salem witch trials. In 1692 Andrew Eliott confessed that he and his co-jurors had been unable to withstand the delusions of the powers of darkness. What do we make of his descendant when his darkest voice comes forward to condemn "Those who suffer the ecstasy of the animals, meaning / Death"?[30] Can Eliot be something of a throwback to the punitive temper of those old New England Puritans, and as such foreign, after all, to the mild-mannered Anglicans, whose faith he adopted?

Hesitation lingers also because the pervasive history of violence against women makes it impossible to be amused by the incitement to sexual violence that accompanies Eliot's obscenity. This violence is not imaginative. It is as banal as Eliot's stabs at anti-Semitism – as banal as evil. Joseph Conrad observed the banality of evil at the heart of *Heart of Darkness*. For Eliot, this 1899 novel confirmed his spectatorial horror as he moved about London, eyeing the substratum of baseness in human nature and piecing together his own "sepulchral city," in the run-up to *The Waste Land*. His alignment of the two works comes in his original epigraph from *Heart of Darkness*, "The horror! The horror!"[31]

To inspect baseness so intently is to shake the barriers of protective sanity. Conrad's narrator, walking about the sepulchral city,[32] has to refrain from laughing in faces full of stupid importance and admits his closeness to breakdown: "I daresay I was not very well at that time."[33] Eliot, as we know, had a breakdown during the last three months of 1921 and completed *The Waste Land* at the sanatorium of Dr. Vittoz in Lausanne. His capacity to be disturbed, like much else in the poem, went back a long way. From 1911, when Eliot was in Paris, through 1912, he was writing what I think of as vigil poems: his speaker lies awake at night tormented by a dark state of mind, questioning the nature of existence.

This crisis of an unquiet soul craving certainty was succeeded by a condition of continuous crisis that Eliot took upon himself in his union with Vivienne. For all the stress of Vivienne's persistent ills and struggles that went on in an overmedicated fog, she supplied Eliot with daily evidence of depletion not unlike his own. As an Englishwoman, Vivienne validated what her transplanted husband perceived: the emptiness of urban routines. Living so close to psychic collapse, she was as sensitive as her husband to the artifice of meaningless control in conforming to so-called civilization. She accompanied Eliot when they walked suburban streets by night, sensing the horror of lives behind decorous curtains. Both, in fact, were susceptible to the surreal. Both were tuned to a high-strung pitch, the frenzy of Eliot's Bolo fantasies a match for Vivienne's frenzy when she threw her nightdress out of a window into Trafalgar Square. "As to Tom's mind, I am his mind," she claimed.[34] Had Eliot's life followed the narrative laid out for him – had he returned to Harvard and become a professor of philosophy and married the well-conducted Emily Hale (who came to see him as the love of her life) – *The Waste Land* as we know it could not have been.

"Worry," as Eliot called this state in confidence to Sydney Waterlow[35] went on from year to year as he accumulated the ragbag of fragments toward a long poem. During his treatment in Lausanne, he found some degree of calm. He was freed there from all marital and work obligations, and he found it relieving to be among other foreigners. In London he had masked his strangeness with an English façade: the office uniform of dark suit, stiff collar, bowler hat, and rolled umbrella. Aiken, visiting after the war, noticed how Eliot had Anglicized himself to a degree that nothing of the American appeared to remain. In turn, Eliot's brother, explaining the breakdown to their mother on December 12, 1921, deduced two causes: Vivienne and expatriation.[36]

Henry reports how impossible it was for his brother "to do creative work (other than the critical) at home." After his day at the bank Eliot came home to a wife's "demand[]" for "attention." Henry puts the entire blame on Vivienne, since he is skeptical about her ills and indifferent to the effect on her of a loveless marriage. As Henry puts it in this letter of December 12, Vivienne "is easily offended if she does not get [attention] well buttered with graciousness and sympathy." In Henry's opinion, his brother would be cured if he could have a little time to himself "to gratify his desire to do creative writing" (Ibid.). This desire was brilliantly fulfilled in the solitude of the Swiss pension in December 1921, as Eliot wrote part V of *The Waste Land*, in a sustained creative burst with hardly a word changed, at the very time of Henry's diagnosis. The second problem was stickier.

"The strain of going out among people who after all are foreigners to him, and, I believe, always must be to an American – even Henry James never became a complete Englishman – has, I think, been to him pretty heavy" (Ibid.). He recalls a despairing confidence from his brother in 1919, breaking through the stiff, conservative mask: how hard Eliot finds it "to live with a foreign nation ... one is always coming up against differences of feeling that make one feel humiliated and lonely. One remains always a foreigner."[37] His caution made him fear to be himself – he might reveal the throbbing tom-tom of a savage. So he disguised himself with protective resemblances. "It is like being always on dress parade – one can never relax. It is a great strain. And society is in a way much *harder, not* gentler. People are more aware of you, more critical, and they have no pity for one's mistakes.... They are always intriguing and caballing; one must be very alert. They are sensitive, and easily become enemies" (Ibid.).

Eliot's friend, Mary Hutchinson, who read *The Waste Land* soon after its completion, said the poem was "Tom's autobiography."[38] Eliot appears to endorse this subjective view of the poem when he claimed that, to him, it was a "personal ... grouse against life."[39]

These statements deprecate the commoner view of the poem as an impersonal social document accumulating evidence against civilization through all the ages: the stagnation of citizens locked into deadening routines of work and coupling. Eliot does define deadness in part by scenes like the crowd flowing to work on the dead sound of the stroke of nine and by the apathy of abused women. Many of his contemporary readers identified with what they took to be modish, postwar disillusion. Eliot resisted this reading, not, I think, because it is invalid, but because these readers missed the fact that the poem also defines deadness by what is *not* dead: the hyacinth girl, the fishmen, Magnus Martyr, the purity of children's voices, a damp gust bringing rain, the message of the thunder and following it, the question or possibility of putting lands in order.

These are hints and guesses of something that is *not* waste and, as such, is anti-wasteland. What I am suggesting is that, in part, *The Waste Land* is defined by a visionary alternative we cannot quite grasp before it fades and eludes us. So, to sink into a waste is to experience this loss of what Eliot terms "reality" and to find ourselves repeatedly trapped in an "Unreal City" (60). Reality, at this point in Eliot's work, remains undefined, implied by its absence. Some fifteen years later, he will find "reality" – after leaving Vivienne in 1933 – in the rose garden of the English country house, Burnt Norton, which he will visit in 1934 in the company of Emily Hale. This visit will evoke a recurrence of the visionary moment associated with the hyacinth girl, "Looking into the heart of light" (41).

In *The Waste Land*, back in 1921, what follows that radiant memory is a collapse into hopelessness, a line in German from the opera, *Tristan und Isolde*, reporting a vacant horizon: no love is coming across the sea. To lose what is anti-wasteland is the very condition of being in the waste. The mass of its inhabitants – the workers crossing London Bridge, the typist and the clerk, the yapping Cockneys in the pub – are too oblivious of their condition to suffer the realization that the poem grants those who enter its ominous silences, marking its repeated loss of vision.

This visionary alternative, I want to suggest, had an older, deeper, and more lasting source in Eliot's biography than what he witnessed in the streets of his adoptive city. That unforgettable alternative continued to reside in the Indian scriptures, in the memory of Emily Hale transformed as hyacinth girl, and going further back in Eliot's memory, to the Gloucester fishermen who lived daily on the edge of mortality.

In other words, the London of *The Waste Land*, from a biographical angle, is less a documentary scene than a projection from an inward deadness, an awareness of which is sharpened by live memories, live desire. Evanescent though they are, memories provide a counterpoise to dead souls and are therefore vital, in every sense, to the poem. A thirst for revelation, which in the end does come, points beyond a poem that has no full stop at the end. Meanwhile, the searcher remains at some interface, jolting ever faster between his "ruins" and an elusive peace, which he can apprehend but not hold.

Is *The Waste Land* in any sense a unified poem? Though the fragmented scenes appear to "[play] with the vagaries of recollection,"[40] the title lays down a comprehensive view. To contrast the multiplicity of London in Virginia Woolf's *Mrs. Dalloway*, the realistic London of a native, is to see more clearly the extraordinary single-mindedness of Eliot's London, the Unreal City a stranger or foreigner might observe.

In this sense the poem is unified by the experience of the poet: a student's solitary search on the outposts of consciousness epitomized by the rousing DA in the Indian scriptures; and the awakening to love for a woman, a love immediately frozen into an icon of memory associated with flowers. This constructed memory is, like DA, posed at a distance: at once in the past and in the wings as an alternative narrative. Last, chronologically, is the poet's transplanted and masked life, locked to a wild wife in an alien metropolis.

This London with its "horns and motors," its creeping rat, sordid sex, and the local pub on the border of Paddington, where Eliot would watch people coming out at closing time (near to the Eliots' cage in Crawford Mansions), came to dominate the poem Pound edited, but the documentary scenes of parts I–III were, biographically, the final overlay. Madame Sosostris, the "clairvoyante" with her tarot cards in part I seems to offer an organizing idea of the dramatis personae in the poem, but biographically this was trivial.

Many years later, in the 1950s, when Eliot's friend, Mary Trevelyan, took him for reminiscent drives around those areas of London on which he had drawn in *The Waste Land*, he mentioned a single visit to a fortune-teller when he was putting the poem together in 1921. He went to dine in Hampstead, he said, or it may have been Primrose Hill, with an unnamed woman he had met at the poetry circle of the Lyceum Club. She had shown him her tarot pack, the only time he had seen one.[41] In the last century there was too much attention to the tarot pack, as to various other dead-end trails, which Eliot laid for busy scholars in some allusions and notes. As Virginia Woolf observes in "The Art of Biography," our challenge is to distinguish the dead fact from "the fact that suggests and engenders."[42]

The most suggestive of the live facts in the biographical background to *The Waste Land* is the priority, both emotionally and chronologically, of Eliot's desire for what was *not* a wasteland. Then, too, the facts of Eliot's expatriate life and his breakdown in 1921 light up a state of being threatened by collapse, externalized in the surreal spectacle of "London bridge is falling down falling down falling down" (426). Eliot appropriated Bertrand Russell's hallucination, provoked by the philosopher's horror at the sight of troop trains of the doomed departing from Waterloo for the trenches. The image spoke to the poet's own state of collapse. I think it had less to do with the Great War, and more with a private situation: a proper Bostonian displaced and shaken by his wife's fling with Russell, repelled by what he calls, during his breakdown, "neurotic carnality,"[43] and propped up (how effectively remains to be seen) by intimations of "Shantih."

NOTES

1 Vera Brittain went up to Somerville College in 1914.
2 T. S. Eliot to Eleanor Hinkley, October 14, 1914, in *The Letters of T. S. Eliot: Volume 1: 1898–1922*, ed. Valerie Eliot and Hugh Haughton, rev. ed. (New Haven, CT: Yale University Press, 2011), 70.
3 Eliot to Conrad Aiken, December 31, 1914, *Letters*, 1, 82.
4 Henry Ware Eliot to Thomas Lamb Eliot, March 7, 1914, *Letters*, 1, 41.
5 Eliot, *The Waste Land: A Facsimile and Transcript of the Original Drafts Including the Annotations of Ezra Pound*, ed. Valerie Eliot (New York: Harcourt, 1971), 45, line 143.
6 In his *Journals 1982–1986* (London: Random House, 1997), Anthony Powell imagines what his mother might have said on meeting Vivienne, 230.
7 Vivienne Eliot to Henry Eliot, October 11, 1916, *Letters*, 1, 172.
8 Russell taught philosophy at Harvard in the spring semester of 1914.
9 The source is an editorial note to *Letters*, 1, 117, where we are told that Eliot studied Sanskrit with C. R. Lanman in 1911–13. "On 6 May 1912, Lanman gave TSE a Sanskrit edition of *The Twenty-Eight Upanishads* (Bombay, 1906), now at King's." Lanman's "hand-written key" includes "'Brhadāranyaka, 220 (v. 1, 2, 3), Da-da-da = *dāmyata datta dayadhvam*.'"
10 Eliot to Bertrand Russell, October 15, 1923, *Letters*, 2, 257.

11 Prefigured by the cry in "Gerontion" (1919): "'We would see a sign!'" (17). What's wanted are "Signs taken for wonders" (17).

12 Eliot refers to this poem in a letter to his new, influential mentor, Ezra Pound, on February 2, 1915, in *Letters, 1*, 94.

13 Eliot to Lytton Strachey, June 1, 1919, *Letters, 1*, 357.

14 See the drafts of "Death by Water" in *The Waste Land: A Facsimile*. See also Eliot's preface to James B. Connolly's *Fishermen of the Banks* (London: Faber and Faber, 1928), a favorite book of Eliot's as a child, originally called *Out of Gloucester* (Freeport, New York: Books for Libraries Press, 1902).

15 Program in the Eliot Collection, Houghton Library, Harvard University.

16 The date is provided in a letter from Eliot to Evdo Mason, February 21, 1936. The Humanities Research Center, The University of Texas at Austin.

17 Lyndall Gordon, *Henry James: His Women and His Art*, rev. ed. (London: Virago, 2012), 134.

18 Eliot, "Fragments: 25," Appendix A, *Inventions of the March Hare: Poems 1909–1917* (London: Faber and Faber, 1996), 314.

19 Weekly book talk in the Toll Hall browsing room at Scripps College, where Emily Hale taught speech and drama. Reported in the magazine *Scripture*, December 12, 1932. Scripps College Archives. Eliot was at that point due to visit her.

20 Eliot to Henry Eliot, September 6, 1916, *Letters 1*, 166.

21 *The Waste Land: A Facsimile*, 13, line 51.

22 Ibid., written across the margin, p. 11.

23 *The Waste Land: A Facsimile*, 12, lines 49–50.

24 Eliot to Eleanor Hinkley, June 17, 1919, *Letters 1*, 365.

25 In *Modernism, Memory and Desire: T. S. Eliot and Virginia Woolf* (Cambridge: Cambridge University Press, 2008, 2011), Gabrielle McIntire points out how, for the moderns, memory "casts its gaze to what is sealed off ... while desire pushes to the future for its realization" (1).

26 Wyndham Lewis to Ezra Pound (before July 1915), in Appendix A, *Inventions of the March Hare*, 305.

27 Gabrielle McIntire, in *Modernism, Memory and Desire*, cites evidence that Eliot sent Aiken one of these verses in 1964, a month before his death (15). I agree with McIntire's conviction that the verses are not "at odds" with Eliot's major work.

28 *Letters, 3*, August 25?, 1927 (660), and Geoffrey Faber's reply on August 27, 1927: "Your remark about Swift's obscenity interests me greatly.... To be obscene in Swift's manner is to separate the lees & the wine – is it not?" (662).

29 Lyndall Gordon, *The Imperfect Life of T. S. Eliot*, rev. ed. (New York: Norton, 2015), 2.

30 "Marina" *Collected Poems: 1909–1962* (1930), 12–13.

31 See also Eliot's use of "horror" amounting, he said, to a mystical experience in his essay, "Cyril Tourneur" (1930) *Selected Essays: 1917–1932* (1932; New York: Harcourt, 1960), 166.

32 The sepulchral city is Brussels.

33 *Youth, Heart of Darkness and The End of the Tether: Three Stories* (London: J. M. Dent, 1902, 1960), 152.

34 Diaries, Bodleian Library.
35 Eliot to Sydney Waterlow, *Letters, 1*, December 19, 1921, 617.
36 Henry Eliot to his mother, December 12, 1921, *Letters, 1*, 613.
37 Eliot to Henry Eliot, July 2, 1919, *Letters, 1*, 370.
38 *The Diary of Virginia Woolf, Volume Two, 1920–1924*, ed. Anne Olivier Bell (London: Hogarth, 1978), June 11, 1922, 178.
39 Quoted by Theodore Spencer in a lecture at Harvard and noted by Henry Ware Eliot. Epigraph to *The Waste Land: A Facsimile*.
40 McIntire, *Modernism, Memory and Desire*, 5.
41 Eliot in conversation with Mary Trevelyan (March 1955). Trevelyan's unpublished memoir, "The Pope of Russell Square."
42 Virginia Woolf, "The Art of Biography," *The Death of the Moth and Other Essays* (1940; London: Hogarth Press, 1942), repr. *The Essays of Virginia Woolf*, ed. Stuart Clarke, vol. VI (London: Hogarth Press, 2011), 187.
43 Eliot to Richard Aldington, November 17, 1921, from London before leaving for the sanatorium. *Letters 1*, 606.

4

BARRY SPURR

Religions East and West in
The Waste Land

I

At the heart of the process of attaining religious understanding, in all belief systems, is the idea of the journey of faith. Even in those religions that prioritize the conversion experience – which occurs for the believer at a specific place and time – this moment of illumination is usually understood as a challenge to pursue the lifelong implications of what was revealed in that singular event. T. S. Eliot's wise men in "Journey of the Magi," having traveled backward through time and reached their destination at Bethlehem, realize – as one of them meditates, long afterward – what had been revealed to them there, after a protracted and difficult journey, marked the start of another arduous process: of dying to worldliness. "I should be glad of another death" (43), one of them muses, appropriately open-endedly as the poem closes.[1] During the years when Eliot's Christianity was becoming publicly known he deprecated any notion that embracing belief amounted to a comfortable end rather than a daunting beginning: "it [is] rather trying to be supposed to have settled oneself in an easy chair, when one has just begun a long journey afoot," he wrote in a letter to Paul Elmer More in 1929.[2]

The concept – philosophical as well as religious – of the quest for the fullness of understanding, in the various ways that it might be configured, and of the formidable obstacles confronting the undertaking, particularly in an increasingly secularized, anthropocentric world, is a theme found in Eliot's earliest and latest poetry. The recurring presence of a quest narrative serves, thereby, as a warning against that common tendency in readings of his poems to make a too-sharp division between works (including *The Waste Land*) written before his embrace of formal Christianity in 1927, when he was baptized and confirmed, and afterward. Eliot himself repudiated the identification of a breach between his earlier and later lives and his creativity: "what appears to another person to be a change of attitude and even a recantation of former views must often appear to the author himself rather as part of a continuous and more or less consistent development."[3]

From Eliot's earliest poems (and, in his pre-Christian corpus, most notably and extensively in *The Waste Land*), the metaphor of the quest for knowledge – both personal and universal – recurs. Repeatedly, the metaphor is revealed in terms of the dual anxiety to know truth and embody it in human lives – in the individual's life and that of the society or culture – and in the recognition that this fulfillment is at best contingent, maybe unattainable, even a delusion. So the "hollow men," in the poem of that name, journeying to Hell, look up longingly to the "perpetual star / Multifoliate rose / Of death's twilight kingdom" (63–5). This Dantean vision of the Virgin, potentially redemptive, is "The hope only / Of empty men" (66–7). That the aspiration is expressed is noteworthy, but it is a hopeless hope, given their infernal trajectory.

Earlier in Eliot's corpus, we find the quest motif introduced in J. Alfred Prufrock's monologue in the opening invitation, "Let us go" (1). Nothing less than the search for the "overwhelming question" (10) of the meaning of human existence impels Prufrock, even if, in his self-satire, he recognizes the unlikelihood of his ability to roll the universe to this point of ultimate interrogation. The poem's imperative opening, promising a journey to enlightenment – possibly through the experience of consummated romantic love (as the poem's title seems to anticipate, until we recognize its irony) – is soon compromised by a series of disappointments, ending in desolation. The length of the monologue is one of the ways in which Eliot represents, poetically, the recurring sense in his work of the protracted struggle to attain meaning and to give poetic expression to it. *The Waste Land* and *Four Quartets* are the best examples of this undertaking in his corpus, as the poet draws together varieties of lived experience with the commitment to articulate this in a language which, in the modernist way, is being constantly, inventively remade to communicate such knowledge to the poet's contemporary audience.

Eliot's search for a spiritual explanation of the "overwhelming question[s]" of human existence developed from his study of Western and Eastern philosophy as a student at Harvard; through the period of his reviewing works for learned journals, and his editing of the *Criterion* – where books on philosophy and religion were regularly noticed – to his acceptance of orthodox Christianity in 1927. Over this period of some twenty years we discern Eliot's process of elimination of various belief systems and, indeed, of disbelief (although he always valued robust skepticism). The student Eliot had immersed himself in the study of Eastern philosophy – for which Harvard was renowned in the early twentieth century – when he returned there, after a year in Paris (1910–11). He took the course in Sanskrit and read the *Bhagavad Gita*. He studied the sacred books of Buddhism and was given, by his instructor, Charles Rockwell Lanman, the "Fable of the Thunder," containing the "DA … DA … DA" passages that Eliot would use in the final section of *The Waste Land*. Some traces of these studies are to be found as late as *Four Quartets* (which Eliot completed during the Second World War). But he was never a Buddhist nor the follower of any Eastern philosophy or religion. Manju Jain puts the matter succinctly when, in referring to Eliot's study of Eastern belief systems, she observes that it "gave him an alternative world view but it did not provide him with a mainstay in his search for a defining belief."[4] Indeed, Eliot's allusions in his poetry to Eastern philosophy and religion are striking because of their rarity, providing different perspectives, or a brief widening of vision, when they do appear, in relation to the Western philosophical, spiritual and religious sources and ideas that, increasingly, from the time of *The Waste Land*, dominate Eliot's poetry, his thought and his life.

II

The very title of *The Waste Land* introduces a major informing myth of the poem – that of the impotent Fisher King of fertility stories, whose land is under a curse and has been laid waste. Linking this to the Grail legend – the Christian story of the cup containing the blood of Christ that had been brought to Glastonbury in England by Joseph of Arimathea – Eliot establishes, as central to the poem's meaning and structure, the notion of journeying for enlightenment and renewal, as signified by the knight's search for this holy relic. Attainment of the Grail will release the land and the people from the curse they are enduring. So the concept and motif of journeying and questing for a religious understanding of human life, with the possibility of a redemptive outcome, is at the heart of *The Waste Land*, in both its themes and techniques, and the ways in which they evolve. This is the reason why, among other elements of its complex character, it is a profoundly religious poem.

From this point of view, the poem's epigraph is unpromising, as the Cumaean Sybil replies to the boys' question, "What do you want?" with the despairing, "I want to die." But this leads immediately into the first section, "The Burial of the Dead," the title of which is taken directly from the liturgical order for funerals in the Anglican *Book of Common Prayer*. Eliot, who did not suddenly appropriate Anglicanism five years later at his baptism in 1927, but for many years before had been taking an interest in its theology, its architecture, and its rich tradition of liturgical and homiletic language, was familiar with the Prayer Book, a lively testament of English prose-poetry, in its early modern splendor.[5] Particularly, he knew that its burial service is initiated and insistently punctuated by the Christian theology of the resurrection of the body. So *The Waste Land*, by summoning the recollection of that liturgy – the phrases and cadences of which would have been familiar, also, to many of the poem's original readers – begins in a condition of tension between mortality (emphasized in the work's title and in its epigraph) and eternal life, the fact of death (even a yearning for it) and the possibility of redemption from death. A series of deaths unfolds in this first section – they are, as it were, corpses brought for poetic burial.

The first death that we encounter in *The Waste Land* is the death of nature, mediated through the reversal of the *reverdie* tradition in poetry, wherein springtime (April) is portrayed as the annual period of fertile renewal, but here, startlingly, as "the cruellest month" (1). Then there is the postwar death of Europe, as expressed by Marie (who reflects on the dissolution of her former aristocratic life in this period of the breaking of nations). The following bridge passage to the next kind of mortality introduces the principal metaphor of the poem, a desert landscape, bereft of life. The invocation to the "Son of man" (20) in these lines is directly biblical (the phrase is used in both testaments; in the New Testament it appears more than eighty times to refer to Christ), so the allusion introduces the Savior, although in the negative context of the speaker's knowledge only of "a heap of broken images" (22), and, what is more, of being shown "fear in a handful of dust" (30). This is a biblical reference again: to the dust from which man was created and to which he will return (Genesis 3:19). What is striking, in other words, is the irony of the invocation to the Redeemer in the course of the enumeration of images of dissolution and anxiety, rather than the resurrection hope at the heart of the Christian faith.

This leads to the death of passion and romance, where disengagement and disappointment dominate, whether in reminiscence of Richard Wagner's *Tristan und Isolde* or the Grail legend where the male plant, the hyacinth, has now, perversely, been appropriated by the female speaker, "the hyacinth girl" (introducing the leitmotif of sexual confusion and dysfunction that recurs in the poem). And "The Burial of the Dead" closes with two more deaths: that of prophecy, as embodied in the flawed Madame Sosostris, and that of the metropolis, in which "death had undone so many" (63). In the process, Eliot mentions, in Madame's divination from the Tarot pack, "The Hanged Man" card, which is missing. At once, the memory of the crucified Lord is summoned, but only as the reader notes his absence. As much later in the poem, when the biblical account of the events on the road to Emmaus is recalled, Eliot weaves into the context of the Grail legend the larger story of the Passion, Death, and Resurrection of Jesus. Denial and absence may dominate such allusions, but the references are there, nonetheless, and the absent presence of their origin haunts the poem with the redemptive possibility of renewed life until its very end.

Embedded, too, in the final strophe of "The Burial of the Dead," with its evocation of the mercantile City – at that time the center of world commerce (another potential corpse for burial, within the larger corpse of London itself, and to be focused on in section IV) – is the reference to the church of Saint Mary Woolnoth, on the corner of Lombard Street and King William Street. Predating the Norman Conquest, rebuilt by William the Conqueror, patched up after the Great Fire, the church was reconstructed from 1716 by Christopher Wren's pupil, Nicholas Hawksmoor, who, over the years, built "the most original church in the City,"[6] with an interior of baroque elegance. It has – John Betjeman observes – a sumptuousness "markedly different from the curves and lightness of Wren."[7] In his "Notes on *The Waste Land*," Eliot points out that the "dead sound" of the chime from Saint Mary Woolnoth, on "the final stroke of nine," was "A phenomenon which I have often noticed" (note 68). Seen by Eliot every day when he was working at Lloyds Bank, it was one of the valued City churches, a number of which, having been declared "redundant," were destined for demolition in these years. In 1926, Eliot led a hymn-chanting procession through the streets of the City, in protest at this, and his campaign was successful in preventing the atrocity.

Eliot made clear in 1921, at the very time he was drafting *The Waste Land*, that the essence of his appreciation of the churches was based on personal experience of the sanctuary they offered in the midst of the deadly grind of business (even as he was also drawn by their historical and aesthetic significance):

> They give to the business quarter of London a beauty which its hideous banks and commercial houses have not quite defaced.... The least precious redeems some vulgar street.... The loss of these towers, to meet the eye down a grimy lane, and of these empty naves, to receive the solitary visitor at noon from the dust and tumult of Lombard Street, will be irreparable and unforgotten.[8]

Later, another City church, Magnus Martyr at London Bridge, by Wren himself (under construction from 1671–6), is brought into the poem at a crucial point in its religious development. Eliot noted of the church that "The interior of St. Magnus Martyr is to my mind one of the finest among Wren's interiors" (note 264). His special appreciation here may well have been combined with his recognition of its role as a leading center of the Anglo-Catholic movement in those days (as, indeed, it continues to be).

The "dead sound" of Mary Woolnoth's chime at "nine" (68) combines the time to start work with the customary time of executions in prison and the time of the archetypal execution, of Christ, at the "ninth hour." All churches are witnesses to the Resurrection, so, in tune with both death and redemption from it, which the liturgical title of this first section initially evokes, "The Burial of the Dead" draws to its close. But not without the cynical satire of resurrection to new life in the speaker's call to Stetson, seen among the City throng, in which he asks the murderer whether the corpse he buried in his garden (in the English style) has come into bloom. This whimsically diminishes, somewhat, the recurrent resurrection allusions prior to this, and the section closes with the recognition that the speaker himself belongs to the same life-denying regime as Stetson: "mon semblable" (76).

III

"A Game of Chess" particularizes the death of London in terms of three of its classes of citizens: upper, middle, and working-class Cockney, and includes a powerful suggestion, also, of the death of femaleness, in a sequence of variously configured fallen women. In terms of the quest motif, the elements of class and gender comprehensiveness indicate the thorough-going quality of the speaker's journey through the desiccated urban wasteland, dissecting its diverse denizens and maladies, while seeking redemption from it and them. The brilliant evocation of aristocratic femininity in the opening 110 lines enacts a spectacular fall from grace by beginning in recollection of Enobarbus's description of Cleopatra, with echoes too of Belinda at her toilet in *The Rape of the Lock* (and rape, indeed, emerges as portrayed in the lady's boudoir, "above the antique mantel" (97)). The language declines as the affectations of appearance are stripped away to reveal the sterility and decay beneath, the ornate Shakespearean pastiche declining and dissolving into "'Jug Jug' to dirty ears" (103).

The bridge passage that follows transports us to another interior, instinct with despair – this time in the context of an overheard and over-heated domestic dispute in which the deranged female voice is met with the disengaged responses (not in quotation marks, possibly suggesting the poet himself, with Vivien as the female speaker) of the man. The "closed car" (136) and the chess game indicate a certain level of privilege and refinement, placing this couple in the urban middle class, with the Cockneys to follow. The febrile pair are "waiting for a knock upon the door" (138). This may be death, which would be a release from such hysteria, or, as the phrase summons another biblical text, and one of the most famous of religious paintings based on it – Holman Hunt's "The Light of the World" – Eliot is also subtly sustaining his theme of the possibility of religious redemption:

> Behold, I stand at the door, and knock: if any man hear my voice, and open the door, I will come in to him, and will sup with him, and he with me.
>
> (Revelation 3:20)[9]

As is well known, the famous Pre-Raphaelite painting (no doubt seen by Eliot in one of its two versions in St. Paul's Cathedral in the City) is a deeply ambiguous, ironic work. The Savior indeed stands waiting and knocking outside, but Hunt's door, overgrown with vegetation, appears firmly, long-standingly, permanently closed. Again, the promise of Christian redemption is recalled, even proffered, only to be disappointed.

In the concluding East End pub scene of this section, fertility of a kind is surprisingly registered (for the first time in *The Waste Land*) in Albert's fathering of Lil's children – five, no less – but his is seen to be a callous, love-less sexuality, indifferent to Lil's welfare: she "nearly died" in childbirth with "young George" (160). Through a crude procedure – "the chemist said it would be all right" (161) – she has aborted her latest pregnancy. Once again, life is touched with death, and female lives, congruent with the dominant theme of this section, are spoiled: even when sexual potency can be stirred, its results are not regenerating but life-denying, and the section (which opened with Cleopatra) closes in reminiscence of another Shakespearean heroine, Ophelia, and her deranged song before her suicide. Those who commit suicide, we remember, have committed the most grievous of sins, despair – in Catholic theology, the sin against the Holy Ghost – and were, in earlier times, buried outside consecrated ground, at crossroads. Eliot stimulates us here, at one of the darkest points of the poem, to question again the possibility of salvation in the culmination of a concentrated catalog of assaults upon the human body and soul, which he dramatizes poetically in this section's three scenes of human decay, with a particular female focus.

IV

In the title of the third section, "The Fire Sermon," the poet enlarges the frame of reference of *The Waste Land* beyond its English and Eurocentric perspectives and references to embrace eastern metaphysical philosophy. In doing so, he places the religious concept and form of the sermon at the heart of the poem. Here, it is the Buddha's homily against sin, the fires of lust and envy, to which Eliot alludes. This comes from the *Maha-Vagga*, "a central text of early Buddhism,"[10] equal in importance to Jesus's Sermon on the Mount in Christianity (Eliot indicates in the "Notes"). Buddha's sermon takes up a trope used throughout the Upanishads and the Vedas and in the *Gita*, but one that has a particular importance to the Buddhist tradition – a trope of fire that refers both to the pain of worldly experience and to the process of purification by which that pain can be overcome.[11]

The significance for Eliot, as revealed throughout his poetry, of the process of purification from sin and, especially, the radical purging of fire, explains his attraction to the Buddha's teaching in this sermon, in combination with the poet's more general familiarity with and study of Eastern philosophy that he undertook during his graduate years at Harvard, when he

> read selected portions of the Vedas and Upanishads in the original ... and more in translation, most likely in the famous Sacred Books of the East series edited by Max Muller.[12]

What follows in this section – what "Tiresias *sees*" – is, Eliot tells us emphatically in the "Notes," "the substance" of *The Waste Land* (note 218). And what is portrayed is lust in action in the copulation of the typist and the "young man carbuncular" (231) (his elevated title, with its Miltonic inversion of substantive and Latinate epithet neatly mocking the low occasion he has initiated). This scene takes place within the setting of the death of London, registered again in the representation of the abandonment of the City and the curtailing of the poet's music, "Sweet Thames, run softly till I end my song" (183), with the death rattle of bones for accompaniment, as scavenging rats creep among naked bodies. The physical gruesomeness of the scene is reminiscent of Hieronymus Bosch's hellscape; the particular focus on the loveless lovemaking, at the twilight hour, recalling that sixteenth-century artist's conception of the Inferno, not as a fantastical horror, but realistic in its detailed wickedness. The indifference of "lovely woman" to what has occurred – judged by the speaker as stooping "to folly" (253) and presenting yet another individual female fall from grace – is "automatic" (255), amoral. Although his expression is characteristically detached, Eliot's speaker is nonetheless registering a judgment, which is intensified by the subsequent plaintive lament over London, "O City city" (259) (and note the variation in capitalization, embracing both the mercantile City and the metropolis, the city, at large).

As the waxing and waning of hopelessness and hope persists, we are taken refreshingly out of doors and into the City parish of St. Magnus the Martyr in Lower Thames Street at London Bridge. This great Anglo-Catholic shrine was known as the fishermen's church, the strong smell of fish from the nearby Billingsgate Market (relocated to the Isle of Dogs in 1982) being ameliorated, within, by an equally strong aroma of incense. The fish harvest festival used to be celebrated there. In these few lines, the poet juxtaposes the degradation of the mechanical sexuality that has gone before with a strikingly attractive scene, animated by the sounds of a mandolin and bonhomie from a bar where the "fishermen lounge at noon" (263). What is described is replete with Christian symbolism. Christ, the king of heaven, made of his fishermen-disciples, fishers of men, and, as earlier in the poem as the Son of Man, he emerges here, implicitly, as the alternative Fisher King of the poem. The fish itself, of course, is an ancient Christian symbol. Yet for all these positive intimations, the speaker nonetheless remains separated from the fishermen's musical conviviality (like Prufrock hearing from the street outside the women "Talking of Michelangelo" "In the room" within, 14, 13).

Then, as we enter the church, the colors of the classical columns in Magnus Martyr, Eliot notes, are "white and gold" (265). These are also two of the liturgical colors of Easter, the very feast of the Resurrection and new life. Commentators on *The Waste Land*, too readily appreciating the lavish decoration of the "Ionian" structures in the church, tend to overlook the arresting polysyllabic adjective that introduces and governs that line: "Inexplicable." The speaker is unable to discern the full meaning of this "splendour," even as he recognizes its beauty. And, immediately after, we are plunged into the Thames itself, which is sweating with "oil and tar". The technique of fragmentation, here as throughout the poem, is a powerful method for registering the pilgrim's inability to sustain, from the point of apprehension to comprehension and consummation, any salvific remedies as he moves through the wasted land. Nonetheless, the possibilities for salvation are there, clearly embedded in the poem's discourse. *The Waste Land* is thus not bereft of religious possibility, even hope. An "Inexplicable splendour" is preferable to none at all.

The abrupt stylistic change to a terse lyricism, punctuated by the Rhinemaidens' refrain, leads to abrupt contrasts of subject – the present, industrially polluted river; then the memory of the Elizabethan Thames, gloriously adorned by the golden royal barge of the Virgin Queen, who, in gliding past the tower, is brilliantly melded with the Virgin herself, with her litany of white and gold (recalling Magnus Martyr, too): "House of ivory ... Tower of gold."[13] But then we return rudely to the present, as the succinct lyricism appropriate to virginal proprieties expands to encompass the distinctly unmaidenly Thames women who have raised their knees by Richmond and at Moorgate. The Rhinemaidens' song peters out in a tart "la la" (306) (read brazenly by Eliot in the Caedmon sound recording) as Romantic-Wagnerian and Virginal-Elizabethan conceptions are set in antithesis with the squalor of contemporary casual liaisons, whether in London or at the not-too-distant seaside resort Margate (echoing and binding with Moorgate).

The moral dimension of the religious quest is clearly represented here, and the judgments are damning, whether of the fires of lust of the Buddha's sermon or those recalled by the great patristic moralist, St. Augustine, in his *Confessions* (as quoted by Eliot in his "Notes"):

"to Carthage then I came, where a cauldron of unholy loves sang all about mine ears."

Eliot indicates that

The collocation of these two representatives of eastern and western asceticism, as the culmination of this part of the poem, is not an accident.

(notes 307 and 309)

So great are the sins that they must be burned out in a refining fire. As in John Donne's famous cry for a forge-like battering and purging to "make me new,"[14] here, too, only a violent refinement and transformation will suffice, as figured in Eliot's repeated, stabbingly insistent "burning" with which the section closes, unpunctuated – leaving the participle and the experience unresolved, perhaps in purgatorial process.

V

In the Western, Christian tradition, epitaphs with monitory and often biblical inscriptions are traditionally inscribed on gravestones and memorial tablets. The fourth part of *The Waste Land*, following the violent imagery of the third section, is in the form of an epitaph, with a gentle rhythm and rhyme. This is a welcome respite in the poem at large. But its consoling accents are deceptive. Unlike the model it recalls (of the conventional gravestone's brief biography accompanied by monitory, but usually encouraging sentiments, typically anticipating the resurrection of the body), "Death by Water" strikingly disappoints. Consistent with the earliest section of the poem, it provides an individual corpse as representative of a larger phenomenon: Phlebas, from the great seafaring trading nation of antiquity, represents for us again the dead commercial heart of the "Unreal City." He is now released from the diurnal round of "profit and loss" (314) but a fortnight on from his death at sea (recalling such as Milton's Lycidas, but pointedly *unlike* him, not raised from a watery grave "through the dear might of him that walk'd the waves").[15] The only rising that is experienced here is the ocean's relentless rising and falling. The phrase "rose and fell" (316) is especially telling in *The Waste Land* where the longed-for hope of resurrection to new life goes to the very heart of the meaning of the poem, personally and universally. The myth of a drowning man seeing all of his existence passing before him is glanced at, but the most important reflection is the speaker's noting that Phlebas, having left behind the endless "wheel" of the ship of commerce, has now replaced it, not with the peaceful stillness of eternity but with the similarly unrelenting whirlpool of the deep. The closing lines, epitaph-like, speak to those still remaining with a warning to consider Phlebas, "once handsome and tall" (321) and now consigned to unredemptive oblivion. We note that the lines are addressed to "Gentile or Jew" (319), to all of humanity. Yet the patent absence of consolation in this section, when it is conventionally expected, paradoxically keeps alive, even heightens, the yearning for such a resolution.

VI

The final section of *The Waste Land*, "What the Thunder Said," coming after the epitaph-like fourth section, is a postlude to the laying waste of the West that the previous sections variously detail. Again, Eliot draws on Eastern legends, thereby accentuating the sense of the fragmentation and exhaustion of Occidental civilization to evoke the cultural and spiritual desuetude he is delineating. The Indian story of the Thunder in the sacred book *Brihadaranyaka-Upanishad* (V, 1) gives this concluding section its title:

> Three groups – gods, men, demons – approach the creator Prajapti and each in turn asks him to speak. To each group he answers "DA." Each group interprets this reply differently.... According to the fable, "This is what the divine voice, the Thunder, repeats when he says DA, DA, DA: 'Control yourselves; give alms; be compassionate.'"[16]

Climatically and climactically, Eliot introduces and then details these Eastern commands and the Western failure of response to them. After so many accounts of disappointment and failure in life, personally and in Western civilization at large, these strange imperatives from another world of culture and human story provide a bracing challenge to the wastelanders.

The rhythm and vocabulary of the poetry now are decidedly incantatory – of a haunting, repetitive chanting kind that is common to both Western and Eastern religious ceremony: as in psalmody, for example. The anaphora of "After" in the opening three lines sets this in motion, as well as emphasizing, in that preposition, the pastness of the domain – its "afterward" quality – which we have now entered, as the poem draws to its close. "After" is also linked to the participants, locations and events of Christ's Passion: his betrayal and arrest, the night of prayer in the Garden of Gethsemane and the "agony" of the Crucifixion. The effects of that death in the natural world are recounted in the New Testament, "reverberation" here alluding to the shaking of the earth (Matthew 27:51). Succeeding "After" in these lines is the repetition of "and" – reminiscent of the manner of accumulating narrative in the Authorized Version of the Bible – which in turn modulates to the bald declaration that "He who was living is now dead" (328).

The principal, initial metaphor of the desert landscape (introduced in the title and particularized in the first section) is recovered now, as the poem, like the poetry itself, returns to an elemental condition, stripped bare of the complexities of sections II to IV. Such a retreat to this place where there is only rock and sand and (literally) no water indicates, in literary terms, not just life *in extremis*, but also, in the tradition of retreat to the desert by Christ and the so-called Desert Fathers, the possibility of spiritual renewal through such a stripping away of worldly connections. The insistent, repetitive call for water, in this verse paragraph, is a cry for both the element itself and its symbolic, sacramental function of purification – "the mystical washing away of sin," as the Prayer Book rite of Baptism has it, and which Eliot was to undergo in a few years' time. Evil spirits haunt the desert places, too, representative of Satan's temptation of the Lord in the wilderness (Luke 4:1 ff.), and the lack of water becomes even more acute with "dry sterile thunder" (342) failing to bring the longed-for rain. Under a delusion stirred by heat and thirst, the speaker imagines he hears the water-dripping song of the hermit-thrush (which, Eliot writes, "I have heard in Quebec Province," note 357), and this stirs a memory of the Grail legend, where the advent of the Hermit is a token of spiritual redemption. Onomatopoeically, to make the reference even more haunting, we too hear that water-dripping song, but to no avail. Yet, as so often in the poem, such allusions, however desperate and, as here, delusional, keep alive the antithetical possibility of redemption.

In the context of this faint hope is the next paragraph's recollection of the scriptural, post-crucifixion experience of the disciples of the resurrected Lord on the road to Emmaus (Luke 24:13 ff.). Cleopas and another disciple meet Jesus but do not recognize him, and Eliot extends this nonrecognition to include a failure even to know whether the figure is a "man or a woman" (364). In scripture, the disciples discuss the sad recent events of Jesus' death and the empty tomb, but it is not until they reach Emmaus, at supper, that they recognize him, in the breaking of bread. Significantly, this famous recognition scene, so often portrayed in art, is left out of Eliot's account, with the verse paragraph concluding with a repetition of its opening query and thereby framed by it. So the redemptive consequences of the two sacraments of the Gospel – Baptism and Eucharist – are denied in these two paragraphs of this section, and the persistent theme of death without resurrection, punctuating the poem as a whole, is now even more decisively registered.

Broadening the scope of the poem and recalling its earlier allusions to the dismemberment of Europe after the Great War and the Spenglerian sense of the decline of the West that emerged from that cataclysm, Eliot succinctly surveys nothing less than the rise and fall of civilizations, with reference to the cities on which they were centered, from antiquity to the present (as represented by London). The context is of bewilderment at the pervasive character of this phenomenon – as captured in an incantatory series of questions: "What ... Who ... What" (366–71) – but all are summarized as "Falling towers" (373), the final adjective of the verse paragraph, "Unreal" (376), being the epithet originally associated with London. Here, it serves as the perfect keynote for the next verse paragraph, which is a surreal vision inspired, Eliot noted (B. C. Southam points out), by

> a painting of the school of Hieronymus Bosch ... [with] grotesque and horrifying visions of Hell, its devils, temptations and torments.[17]

Animated again by the biblical incantation on "And" (used repeatedly in the Authorized Version translation to begin sequences of verses), the verse paragraph includes more images of a world turned upside down and reduced to emptiness and exhaustion. That emptiness notably characterizes the chapel, in the following lines, as the frame of reference narrows again to concentrate on the approach to the Chapel Perilous, which is the final stage in the Grail story – perilous because the knight's courage would be tested there by the horrors contained within. But Eliot's version is bereft even of these: it is "empty ... only the wind's home" (388). Harmless, it is also devoid of a challenge over which the questing knight could triumph: "Dry bones can harm no one" (390). But a cockerel is there and his call is heard, heralding morning and signaling to ghosts and spirits that, as darkness is passing, they must too. The cockerel also recalls the Passion story, as Eliot conflates, in this verse paragraph, episodes from his two principal sources, the Bible and the Grail legend. Jesus foretells that his disciple, Peter, will deny knowledge of him when he is under arrest prior to his trial:

> Verily I say unto thee, That this day, *even* in this night, before the cock crow twice, thou shalt deny me thrice.
>
> (Mark 14:30)

Eliot is establishing the concept of three denials, which he will combine with the three commands of the Thunder as the poem draws to its close, succinctly drawing together Western and Eastern spiritual traditions.

Stunningly, at this point of desperation and dryness, rain falls – but not, it maddeningly turns out, in the wasted land: rather, a world away, over the sacred Ganges and the holy mountain Himavant in the Himalayas. And this transition to that other world leads to the three commands of the Thunder, signaled by the section's title, as the monitory voice from the

East is countered by the three failures of the wastelanders to fulfill them (as anticipated in the earlier allusions to Peter's triple denial of Jesus, when the cock crows). To the command to give (*"Datta,"* in Sanskrit), the wastelanders have merely given in to such as lust (as detailed in several preceding episodes in the poem, especially in its third section); to the command to sympathize (*"Dayadhvam"*), the response has been an utter failure of empathy in the prison-like isolation of each individual, reminiscent of the pride and selfishness of Coriolanus in Shakespeare's play of that name. Finally, *"Damyata"* (control) reveals the regretful disappointment of mastery, as figured in imagery from yachting (a favorite pastime of the youthful Eliot). The contingency of the imagined heartfelt response to such adroit control – in a romantic setting, at sea, what is more (making the reflection even more poignant) – touches on a recurring motif in *The Waste Land*: the promise of fulfillment, doomed to disappointment. The absence of punctuation at the end of this last statement of failure leaves it, nonetheless, suspended in an air of irresolution, gesturing, possibly, to a future beyond the poem where such incapacity – failure of control – and the concomitant frustration of those who might have responded to such mastery may be resolved.

The Waste Land closes, Babel-like, in a lunatic confusion of tongues from which emerges, again, the haunting threefold command: "Datta. Dayadhvam. Damyata" (432), precisely matched with the repeated incantatory enunciation of "Shantih" (433), the Sanskrit word that "serves as a formal ending to an Upanishad" (note 433), the poetic dialogs and commentary that follow the Vedas, the ancient Hindu scriptures. Eliot's final note tells us that the Western equivalent to this word is "The Peace which passeth understanding." This recalls not only St. Paul's words to the early Christians (Philippians 4:7) but the liturgical conclusion to several of the rites in the *Book of Common Prayer*. A poem richly informed by religious traditions, Western and Eastern, thus closes appropriately in the incantatory language common to the spirituality of both worlds, even as the mysterious Eastern borrowing here finishes the poem with a challenge, as daunting as it is haunting, to revive the exhausted wells of Western Christianity and, thereby, Western civilization.

NOTES

1   "Journey of the Magi," *The Complete Poems and Plays of T. S. Eliot* (London: Faber and Faber, 1969). All subsequent references to Eliot's poetry are to this edition.

2   Eliot to Paul Elmer More, August 3, 1929, in T. S. Eliot, *The Letters of T. S. Eliot, Volume 4: 1928–1929*, ed. Valerie Eliot and John Haffenden (London: Faber and Faber, 2013), 567.

3   Eliot to Paul Elmer More, March 27, 1936, quoted in Kenneth Asher, *T. S. Eliot and Ideology* (Cambridge: Cambridge University Press, 1995), 9.

4   Manju Jain, *T. S. Eliot and American Philosophy: The Harvard Years* (Cambridge: Cambridge University Press, 1992), 111.

5   For a full account of Eliot's Christian faith and practice and its influence on his work, see my *Anglo-Catholic in Religion: T. S. Eliot and Christianity* (Cambridge: Lutterworth, 2010).

6   [Unnamed author] *London: Everyman Guide* (London: David Campbell, 1993), 149.

7   *The City of London Churches* (Pitkin: London, 1973), 26.

8   "London Letter," *The Dial*, May 1921, 690–1.

9   *The Holy Bible* [Authorized Version, 1611], Oxford: Oxford University Press, n.d. Subsequent references to the Bible are from this edition.

10 Cleo McNelly Kearns, *T. S. Eliot and Indic Traditions* (Cambridge: Cambridge University Press, 1987), 75. Kearns's study is the authoritative account of the influence of Eastern philosophy on Eliot's thought and poetry, with a reading of *The Waste Land* at large with reference to that influence.

11 Ibid., 75–6.

12 Ibid., 31.

13 Litany of the Blessed Virgin Mary: "Tower of ivory, pray for us. House of gold, pray for us."

14 John Donne, Holy Sonnet XIV, "Batter my heart," line 4. *The Norton Anthology of Poetry*, ed., Margaret Ferguson, Mary Jo Salter, and Jon Stallworthy, 5th ed. (New York: Norton, 2005), 320.

15 John Milton, "Lycidas," line 173. *The Norton Anthology of Poetry*, ed., Margaret Ferguson, Mary Jo Salter, and Jon Stallworthy, 5th ed. (New York: Norton, 2005), 414.

16 B. C. Southam, *A Student's Guide to the Selected Poems of T. S. Eliot* (London: Faber and Faber, 1968), 92.

17 Ibid., 91.

5

DAVID E. CHINITZ AND JULIA E. DANIEL

Popular Culture

In 1970 Leslie Fiedler cited Eliot's quotation of a 1912 popular song, "That Shakespearian Rag," in part II of *The Waste Land* as an early evocation of jazz rhythms in high culture. Did this mean that Eliot heralded the postmodern tendency, celebrated by Fiedler, to "cross the border [and] close the gap" between high art and popular culture?[1] Evidently not, for Fiedler also reiterated the longstanding critical bromide that Eliot's quotation of the song is a purely satirical maneuver. According to Fiedler, "Eliot is mocking a world he resents" (482) – the world of popular culture – and though Eliot may have been technically innovative in his adaptation of popular material, he used it only to make the same old point: that popular culture is a vapid debasement of high culture and very likely a threat to it. Such was the critical consensus from the 1930s through the end of the century: popular culture in *The Waste Land* "exists as an index of the degradation of the modern age."[2] This view erases the complexity of Eliot's relations with popular culture and makes an interesting aspect of his work far less compelling. Eliot was neither in theory nor in practice an unalloyed opponent of popular culture and reflexive defender of autonomous high art. He was rather, as David Chinitz has demonstrated elsewhere, "productively engaged with popular culture" throughout his career, and his response to it varied considerably, depending on the cultural phenomenon in question.[3]

Any study of popular culture in *The Waste Land* must therefore take into account the specific characteristics and cultural contexts of the elements with which the poem engages. Our analysis investigates Eliot's treatment of two categories that together constitute popular culture as an object of study: the *popular arts* – expressive forms such as music and film – and *lived culture* or popular practices, including those involving popular recreation, women's fashion, and the use of automobiles. Rather than cataloging every reference to popular culture throughout *The Waste Land*, we offer a deep reading of key moments in "The Burial of the Dead" and "A Game of Chess" to demonstrate Eliot's nuanced and varied treatments of both the

69

popular arts and lived culture. This approach enables us to recuperate in detail the sociohistorical situation of iconic and diverse elements of popular culture, from jazz to perfume, and to understand how Eliot's representation of these forms comments on their wider cultural significance, whether for good or ill.

Although a thorough examination of the history and meaning of the term "popular culture" is beyond the scope of this chapter, a brief discussion will clarify its boundaries. To begin with "culture": in the "most widespread" usage of this term, as Raymond Williams notes, it refers to "the works and practices of intellectual and especially artistic activity."[4] Scholars across disciplinary boundaries, however, now typically understand culture in a more expansive sense as "an entire way of life" comprising "all the characteristic activities and interests of a people." The definition just quoted is, in fact, Eliot's own, from his *Notes towards the Definition of Culture.*[5] That book was influential in promulgating the modern, sociological understanding of culture, though Eliot has been criticized, not unjustly, both for slipping at crucial moments from this broad understanding into a narrower, more aesthetic one, and for not realizing quite how much "all the characteristic activities and interests of a people" comprehends. Eliot exemplifies his definition by mentioning "Derby Day, Henley Regatta, Cowes, the twelfth of August, a cup final, the dog races, the pin table, the dart board, Wensleydale cheese, boiled cabbage cut into sections, beetroot in vinegar, nineteenth-century Gothic churches and the music of Elgar" (104). While granting that "[a]ny list would be incomplete," Williams observes the "pleasant," almost romantically folkish character of Eliot's "miscellany," which is limited to "sport, food and a little art" – in short, to typical features of "English leisure."[6] He notes that the " 'characteristic activities and interests' " of the English people would in fact "also include steelmaking, touring in motor-cars, mixed farming, the Stock Exchange, coalmining and London Transport" (234). As we will see, although Eliot's list of colorful examples neglects such seemingly pedestrian elements of lived culture, his poetry directly engages them.

"Popular culture" has been conceived historically in several incompatible ways, but here we will be concerned with culture in the broad, sociological sense just discussed – that is, with an "entire way of life," excluding only its high culture.[7] Earlier studies of literature in relation to popular culture tended to analyze the representation of expressive culture or the ways in which authors draw upon structural elements or aesthetic principles found in the popular arts. Most of the scholarship that has been published to date on popular culture in Eliot's work has been of this type. The purview of literary critics has expanded in recent years, however, to include a much wider variety of cultural phenomena, from fashion to advertising to gardening styles. Following the same trajectory, this chapter briefly surveys recent criticism on the popular arts in *The Waste Land* before turning to some case studies exemplifying the significant and still largely overlooked presence of lived culture in the poem.[8]

Popular Arts in *The Waste Land*

From the perspective of the early twenty-first century, the assumption that Eliot consistently invokes the popular arts only to disparage them appears increasingly quaint – a relic of two bygone eras in literary and cultural criticism. In the middle of the last century, when Eliot's reputation and influence were at their peak, it flattered critics' own prejudices against popular culture to range the venerated writer on their side. Beginning in the 1970s, it flattered criticism's newfound enthusiasm for popular culture, as well as its compulsive iconoclasm, to condemn Eliot as a cultural elitist. The figure of T. S. Eliot as the great champion of high culture and the implacable enemy of all else was indispensable to both generations.[9] For all the adulation of the New Critics and the derision of the postmodernists, these antagonists, as far as the subject of Eliot and popular culture is concerned, now appear "folded in a single party."[10]

Contemporary criticism is increasingly aware that Eliot responded to the popular arts of his time in a variety of ways. The recent emergence of a serious scholarly discussion of *The Waste Land* and film exemplifies the current situation. Susan McCabe refers to *The Waste Land* as the "quintessential montage poem," positing that it employs "cutting-edge methods of cinematic dissociation," albeit for politically regressive purposes.[11] Avishek Parui argues that *The Waste Land* "showcases a mode of seeing that combines the mythic and the cinematic," while David Trotter finds an "affinity with cinema [that] went a great deal deeper than any belated discovery of montage technique in his poems would suggest."[12] Despite their differences, these critics all recognize cinema as an expressive form belonging to Eliot's world – one from which he did not, after all, thoroughly dissociate himself. None of them even feels the need to refute the old view to the contrary, though Trotter does express surprise that his contemporaries have overlooked the richness of Eliot's relations with cinema (125). The conversation takes Eliot's engagement with popular culture as a given.

The relation of *The Waste Land* to various genres of music has garnered most of the recent critical attention. Sebastian Knowles, Jonna Mackin, Ronald Schuchard, and David Chinitz, among others, have analyzed, from diverse points of view, the influence of the English music hall on Eliot's thought and poetry, with attention to the text and context of *The Waste*

Land.[13] Observing the racialized provenance of several songs alluded to on the deleted first page of the poem's manuscript, Michael North finds in the minstrel show an "unexpected prototype for Eliot's experiments" with the "techniques of quotation and juxtaposition."[14] Chinitz has linked these song references with an erotic melancholia running through Eliot's early poetry and reflecting a distorted version of a romantic topos common in fin-de-siècle and early twentieth-century popular song.[15] These last two analyses draw freely on the text of the unedited *Waste Land*, arguing that it exposes impulses and associations that were always present, if camouflaged, in the published version of the poem.

As North notes, comparisons of Eliot's poem to jazz were "almost ritualistic" among both the early detractors of *The Waste Land* and the young American modernists who first adulated the poem.[16] The relation was taken as a matter of course by both sides. Early readers' responses to the poem – and the modernist art it epitomized – generally mirrored their feelings about jazz as a cultural phenomenon; only later was the poem disentangled from and deployed against the popular. Recent work by such critics as Juan Antonio Suárez and Chinitz has analyzed the association between *The Waste Land* and jazz in both cultural-historical and stylistic terms.[17]

As even this short survey makes clear, we know too much now about Eliot's complex relations with popular music to dismiss his "Shakespeherian Rag" (128) as mere mockery. The allusion is *teasing*, certainly: as Edward Brunner comments, it "pretends to be scandalized by the vulgarization of Shakespeare."[18] Yet it appears at almost the exact center of "A Game of Chess," the section of *The Waste Land* that opens by rewriting Shakespeare's Cleopatra and ends by rewriting his Ophelia. The allusion, in this context, is self-referential: the poem itself pastiches and even vulgarizes Shakespeare, making Cleopatra a neurotic middle-class Englishwoman and relocating Ophelia to a working-class pub. No doubt Eliot does this with less relish than the lyricists Gene Buck and Herman Ruby, who, with composer David Stamper, wrote "That Shakespearian Rag" for the 1912 Ziegfeld Follies. Yet his treatment of the song is clearly playful – especially in its refashioning of the original lines "That Shakespearian rag / Most intelligent, very elegant." His insertion of four consecutive exclamations of "O" and of the extra syllable in "Shakespeherian" jazzes up the song, exploiting scat and syncopation to produce energetic new rhythms.[19] Chinitz has characterized Eliot's treatment of the lyric as "quizzical [and] elusively ironic" – a species of camp.[20]

The quotation materializes as the response of a morose, possibly shell-shocked character to his voluble, possibly hysterical wife, and, like his other "responses," appears to be thought but not spoken. Goaded by his silences, the woman harries him with the question "'Are you alive, or not?

Is there nothing in your head?'" (126). The word "But" and the lines of song follow, suggesting that there is indeed nothing there but this lyric. If any vital spark smolders in this survivor of "rats' alley" (115), it is apparently here in the song. Brunner thus traces a thread of resilience, and even of "redemption," through this quotation to other uses of popular music in *The Waste Land*.[21]

T. Austin Graham, by contrast, finds the song's unbidden invasion of the man's mind symptomatic of the increasing pervasiveness of music in the age of mechanical reproduction[22] – a theme he finds replayed in Eliot's earlier poems as well:

> Eliot's use of popular song is frequently anxious and eerie, and it cannot be separated from his concerns over recording technology and mechanical methods of distributing music; from his understanding of music as an increasingly commodified product in a commercial culture; and from his sense that the human auditory process has been altered, perhaps irrevocably, by a new and ever more cluttered sonic environment. (57–8)

When Eliot's typist "puts a record on the gramophone" (256), Graham argues, she is cultivating this sonic clutter. Preferring not to think about the cheap sex in which she has just engaged – her mind permits itself only one "half-formed thought" (251) on that subject – she deliberately fills the mental void with "canned music" (66). The typist thus exemplifies "the alienated, unsatisfied music listener" produced by "mechanized cultural abundance" (66–7). As Graham is quick to add, Eliot's misgivings are directed not at popular music itself but at its place in a new cultural economy. The two are hard to separate in practice, however, for popular music's connection to mechanization and commercialism is arguably the defining feature that separates it from antecedent and ostensibly more organic "folk" music.[23] In his eulogy for the music-hall superstar Marie Lloyd, Eliot criticizes the rise of the gramophone and other technologies of mechanical reproduction for fracturing the sympathetic relationship between performer and audience.[24] This rift probably accounts to a considerable extent for Eliot's ambivalence toward the popular arts to which he was otherwise obviously attracted. His response to many features of lived culture, as *The Waste Land* shows, was somewhat less mixed.

Lived Culture in *The Waste Land*

If *The Waste Land* flickers and rings with the ambivalent presence of film and music, so too is it full of the din, grit, and odor of the everyday, especially in Eliot's expansive inclusion of relatively new or recently modernized elements of lived culture. By investigating the historical and social contexts of several of these popular practices, we seek at once to recover their unique auras of modernity and to render Eliot's specific embedded critiques of these new forms legible to contemporary readers. We begin with horoscopes and fortune telling, as seen in "The Burial of the Dead," to show that, from nearly the beginning of the poem, Eliot turns to this ancient and yet newly commoditized and regulated practice to present both the persistence and the degradation of ritual form in its modern, popular incarnations. We then move to office and automotive culture, as well as to perfumery, in "A Game of Chess." Our readings demonstrate Eliot's engagement in poetry with some of those elements of lived culture that Raymond Williams accuses him of overlooking in his prose, and they reveal that what Eliot critiques in these elements is a perceived loss of authenticity as they undergo modernization.

In crucial ways, *The Waste Land* explores what Eliot understood to be the lost ritual roots of the lived culture of his time, while also criticizing the threat of mechanization and commodification to cheapen both ritual practice and human practitioner. One of the most emphatically ritualistic gestures early in the poem, the reading of the tarot, comments with a mix of anxiety and assurance on the considerably popular, yet increasingly regulated, practice of consulting fortunetellers.[25] Critics have read Madame Sosostris's words of warning, "One must be so careful these days" (59), as demonstrating anxiety or even paranoia about the control of sacred knowledge. While such scholarship emphasizes the mystical pedigree of this divine communication as the main reason for caution, Brian Diemert relates the air of concern surrounding the practice to the more mundane sphere of consumer habits and business regulations. New legislation sought to curtail the public's appetite for fortunes, a proclivity some thought dangerous to wartime morale, by labeling horoscopes as a form of fraud. The particular care shown by Madame Sosostris is thus symptomatic of a culture in which prophesies have devolved into black-market commodities. Delivering the horoscope by hand, as she proposes, would sidestep charges of mail fraud, though she might still be brought up on general charges of practicing divination for profit. Fortune tellers ran the risk of accidentally sharing their esoteric wisdom with undercover officers, and the *Times* often published arrest reports and covered the trials of these latter-day sibyls. Sosostris's concern originates thus from anxieties about authenticity and audience fundamentally shaped by new cultural attitudes and regulations: will her words reach the intended customer or will she be punished (and published) as a fraud? Is she in fact a fraud? The public figure of the fortuneteller hovered somewhere between priestess and charlatan. The scathing comments of trial judges cast fortunetelling as a nearly comedic act of deception, while the very need for prosecution testified to a booming underground industry catering to a public who took divination seriously. Eliot's evocation of this split public sentiment toward fortune tellers contributes to *The Waste Land*'s atmosphere of anxiety and ambiguity. Sosostris in some ways seems the charlatan, with her overblown mystical credentials standing in laughable contrast to her all-too-human cold. Yet for all her sniffling and fretting, she still manages to inhabit her role as priestess, as her "wicked pack" (46) correctly divines how the poem will unfold. As such, she stands as an example of a popular practice gone awry and yet also as a reminder of its ritual pedigree.

While Eliot's response to such popular practices as fortunetelling is mixed, his presentation of mechanized or mass-produced *objects*, and the cultural habits they enable, is mostly apprehensive, especially when they replace an earlier artisanal form or induce dissociation, whether between man and woman, person and place, or senses and self. Both the typist's flat and the lady's toilette in "A Game of Chess" are cluttered with such objects, from the gauche array of food in tins to the bijoux of small perfume bottles, and therefore they serve as excellent case studies in the ways Eliot critiques the lived culture that accrues around these thoroughly modern goods.

The typist episode in particular lends itself to such a study, since her profession and her flat capture the experience of everyday living for the contemporary working woman. One of the new qualities of this lifestyle was an abundance of mass-produced conveniences, like the prepackaged food, gramophone, typewriters, and taxi that situate Eliot's typist in an atmosphere of mechanized decadence. Lawrence Rainey places the typist in the context of her modern vocation, one in which young women were equated with the new technology they used, to the point of being referred to as "typewriters" as well as typists. They epitomized "an interlocking grid of new communications and storage and retrieval technologies" – a "new office culture" with which Eliot was intimately familiar during his employment at Lloyds Bank.[26] Rainey also marks the rise of both popular literature featuring typists as romantic protagonists and journalistic exposés revealing the low wages, poor diets, and cramped living conditions of these working girls. Eliot plays on these conventions and social concerns in portraying his typist, who, like her literary and real-life counterparts, eats tinned food and uses her divan as a bed in her one-room flat. The lack of intimacy in the typist's sexual encounter with the clerk also occurs on a stage that precludes privacy, rendering the typist overexposed and vulnerable before she suffers his first gropes. Not only is the clerk met by piles of her undergarments on the divan, but even more of her delicates are "Out of the window perilously spread," making public her private lingerie (224). In these details, Eliot presents the very environment of the flat as one of violation and links the distress of the scene directly to the new office culture and to the habits of living it generates far beyond the office walls.

Eliot similarly critiques new changes in British automotive culture, particularly the rise of the taxi and the closed car, which he represents as divorcing drivers and passengers from each other, their local environment, and even their sense of self. After bemoaning the gramophone's ubiquity in his tribute to Marie Lloyd, Eliot goes on to criticize a future in which "every horse has been replaced by 100 cheap motor-cars" (407–8). Eliot's nostalgia for the absent horse translates into broader concerns about automotive mechanization in the typist episode, where "the human engine waits / Like a taxi throbbing waiting" (216–17). Horse-drawn taxis still shared the road with their motorized counterparts in London in the late teens – the last license for a horse-drawn cab was granted as late as 1947 – although the trend toward replacement was already clear. The taxi became a prominent icon of modern city living, combining as it did the latest automotive developments with a uniquely urban convenience.[27] Like the typist, the taxi driver became synonymous with the technology of his trade. In *The Waste Land*, Eliot replaces the human operator with an anthropomorphized waiting engine, effacing the presence of the driver within his idling vehicle. As with the gramophone and the typewriter, the taxi also breaks traditional chains of agency. It is a vehicle directed not by the driver but by the passenger, splitting purpose and motion, volition and capability across the back of a seat.[28] If the human engine is like the waiting taxi, it is trapped in a humming stasis while caught between two lives – that of the driver and the as yet nonexistent patron. In other words, this "human engine" lacks a coherent engineer and so captures in miniature the sense of a fractured self. Ultimately, what is lost in all this mechanical throbbing, and in the new automotive culture more broadly, is the beating of a heart, whether that of the driver, the passenger, or the now defunct horse.

That Eliot laments the rise of "cheap motor-cars" in his essay on Marie Lloyd is typical of debates within the English automotive world at the time. As Rudy Koshar illustrates, English designers and motorists worried over the influence of Ford's mass-produced vehicles on their more artisanal, "low-volume production ... designed to appeal to a multiplicity of middle-class tastes and preferences."[29] Eliot's anxiety about the availability of "cheap" models thus encompasses fears about class, nationality, and craftsmanship. Cars appear early on in *The Waste Land*, as the taciturn husband in "A Game of Chess" promises "a closed car at four" in case of rain (136). That it is only "a" car may suggest that this is also a taxi, summoned to whisk the couple away for some diversion from their tedious afternoon. However, the car's inclusion in a list of banalities used to fill the hours reduces it to just another aspect of that daily tedium. By withholding the car's destination, Eliot adds the couple to the list of travelers in *The Waste Land* whose wanderings never alleviate their restlessness: where they are going does not matter, because their lives will remain the same. A crucial detail that Eliot does provide, however, is that this car is "closed." While contemporary readers might find this descriptor unremarkable, it in fact signals a recent modernization of the automobile that directly contributes to Eliot's ritualistic presentation of seasons and water in the poem. Originally, open touring cars were the playthings of the elite, who used them primarily for pleasure drives in the country. However, Ford altered these driving habits with the introduction of the closed, or hard-top, car in 1915. Ford's advertising for the closed car targeted middle-class drivers who craved comfort and conveniences, particularly preserving their clothing from the elements.[30] No longer merely a diversion for sunny afternoons outside the city, driving was becoming the fashionable way to get around on any day, anywhere, and car manufacturers abroad eagerly patterned new closed vehicles on Ford's model. In "A Game of Chess," Eliot implicitly criticizes the lack of contact with the environment in the sealed-off interior of the car. In *The Waste Land*'s parched landscape, the hope of coming rain represents the fulfillment of the fertility ritual as well as a desperately needed reinvigoration of culture. By treating the rain as a mere inconvenience easily avoided in a trendy closed car, the couple demonstrates the deadening effects of a popular automotive culture that severs people from the particulars of places and seasons.

In spite of their class differences, the cultural environments of the affluent lady in "A Game of Chess" and the typist in "The Fire Sermon" overlap in more than their shared references to automotive culture. Just as Eliot lingers over the typist's "drying combinations" (225), he pauses to describe the clutter on the woman's dressing table. Her perfume in vials mirrors the typist's food in tins, another organic product once made by hand reduced to a fabricated approximation. Amid the lady's baroque toilette can be found a variety of dainty perfume containers, whose contents disorient the senses: "In vials of ivory and coloured glass / Unstoppered, lurked her strange synthetic perfumes" (86–7). The very strangeness of these insidious perfumes is due in part to their synthetic nature, a recent advancement in perfumery that radically altered the cultural practices surrounding this highly sexualized and class-encoded consumer good. Eliot here specifically uses the technical term "synthetic," a word popularized in the perfume industry in the late teens with the creation of fabricated scents. Before the early 1900s, perfume was an artisanal product created by individual perfumers who hand-blended expensive botanicals into signature aromas. These artisans carefully guarded their craft – one with a pedigree running back to ritual practices in the ancient world, where expensive tinctures made choice offerings to the gods (as well as practically masking the odor of less aromatic sacrifices). Etymologically, the word "perfume," which means "through the smoke," derives from perfume's use in rites involving burning. In "A Game of Chess," Eliot evokes perfume's ritual history as it literally contributes to the smokiness of the room. The clean breeze "That freshened from the window" (90) does nothing to alleviate the floral stench; it actually worsens the smell by "Stirring" the air (93). Perfume becomes *per fume*, a scented smoke that ascends to the heavens – or fails to ascend, in this case, as the aromas, combining with smoke from the candles, are caught in the room's ornate ceiling. Like the closed car, the cramped room seals its inhabitants in, leaving them to suffocate amid chemicals that have "drowned the sense in odours" (89). Another of perfume's traditional ritual applications is the anointing of the dead, and in "A Game of Chess," the lady's implied act of self-anointing adds to the funerary tone of the scene.[31] In its sense-muddling manifestations throughout the overwrought room, the perfume is alternately a threatening sea, a smoldering burnt offering, and sacred oil for this act of extreme unction.

These are no ancient unguents, however, but thoroughly modern potions. In 1882, the Parisian manufacturer Houbigant produced "Fougère Royale," the first perfume that incorporated synthetics, thus moving the art of perfumery into the arena of the laboratory.[32] By 1900, the vast majority of perfumes featured synthetics in their blends, and the trade had transformed into a booming industry seemingly overnight. The use of synthetics made perfume significantly less expensive, and it soon found its way to the masses over department store counters. These perfumes enjoyed immense popularity throughout the twenties and thirties, thanks to the marriage of synthetic perfume's affordability and an expanding class of working women with disposable income, like Eliot's typist. The "vials of ivory and coloured glass" (86) were also part of the trade, as the mechanization of mould-blown glass, along with the invention of the automatic bottle-making machine in 1891, enabled perfume bottle designers, like the famous René Lalique, to create dazzling containers in bulk and at a reasonable price.[33] Lalique's crystal pieces were crafted without lead, resulting in a cheaper, more malleable glass, as well as the signature milky coloring that distinguished the brand. The lady's ivory bottle in *The Waste Land* may refer to this white-tinted, machine-molded frosted glass, which had become massively popular. "Ivory" would then serve as an adjective in Eliot's line, one that describes the frosted finish on the bottles. Alternatively, the word may refer to a bottle made of ivory celluloid, also known as French Ivory or Ivorine. Celluloid was patented in 1870 and soon became a ubiquitous industrial material thanks to its malleability and relative affordability. French Ivory, one of celluloid's many manifestations, was used as a pre-molded ivory, tortoiseshell, or horn replacement for many luxury and personal items that once would have been hand-etched, including billiard balls, fountain pens, umbrella handles, and perfume bottles. The lady's "ivory," now a noun, might then be one of the many popular French Ivory containers commonly used in art deco designs for perfume bottles and women's dressing table sets. The opacity of Eliot's phrase, like the ivory vial itself, makes it difficult to tell whether her table represents a mix of the old and the new, with genuine antique ivory flasks alongside glass containers from the department store, or a thoroughly modern cosmetic set made of the newest materials in the latest fashion. In either case, in the description of this fragrant still life, Eliot's readers would have recognized a changing industry that blurred the boundaries between art objects and machine-made consumer commodities.

The many scents lurking in these containers add to the atmosphere of decadent excess. Just as the interior of the room is heavily encrusted with décor, the air is saturated with the chemical approximation of fresh flowers and spices. "Unguent, powdered, or liquid" (88) refers to the different vehicles for these synthetics: a lotion, a talc-based powder, or a liquid to be daubed on the skin or atomized. To compound the effect, Eliot matches this triad of scent vehicles with a trio of disorienting effects: "troubled, confused / And drowned the sense in odours" (89). The proliferation of artificial odors not only overwhelms the speaker but also testifies to the lady's anxiety before she even speaks. Just as she barely manages to hide her terror behind the facade of conversation, she also anxiously masks the odor of her body in a cloud of store-bought aromatics.[34] Much as with the gramophone and the taxi, Eliot faults this popular consumer good for the scented fog it imposes between not only the lady and the gentleman but also the lady and her bodily self.[35]

Eliot engages as a poet with a variety of cultural phenomena comparable to that of Raymond Williams's expansive list, interweaving expressiveness and commodification, leisure and labor, art and the everyday, to represent the texture of modernity. On the whole, *The Waste Land* is critical of popular culture, although, as we have seen, it draws significant distinctions as well, revealing an ambivalent warmth for the popular arts and a greater skepticism toward lived culture, with Eliot's strongest condemnation reserved for objects and practices seen as obstructing or perverting authentic experience. We conclude here by returning to the impetus behind this project: the hope that our sampling of popular culture in *The Waste Land* will demonstrate the broader prospects of approaching the poem through an inclusive notion of popular culture. A great deal of work remains to be done on how Eliot portrays and comments on the lived culture of his moment particularly. The preceding discussion of perfume could be extended to cosmetic culture more broadly and its role in the lives of women who sought to make themselves "a bit smart" (142). Similarly, Beci Carver has recently analyzed the social and commercial life of lingerie by paying attention to the typist's surprisingly old-fashioned undergarments.[36] Her analysis opens up the possibility of reading fashion in *The Waste Land* more generally, down to the silk hats and handkerchiefs. One could also explore, for instance, the gastronomical *Waste Land*, complete with cups of coffee, hot gammon, currants, picnics, and canned edibles, or the economic *Waste Land* suggested by commuters, clerks, fishmongers, loitering heirs, Smyrna merchants, and trade wars. Such scholarship will not only provide new points of entry into the poem but add to our understanding of Eliot as a commentator on and consumer of popular culture.

NOTES

1 Leslie Fiedler, "Cross the Border – Close the Gap," *A New Fiedler Reader* (Amherst, NY: Prometheus, 1999), 482.
2 Jon Thompson, *Fiction, Crime, and Empire* (Urbana: University of Illinois Press, 1993), 35.
3 David E. Chinitz, *T. S. Eliot and the Cultural Divide* (Chicago: University of Chicago Press, 1993), 12–13.
4 Raymond Williams, *Keywords: A Vocabulary of Culture and Society* (New York: Oxford University Press, 1976), 80.
5 T. S. Eliot, *Notes towards the Definition of Culture*, in *Christianity and Culture* (New York: Harcourt, 1968), 116, 104.
6 Raymond Williams, *Culture and Society 1780–1950* (New York: Columbia University Press, 1983), 234.
7 For a useful, authoritative (though not neutral) discussion of various definitions, see John Storey, *Cultural Theory and Popular Culture: An Introduction*, 6th ed. (Harlow, Essex: Pearson, 2012), 5–13 passim, and his *Inventing Popular Culture: From Folklore to Globalization* (Oxford: Blackwell, 2003). Regarding our own model, we are cognizant of the checkered history of definitions of popular culture as the "other" of high culture, which have often been deployed to denigrate the popular. No such valuation, of course, is intended or implied here. We are also keenly aware of the problematics of the high-low binary, but we trust it is clear that we are making no strong claims for it. Its function here is essentially heuristic. Critics of *The Waste Land* have written at length of Eliot's allusions to Dante and Ovid, while they have said little of his references to motor-cars and jazz. We begin to redress that imbalance.
8 The distinction between expressive and lived culture presents problems of its own, particularly in the way it reifies the postindustrial severance of aesthetics

from utility. However, given the aforementioned history of criticism on popular culture in *The Waste Land*, it does provide a useful structure for this analysis. Indeed, our attention to lived culture has the benefit of elucidating many of the aesthetic qualities of purportedly mundane and utilitarian objects and practices, like the purchasing and collecting of perfume bottles.

9 Chinitz, *T. S. Eliot*, 158–67.

10 Eliot, *Complete Poems and Plays, 1909–1950* (New York: Harcourt, 1971), 143. Poems will be cited hereafter parenthetically by line number.

11 Susan McCabe, *Cinematic Modernism: Modernist Poetry and Film* (Cambridge: Cambridge University Press, 2005), 14, 46.

12 Avishek Parui, "'The Nerves in Patterns on a Screen': Hysteria, Hauntology and Cinema in T. S. Eliot's Early Poetry from *Prufrock* to *The Waste Land*," in *Film and Literary Modernism*, ed. Robert P. McParland (Newcastle upon Tyne: Cambridge Scholars, 2013), 103–4; David Trotter, *Cinema and Modernism* (Malden, MA: Blackwell, 2007), 153.

13 Sebastian D. G. Knowles, "'Then You Wink the Other Eye': T. S. Eliot and the Music Hall," *ANQ* 11, no. 4 (1998), 20–32; Jonna Mackin, "Raising Life to a Kind of Art: Eliot and Music Hall," in *T. S. Eliot's Orchestra*, ed. John Xiros Cooper (New York: Garland, 2000), 49–64; Ronald Schuchard, *Eliot's Dark Angel: Intersections of Life and Art* (New York: Oxford University Press, 1999), chapter 5; Chinitz, *T. S. Eliot*, 46, chapter 3.

14 Michael North, *The Dialect of Modernism: Race, Language, and Twentieth-Century Literature* (New York: Oxford University Press, 1994), 85–7.

15 David E. Chinitz, "In the Shadows: Popular Song and Eliot's Construction of Emotion," *Modernism/modernity* 11, no. 3 (2004): 451–62.

16 Michael North, *Reading 1922: A Return to the Scene of the Modern* (New York: Oxford University Press, 1999), 146.

17 Juan A. Suarez, *Pop Modernism: Noise and the Reinvention of the Everyday* (Urbana: University of Illinois Press, 2007), 138–9; Chinitz, *T. S. Eliot*, 38, 41–9.

18 Edward Brunner, "Stepping Out, Sitting In: Modern Poetry's Counterpoint with Jazz and the Blues," in *The Oxford Handbook of Modern and Contemporary American Poetry*, ed. Cary Nelson (New York: Oxford University Press, 2012), 223.

19 Ibid., 223–4; T. Austin Graham, *The Great American Songbooks: Musical Texts, Modernism, and the Value of Popular Culture* (New York: Oxford, 2013), 63–4.

20 Chinitz, *T. S. Eliot*, 49.

21 Brunner, "Stepping Out," 224–5.

22 Graham, *The Great American Songbooks*, 65.

23 Michael Coyle, "Popular Culture," *A Companion to Modernist Poetry*, ed. David E. Chinitz and Gail McDonald (Oxford: Wiley-Blackwell, 2014), 81–4.

24 Eliot, "Marie Lloyd," in *Selected Essays*, new edition (New York: Harcourt, 1964), 407–8.

25 Brian Diemert, "The Trials of Astrology in T. S. Eliot's *The Waste Land*: A Gloss on Lines 57–9," *Journal of Modern Literature* 22, no. 1 (1998), 175–81.

26 Lawrence Rainey, "Eliot among the Typists: Writing *The Waste Land*," *Modernism/modernity* 12, no. 1 (2005): 65. doi: 10.1353/mod.2005.0049.

27 As Malcolm Bobbitt has documented, taxis persisted as a mainstay in the London landscape despite the advent of affordable public transportation, and different companies touted the newest models to attract customers. Malcolm Bobbitt, *Taxi! The Story of the London Taxi Cab* (Poundbury, Dorset: Velcoe, 1998), 10–15. For more on London taxi culture, see Bill Munro, *A Century of London Taxis* (Ramsbury, Wiltshire: Crowood, 2005).

28 Motorized taxis shared many common elements with their horse-drawn predecessors. The driver/passenger split is of course to be found in both; however, this dynamic is compounded for Eliot by its inclusion in the mechanized environment of the car. As with "closed" cars and covered hansoms, to be discussed in this chapter, the poet sometimes casts long-established qualities as part of the modern problem.

29 Rudy Koshar, "Cars and Nations: Anglo-German Perspective on Automobility between the World Wars," in *Automobilities*, ed. Mike Featherstone, Nigel Thrift, and John Urry (London: Sage Publications, 2005), 130.

30 See, for example, "Ford Closed Car Advertisement" (1924), *America on the Move*, National Museum of American History: Transportation Collection, accessed December 4, 2013. http://amhistory.si.edu/onthemove/collection/object_502.html.

31 Funerary applications of perfumes are various and widespread. Roy Genders traces them back to ancient Rome: "The early Romans buried their dead, but later cremation on a funeral pyre of scented woods was the custom: the bones and ashes were gathered up and mixed with perfumes before being placed in a decorative urn." *Perfume through the Ages* (New York: Putman, 1972), 86.

32 There is some debate about how to date the emergence of synthetic perfume. In 1855, essence of Mirbane was first synthesized, soon followed by Bitter Almond in 1869 and Vanillin in 1875. Perfumers began experimenting with these chemicals before officially introducing them to the market, but most scholars consider the unveiling of Fougère Royale the watershed moment for synthetic perfumery. Our account here is especially indebted to Aytoun Ellis, *The Essence of Beauty: A History of Perfume and Cosmetics* (New York: MacMillan, 1960), and Julia Muller, *The H&R Book of Perfume* (London: Johnson, 1984). For more on the social history and production of perfume, see Genders, *Perfume*.

33 The feminine, floral, and highly organic styles of early Art Nouveau bottles in the teens were soon overshadowed by sleeker, more urban Art Deco designs in the twenties, such as Lentheric's architectural container for "Miracle" and Jean Patou's minimalist bottle and packaging for "Le Sien." On the development of bottle styles and perfume marketing, see Jacquelyne Y. Jones North, *Commercial Perfume Bottles* (Westchester, PA: Schiffer, 1987).

34 As Maud Ellmann notes, the deleted Fresca episode of *The Waste Land* manuscript makes a cruder but essentially similar suggestion in the lines "Odours, confected by the cunning French, / Disguise the good old hearty female stench" (40–1). Ellmann, "Eliot's Abjection," in *Abjection, Melancholia, and Love: The Work of Julia Kristeva*, ed. John Fletcher and Andrew Benjamin (New York: Routledge, 1990), 194–5; Eliot, *The Waste Land: A Facsimile and Transcript of the Original Drafts Including the Annotations of Ezra Pound*, ed. Valerie Eliot (New York: Harcourt, 1971), 39.

35 As Laura Frost has shown in *The Problem with Pleasure: Modernism and its Discontents* (New York: Columbia University Press, 2013), 37–42, Eliot's concerns were not a merely personal preoccupation: the moral implications of perfume had been a matter of concern for social thinkers since the 1880s.

36 Beci Carver, *Granular Modernism* (Oxford: Oxford University Press, 2014), 126–8.

PART II

Poetic Techniques and Methods

6

MICHAEL LEVENSON

Form, Voice, and the Avant-Garde

Consider, to begin, the late essay on "The Three Voices of Poetry," where Eliot makes some brisk distinctions. The first voice is that "of the poet talking to himself – or to nobody;" the second is "the poet addressing an audience, whether large or small;" and the third "is the voice of the poet when he attempts to create a dramatic character speaking in verse."[1] Eliot, laying out a taxonomy of possibilities, presents voice as *address*: the directedness of speech toward an audience or through a character, inside or outside the work, real or fictional. Such taxonomy has been a temptation, but the concept of voice remains notoriously elusive, largely because it bears the burden of so many interests. It gives a name for identity (as in "finding one's own voice"), but also indicates the mode of an entire work or performance (as in "the voice of Joseph Conrad's *The Secret Agent*"). It can take a divine referent: "the voice of God;" but just as often a political one: "the voice of the people." Use of the term, moreover, remains suspended between figural and literal meanings; a "strong voice," for instance, suggests both force of character and vibrant pitch. James Fenton insists on the social and material effects of audibility, characterizing poetry as "language to which a special emphasis has been given," by relying on such means as "raising the voice in order to be heard above the crowd; raising the voice in order to demonstrate its beauty and power; chanting the words; reciting the words rhythmically; punctuating the units of speech (what will become the lines of the poem) with rhymes; setting the words to tunes; or setting the words to tunes and singing them in unison, as in a drinking song."[2] All of these registers pertain to the workings of *The Waste Land*. We only have to recall the early title ("He Do the Police in Different Voices" – Charles Dickens's fond description of Sloppy in *Our Mutual Friend*) – to meet the range of implications, including performance (the doing), polyphony (the differences), and physicality (the voices Sloppy enunciates with gusto). Our subject being form, voice, and the avant-garde, it will be good to recognize at the outset that voice not only assumes form, but can also be form-disturbing and form-breaking, and that as Eliot pondered and practiced these effects, he located his place within the literary avant-garde more persistently and more variously than we have inclined to suppose.

I

The turn of the twentieth century was a moment of noisy modernity. The rise of a mass journalism, often given to hectoring pronouncement; the high-toned speechifying of bourgeois society; the public demands of suffragettes and the working class; the chug of urban transport – all bear on lyric tone. Eliot reflected on the audible pressures of new technologies: "Perhaps the conditions of modern life (think how large a part is now played in our sensory life by the internal combustion engine) have altered our rhythms."[3] Rhythm was indeed decisive to his early impetus toward poetry, but no more than the experiments in tone. Eliot's encounter with the first significant literary avant-garde, the French poets who came to be called Symbolists, was for him, unlike for W.B. Yeats, an encounter with tonal transformation in the age of modern noise. His celebrated discovery of Arthur Symons's early study, *The Symbolist Movement in Modern Poetry*, has rightly been called decisive. It led him not only to two generations of risk-taking poets – Jules Laforgue initially most important among them – it also opened unsuspected dimensions of voicing. If the story of Eliot's turn to Laforgue is well known, less so is the mediating text from Symons, which was itself an exercise in the naming of voices. For Laforgue, Symons writes,

> Verse and prose are alike a kind of travesty, making subtle use of colloquialism, slang, neologism, technical terms, for their allusive, their factitious, their reflected meanings, with which one can play, very seriously. The verse is alert, troubled, swaying, deliberately uncertain, hating rhetoric so piously that it prefers, and finds its piquancy in, the ridiculously obvious.[4]

Symons evokes the "ironical lilt" of the arch manner, its "icy ecstasy," "artificial through its extreme naturalness," refusing "the old cadences, the old eloquence" (298). The strain in the critical language is revealing. The mobility of Laforgue's manner tests Symons's ability to describe it: the rapid shift from detachment to despair, from chill irony to chastened earnestness. It is this aspect of poetic voicing, the instability of its tonalities, that taxonomies have often resisted or avoided, including Eliot's own taxonomy. To return to Symons is to summon back a moment of opportune unsettlement, with Pater as its epitome, that saw the evocation of fugitive tones as retreat in the service of a literary advance, at once burden and glory.

The Waste Land consummates more than ten years of Eliot's labor in voice. The extent of its challenge can be broached by setting its beginnings against its endings, that is, the opening of each of the five sections against their closing lines. These openings are, in each case, descriptive utterances, making no overt reference to a speaker.

> April is the cruellest month, breeding (1)

> The Chair she sat in, like a burnished throne,
> Glowed on the marble (77–8)

> The river's tent is broken (173)

> Phlebas the Phoenician, a fortnight dead,
> Forgot the cry of gulls (312–13)

> After the torchlight red on sweaty faces (322)

Each declaration points outward toward a condition of the world – a move that reveals an aspect of voicing in *The Waste Land* too easily overlooked. Here the poem accepts a documentary vocation, where speech becomes the assertion of fact through simple syntax and vocabulary, and scenes are surveyed from an apparently detached and all-seeing vantage point. Already, however, the dislocations of perspective show themselves. The startling word "cruellest," the simile of the "burnished throne," the metaphor of the "river's tent" – these suggest a break in the neutrality of view, the stirring of a manner or attitude. They prepare for a contrast that becomes clearest when we set these opening lines against those closing each section.

> "You! hypocrite lecteur! – mon semblable, – mon frère!" (76)

> Good night, ladies, good night, sweet ladies, good night, good night. (172)

> O Lord Thou pluckest

> burning (310–11)

> Consider Phlebas, who was once handsome and tall as you. (321)

> Shantih shantih shantih (433)

The sections close with forcefully accented speech, no longer oriented toward description, but emitted now from a discernible location and an angle of vision. This movement from the documentary eye to a strong personal statement marks a broad track of voicing through the poem. Patience in laying out a scene – a dressing room, a spring or autumn landscape, a drowning – gives way to the outburst of an individual cry, or warning, or prayer. Moreover, these transitions repeat locally within the five sections, yielding a tonal rhythm that repeatedly passes from gnomic generality to ardent utterance.

Much of the critical argument over *The Waste Land* – whether to take it as a work of political and social engagement or as the confession of a traumatized émigré – turns on the emphasis given to these inflections. But it is worth stressing that between the distant poles sound modulated middle tones, where neutrality transforms into the signature accents of individuality. The rotund sounds of the first three lines change force, as well as rhythm, from the moment the first-person plural pronoun enters at line five, and the sounds continue to alter as the plural becomes singular, becomes Marie.

"Subjectivity in Language" is Émile Benveniste's phrase,[5] intended to capture the capacity of rule-governed discourse to organize around personhood. Words can circulate as detached and disinterested signs, but then they become assimilated to the interests and lived experience of individuals. The second stanza of the poem begins with biblical magniloquence, which then resolves into the prophetic "I" who "will show you fear in a handful of dust" (30) – an "I" that transmutes into the dramatic my (*"Mein"*) of Richard Wagner's *Tristan und Isolde*, only to turn again into the personal memory of a living speaker. The poem thus repeatedly raises the stakes for subjectivity in tone, first by moving from the objectivity of language into the realm of personal utterance, and then by shifting among persons, so that intonations that suggest one (kind of) character modulate into suggestions of another. Often we might better speak of "voicing" rather than "voice" in the poem, since the acts of speech pass too quickly to establish any stable personhood.

The shifting scenes in *The Waste Land* have typically been described in terms of montage. Here the cinema has been the leading model, especially the cinema of Sergei Eisenstein, with its methods of assemblage built upon quick cutting among points of view. But an advantage in listening to the voices in the poem is that they give an alternative to visual metaphors, which imply cleaner outlines than the poem in fact preserves. The overlapping reverberations and interpenetrating echoes display the indeterminacy of boundaries around persons, a point that Eliot famously emphasizes in his annotation on "character" in *The Waste Land*: "Just as the one-eyed merchant, seller of currants, melts into the Phoenician Sailor, and the latter is not wholly distinct from Ferdinand Prince of Naples, so all the women are one woman, and the two sexes meet in Tiresias" (note 218). The trope of "melt[ing] into" fits the pattern of interfering waves of speech.

Furthermore, voice often emits its sound only through mediating allusion or direct quotation. When the poem summons Edmund Spenser near the opening of "The Fire Sermon" with its apostrophe to "Sweet Thames" (176), it willfully confuses the relation between speech and speaker. The line evokes the occasion and the music of "Prothalamion," but it also expresses *The Waste Land*'s contemporary concern with the loss of innocence before the predations of moneyed sexuality. The "I" that stands inside Spenser's line must find connection to the series of "I" utterances before and after. "The Fire Sermon" also ends by borrowing its "I"s from earlier texts, in this case from Augustine and the Buddha, who not only preach horror at the spiritual failures in our sexuality, but who also bring the poem's compounding of voices to perhaps its highest pitch. Like the "I" extracted from Spenser's "Prothalamion," Augustine's "I" ("To Carthage then I came," 307) is at once a narrative pivot in Eliot's poem and a sign pointing back to its source in the *Confessions*. Because *The Waste Land* relies so heavily on quoted speech with the first-person pronoun, the force of the utterance is brought into question. What makes the issue pointed is that the poem includes other "I" utterances that exist outside the network of quotations and that convey a tone of desperate immediacy. "I was neither / Living nor dead" (39–40) and "I have heard the key / Turn in the door once and turn once only" (411–12) imply accents of direct speech. An emphasis on these phrases leads to a view of the poem as an anguished confession.

The difficulty is that the apparently direct utterances merge ("melt into") the quoted speeches, so that the ring of authenticity becomes only one style among many. Eliot thus prefigures themes within the sociolinguistics of Mikhail Bakhtin – in particular the saturation of all speech by the inherited and authoritative tones of the past. But whereas Bakhtin enshrines forms of resistance to the dominant conventions that weigh heavily on language, Eliot appropriates, rather than resists, convention.[6] He makes a resource of the unsteady relation between speech in the putative present of modern London and the echoes that vie to say "I." The effect is to create a theatrical aura around even the most searing moments of outcry ("I think we are in rats' alley," 115) – a moment often interpreted as a direct reference to the horrors of trench warfare during World War I.

The poem, it should be clear, distributes its voicing over a wide range of discrete speech acts: interrogation ("'Has it begun to sprout?'" 72), demand ("'Think,'" 114), wish ("your heart would have responded," 420), apology ("I can't help it," 158). But the central act of speech is testimony. Repeatedly, throughout the poem, characters turn back to their past, distant or near, and testify to loss, glimpsed possibility, and failure ("And I was frightened," 15; "I knew nothing," 40; "'Well now that's done: and I'm glad it's over,'" 252; "These fragments I have shored against my ruins," 430). Centrally, these acts of retrospection and witness derive from sexual violence. The most propulsive voicing in *The Waste Land* is not human voicing at all, but the "inviolable voice" of Philomel, crying as the nightingale (101). Broached briefly in "A Game of Chess," the scene of violence unfolds at the end of "The Fire Sermon," where the successive speeches of the Thames-Maidens give the debased fulfillment of the motif. The first of them gives the austere brevity of weary testimony: "By Richmond I raised my knees/ Supine on the floor of a narrow canoe" (294–5).

Not passively to endure the degradation of sexual victimage, but to convert it into words and to achieve the dignity of speech after trauma – this is Philomel's example. Taken up again by many figures, it stands as the primal voicing of the poem.

II

Imagism, devised and promoted by Ezra Pound, gave Eliot his first encounter with a living avant-garde. The movement's early famous proposals were terse and polemical, intended to transform the course of modern verse by revising the root elements of lyric style. "Direct treatment of the 'thing' whether subjective or objective;"[7] "Go in fear of abstractions" (5); "Use no superfluous word" (4). The result would be a purified voice, free from the taint of "rhetoric" (the curse of the nineteenth century), capable of producing the rigorous and bounded Image: "an intellectual and emotional complex in an instant of time" (4). Energy being the central virtue, Pound calls for the "sudden liberation" poetry will achieve when it overcomes rhetoric.

Eliot appeared on the London scene after these doctrines had been elaborated. As Pound admiringly noted, he had already "modernized himself" – most notably through reading, and listening to, the poetry of Laforgue. But while Eliot shared a close collaboration with Pound during the next decade, including of course the collaboration on The Waste Land, he kept apart from the program of Imagism, which in 1914–15 transformed to the program of Vorticism. He accepted the value of energy (his preferred term being "intensity")[8] but he saw it, not as present in a single autonomous image, but as the outcome of a situation, dramatic and narrative. Not the image but the scene gives the context in which Eliot's voices sound. "The Love Song of J. Alfred Prufrock" and "Portrait of a Lady" lay out the early versions, which stage personal relations within carefully designed spaces, offering confined and decorated interiors as the fit arenas for uttered agony. What Eliot took from the Elizabethans, as well as from Robert Browning, was the resource of dramatic context. The Waste Land is the culmination of this subtle practice: it offers, not discrete images, but a series of small-scale scenarios. Marie, Madame Sosostris, the typist, the hyacinth girl, the Thames-Maidens, all live within dramatic plots that shadow forth – briefly but just long enough to evoke a narrative that must arrive in spoken utterance.

The speech of women, we have seen, epitomized by the cry of Philomel, constitutes an originary voicing in The Waste Land. And the primal failures of sexuality, its inhibitions as well as its violence, are the recurrent topic of these micro-scenarios. Women who have been stymied and degraded ("It's them pills I took, to bring it off," 159), or trapped in empty erotic tedium ("that's done," 252), or lost within marriage ("'My nerves are bad to-night,'" 111) speak within the pattern Eliot articulates in the *Hamlet* essay; that is, as if their words were "automatically released"[9] by the brief narrative sequences that contain them. The references to past texts and episodes prepare the scene for the moments of cry and call; tradition provides an orchestral surrounding for the searing solitary voices.

III

Tradition lengthens in one dimension, collecting sounds of the past, even the far distant past, while the city extends horizontally, mixing human voices with other sounds of modernity: the traffic, the crowd, the gramophone. In this latter aspect, Eliot's new work stands in revealing analogy to the experiments of Guillaume Apollinaire in Paris, which he had been recently reading, with their own scenic miniatures placed within a mobile urban panorama. Apollinaire's poem "Hôtels" from the volume *Alcools* begins,

> La chambre est veuve
> Chacun pour soi ...
> Le patron doute
> Payera-t-on
> Je tourne en route
> Comme un toton
> Le bruit des fiacres
> Mon voisin laid[10]

("The room's available / To each his own / ... The owner doubts / You'll pay / I spin round / Like a little top// The carriage noise / My ugly neighbor"; my translation).

Eliot's work often comes close to Apollinaire's open form, with its quick-breathing short lines and its continually shifting gaze, its responsiveness to noise as ineliminable in any scene, and its intense consciousness of the separate human atoms that compose the urban crowd. Walter Benjamin is the indispensable theorist of this situation of modernity, the sudden decomposition of the crowd into its particulars, the recognition of the "one" amid "so many," each with a voice of its own (like the "demotic French" of Mr. Eugenides, 212).[11] As Benjamin saw, and as Eliot and Apollinaire reimagined, the metropolis is an ongoing transaction between bounded containers (rooms and bodies) and the unbounded spaces (crowds, scents, and spectacles) that wash against them. Voice and noise make the connecting medium. They give the sound of the unsleeping urban community but also that of separate persons, testifying to singular histories. "Maintenant," writes Apollinaire, "tu marches dans Paris tout seul parmi la foule / Des troupeaux d'autobus mugissants près de toi roulent." ("Now you walk in Paris alone among the crowd / Herds of lowing buses roll past you," my translation).[12] At the end of "The Burial of the Dead," Eliot conjures the scene in this way: "There I saw one I knew, and stopped him, crying: 'Stetson!' " (69).

This last line suggests the still more disruptive turn that *The Waste Land* will take. Even as the poem, like Apollinaire's "Zone," accepts the values of density and velocity, it disbelieves in the reciprocity of voice. The speaker hails Stetson, but no voice replies. Indeed the absence of dialogue must stand as one of the signal formal aspects of the poem. Conditions of exchange are prepared: a speaker turns toward an auditor, utters resonant words, which elicit no (overt) response. Most often, the listener never comes into view, but sometimes the failure of contact is heightened, as in the so-called nerves dialogue in "A Game of Chess," by the gap between thought and speech with the repetition of "nothing ... Nothing ... nothing" (122–6). The single example of audible dialogue occurs in the pub sequence at the end of the section, but even it appears only through the resources of soliloquy. "I" speaking in the present records a conversation with "Lil" in the past, and in so doing, transforms exchange into testimony – almost as a formal seal on the dominance of monologue.

As strong as any formal principle in the poem is the asymmetry of these monologic voices. *The Waste Land* represents speech on more than one level, in line with Eliot's early principle that "life goes on different planes."[13] The poem's "characters," especially its women, remain caught within the trammels of sexual violence and traumatic testimony. But the voice that moves among their plights enjoys freedom from their necessities. At telling moments, the register changes fundamentally, as a speaking voice detaches itself from the noise below. For instance, the exclamation at the end of "The Burial of the Dead" –

'You! hypocrite lecteur! – mon semblable, – mon frère!' (76)

– breaks the frame of the literary work. It does so, first, through a direct quotation from Charles Baudelaire that brings us into another poem, and then uses its source to address the reader. We are expelled from *The Waste Land*, forced into consciousness of our relation to text and writer. Among "The Three Voices of Poetry," Eliot distinguishes the voice of character from the voice of the poet who addresses the audience. In making that transition here, the poem moves onto another level of discourse, where we are no longer asked to inhabit a text but to take up an attitude toward it.

"These fragments I have shored against my ruins" (430) – the radiant utterance not only names a desperation and a resolve; it also assesses the poem to which it belongs. It stands out as an act of commentary wrested from the din of other voices, a meta-reflection that has never ceased to influence how the poem is read. As such, it belongs alongside the other grandly voiced meta-reflection, the speech of Tiresias in "The Fire Sermon."

> I Tiresias, old man with wrinkled dugs
> Perceived the scene, and foretold the rest –
> I too awaited the expected guest (228–30)

"I Tiresias" is pronoun and proper name, a voice of self-consciousness striving to articulate itself within a world of inarticulate impulse. The typist and the clerk are carried to their hollow clutching by the evening hour that impels them, while the task of speech for Tiresias is to see, to foresuffer, to foretell, in order to ascend from such blind experience to knowledge. Eliot's note articulates the difficult intention: "Tiresias, although a mere spectator and not indeed a 'character,' is yet the most important personage in the poem, uniting all the rest ... the two sexes meet in Tiresias. What Tiresias *sees*, in fact, is the substance of the poem" (218).

The thought is persistent in Eliot of the named figure who cannot be contained by the category of character. Years later, in reflecting on *The Family Reunion*, he wrote of moments when his actors had to speak "beyond character:" "the speakers have to be presented as falling into a trancelike state in order to speak" their lines.[14] This different (higher) level brings a different voice: solemn, incantatory. In place of desperation ("Speak") or depression ("glad it's over") or scorn ("hypocrite lecteur"), there arrives Tiresias's tone of weary vision and acceptance, the equanimity of inevitability. But an unsettling challenge of the poem is its refusal to sustain the voices of recognition. *The Waste Land* breaks its frame only to return to it. Tiresias appears at the center of the central section, but once he has spoken, the poetry returns to the "characters," who struggle as before. The incantatory voice delivers its wisdom and then recedes. Yet, the force of incantation appears in another form, in lines that Eliot would soon describe as the only "*good* lines" in the poem ("The rest is ephemeral").[15] These belong to the "'water-dripping song'" (Eliot's note 357) of part V: "If there were water we should stop and drink / Amongst the rock one cannot stop or think" (335–6). The "we" subject of these late lines gives voice to desire as it takes on the simplicity of need – need beyond the city and its modernity. Much of its haunting force is that it no longer emanates from individuals, angular in their separately coiled desires, but from a shared simple need for water.

From early in his critical career, Eliot engaged nervously with the plays of Maurice Maeterlinck, which stood in the early years of the twentieth century as triumphs of Symbolist drama. In the late essay "Poetry and Drama," he refers to the plays "so much admired in my youth, and now hardly even read, by Maeterlinck" (82). Two essays from *The Sacred Wood* had acknowledged the playwright's prominence, even as they deride him for straining at the limits of language: "Some writers appear to believe that emotions gain in intensity through being inarticulate."[16] Yet, Eliot's "intensity" in part V owes a significant debt to the precedent of Maeterlinck's experiments at a slightly earlier stage in the history of the avant-garde. Here are lines from *The Blind*, marking the characters' dawning recognition that they are lost and abandoned. Although they have not yet realized the fact, the priest who has led them on an excursion to a forest has died in their midst. They begin to speak into the dark.

> SECOND MAN BLIND FROM BIRTH
> I hear nothing coming.
>
> THIRD MAN BLIND FROM BIRTH
> It is time to go back to the Asylum.
>
> FIRST MAN BLIND FROM BIRTH
> We ought to find out where we are.
>
> SECOND MAN BLIND FROM BIRTH
> It has grown cold since he left.
>
> FIRST MAN BLIND FROM BIRTH
> We ought to find out where we are!
>
> VERY OLD BLIND MAN
> Does any one know where we are?[17]

The play sustains this plaintive chant, which, for all of Eliot's published disdain, leaves a strong tonal mark on *The Waste Land*, as on "The Hollow Men" a few years later. One of the most striking turns in the poem is the emergence of a Maeterlinckian "we" near its end, the plural pronoun through which separate selves testify to a common predicament. It stands beyond the small-scale "we" of personal relatedness, as in Marie's "when we were children" (13) or the use in the nerves-dialogue: "I think we are in rats' alley" (115). In part V, "we" has become fully transpersonal.[18] No one can retreat from its inclusive voice.

> DA
> *Datta*: what have we given?
> My friend, blood shaking my heart
> The awful daring of a moment's surrender
> Which an age of prudence can never retract
> By this, and this only, we have existed (400–5)

As in the water-dripping song, the passage evokes the shared agony, invisible beneath the apparatus of modernity. We are told that the wound cannot be found in our obituaries or memories. Where then is it? The poetry will not directly say, no more than it can name the feeling behind the search for water. Eliot criticized Maeterlinck, as he did the Shakespeare of *Hamlet*, for summoning "the emotion which cannot be expressed" ("'Rhetoric'" 84), but this is the risk that *The Waste Land* accepts, as it approaches conclusion. The voice of the first-person plural takes on the sonorities of Symbolism, less now the Symbolism of voice-changing Laforgue and more that of Stéphane Mallarmé, who inspired both Maeterlinck and Eliot to exploit the resources of indeterminacy. In the last part of *The Waste Land*, the poem leaves the city, enters an uncertain landscape, and assumes the voice of Symbolist inquiry into signs without referents.

> Who is the third who walks always beside you? (359)
>
> What is that sound high in the air (366)

IV

This portentous voice, however, contends with another, a more recent sound that Eliot also heard with suspicion and interest, namely the noise of Dada. Within the succession of movements that flared during the pre-war and wartime years – cubism, futurism, vorticism, expressionism – dadaism stands out as a belated eruption resisting both the violent world and its avant-garde predecessors. For the young artists who gathered in Zurich in 1916, the pre-war avant-garde was naively utopian. Their only radical gesture was to give up the high ambition to transform the world through art. Meaning is a dangerous daydream. Expression is a ruse.[19] In their place should stand the exuberance of non-sense and antic gesture – as in Hugo Ball's work of 1916, "Karawane," which makes a new language out of old sounds and whose first lines are these:

> jolifanto bambla ô falli bambla
> *großiga m'pfa habla horem*
> égiga goramen
> higo bloiko russula huju[20]

Eliot encountered Dada in its Parisian incarnation, and in the spring of that gestating year 1921 he published an essay entitled "The Lesson of Baudelaire" in Wyndham Lewis's new journal, *The Tyro*. A brisk effort to rewrite the responsibilities of modern literary voice, it begins with a glance of disdain at "certain intellectual activities across the Channel, which at the moment appear to take the place of poetry in the life of Paris."[21] But Eliot immediately acknowledges that those on his side of the channel must develop "an intelligent point of view" toward the events (4). Dada, he writes, is distinctly French; it cannot be "directly applicable in London," because it is the product of a small public "formidably well instructed in its own literary history, erudite and stuffed with tradition to the point of bursting" (4). These phrases, however, might equally serve as a description of Eliot's own small milieu, as of the poem that would soon startle it.

The argument of the brief essay is that the test of art "depends upon the extent to which it is a moral criticism" (4). The noises of Dada must be measured against the precedent of Baudelaire, who saw that what mattered was "the problem of good and evil." Indeed, Eliot concludes by quoting the line that will close part I of *The Waste Land*: "Vous, hypocrite lecteur" (4). The short text is long enough to show Eliot's half-reluctant attentiveness to dadaism, much as his reading of Jean Epstein's *La Poésie d'aujourd'hui* shows his close awareness of French avant-garde poetry.[22] These recognitions belong alongside another, namely, his fascination with the latest turn in James Joyce's *Ulysses*.

In the spring of the year, Joyce had sent Eliot drafts of three late episodes: "Oxen of the Sun," "Circe," and "Eumaeus." In the letter accompanying their return, Eliot described the new work as "superb – especially the Descent into Hell ["Circe"], which is stupendous.... I wish, for my own sake, that I had not read it."[23] All of *Ulysses* belongs within the history of avant-garde tonality, but the late chapters hold a special place. As Joyce approached the end, he became increasingly aware of the brazen experiments of the young and, it seems clear, inspired by their radicalism. "Circe," in its gestural theatricality and psycho-dramatics – the shattering of the lamp as Stephen confronts his dead mother, Bloom reduced to masochistic groveling as he becomes a female body – has been seen as Joyce's strong rereading of expressionist drama. The connection is important. But a fuller account brings Joyce in relation to Dada. In mid-1920 he wrote teasingly to his brother Stanislaus, asking him to deny the rumor "That I founded in Zurich the Dadaist movement which is now exciting Paris."[24] The tone registers Joyce's distance, but also his interest, and without denying the "expressionism" of "Circe," we might better recognize the dadaist stimulus behind its wilder performances. The indifference to fine writing or to decorum of any kind, the comic excess (in speech, sex, and violence), the assault on readerly norms and tastes, the extravagant play with improbability – the talking soap, the camel that plucks a mango, the End of the World as an octopus in a kilt – these must be seen as part of the Paris Dada carnival of 1920–21 that Joyce watched with detachment and curiosity. Joyce was no dadaist, merely a ruthless exploiter of its tactics, especially its willingness to release literary voice to the broadest, loudest register.

To follow Eliot's relation to Dada, then, we need to move by way of the apparent detour that is Joyce. The example of *Ulysses*'s later episodes, the "stupendous" "Circe" above all, brought conviction to the Dada voicings in *The Waste Land*. First among them is the phoneme "Da" itself, the thrice-repeated sound of the thunder in part V, which in 1921–2 (and in the context of Eliot's meditations in *The Tyro*) cannot have failed to evoke dadaism. If "The Lesson of Baudelaire" is that the avant-garde will matter only insofar as it offers "moral criticism," the poem enacts this thought by following the bare sound of "Da" with the stern injunctions of a religious ethics: Give, Sympathize, and Control. Yet these telling instances also suggest some of the radically disruptive aspects of voice in the poem: the way moral criticism is always *subsequent* to sounds that shatter meaning. What Eliot took from his encounter with Dada was a capacity to listen to noise.

"Fragments" remains our usual name, as it was Eliot's name, for the elements that compose *The Waste Land*. But the word should not suggest that "wholes" are merely waiting to reassemble. The provocation of the eruptive sounds is immediate: they strike the ear (by way of the eye) before there is time for interpretation, and the velocity of the rhythms means that each yields to the next without the security of context, or the comfort of a consistent tone. The dadaist sound is precisely one that cannot be predicted by the sound that came before – a condition that unsettles the entire poem (in the "Shakespeherian Rag" (128), in Augustine and the Buddha, in the cry of Philomel), and then, aggressively, in these late lines:

> London Bridge is falling down falling down falling down
> *Poi s'ascose nel foco che gli affina*
> *Quando fiam uti chelidon* – O swallow swallow
> *Le Prince d'Aquitaine à la tour abolie* (426–9)

Before and after these lines, the poem again gives the promise of meta-commentary ("Shall I at least set my lands in order?" 425; "These fragments I have shored against my ruins," 430), and it ends with words of "moral criticism:" the ethics of thunder and "shantih." This is what Eliot has drawn from Baudelaire, that poetry must encounter good and evil. Yet the ethical frame around the quoted lines cannot disarm their challenge. The different languages create their own violent dislocation of sound, and the quoted texts impose a variety of rhythms. A near century of criticism has not been able to enclose these provocations within a circle of interpretation: the sounds keep leaking out. Among the many tonalities, our last two ring out strongly and competitively at the end: the insurgent dadaist voice of non- or not-yet meaning, and the Symbolist voice that draws upon Maeterlinck, Mallarmé, and, decisively, Baudelaire, to evoke a transpersonal realm of moral extremity. These voices meet but never harmonize. The poem is noisy to its end: murmuring, chanting, reciting, laughing, accusing, praying.

NOTES

1 T. S. Eliot, "The Three Voices of Poetry," *On Poetry and Poets* (New York: Noonday Press, Farrar Straus & Giroux, 1957), 96.

2 James Fenton, *An Introduction to Poetry* (London: Penguin, 2002), 10.

3 Eliot, "Introduction" to Charlotte Eliot, *Savonarola: A Dramatic Poem* (London: R. Cobden-Sanderson, 1926), xi.

4 Arthur Symons, *The Symbolist Movement in Literature* (New York: E. P. Dutton: 1919), 297.

5 Emile Benveniste, *Problems in General Linguistics*, trans. Mary Elizabeth Meek (Coral Gables, FL: University of Miami Press, 1971), 223–30.

6 M. M. Bakhtin, "Discourse in the Novel," *The Dialogical Imagination*, ed. Michael Holquist, trans. Carol Emerson and Michael Holquist (Austin: University of Texas Press, 1981).

7 Ezra Pound, "A Retrospect," *Literary Essays*, ed. T. S. Eliot (New York: New Directions, 1935), 3.

8 Ezra Pound [as B. H. Dias], "Art Notes," *New Age* 26 (January 29, 1920): 205–6.

9 Eliot, "Hamlet," *Selected Essays* (1932; London: Faber and Faber, 1999), 145.

10 Guillaume Apollinaire, *Alcools, Oeuvres Poétiques* (Paris: Gallimard, Bibliothèque de la Pléiade, 1956), 147.

11 Walter Benjamin, *Charles Baudelaire: A Lyric Poet in the Age of High Capitalism*, trans. Harry Zohn (London: Verso, 1997).

12 Apollinaire, *Alcools, Oeuvres Poétiques*, 39.

13 Eliot, "Mandarins 3," *Inventions of the March Hare: Poems 1909–1917*, ed. Christopher Ricks (London: Faber and Faber, 1996), 21.

14 Eliot, "Poetry and Drama," *On Poetry and Poets*, 88.

15 Eliot to Ford Madox Ford, quoted in *The Waste Land: A Facsimile and Transcript of the Original Drafts Including the Annotations of Ezra Pound*, ed. Valerie Eliot (London: Faber and Faber, 1971), 129.

16 Eliot, "Rhetoric and Poetic Drama," *The Sacred Wood: Essays on Poetry and Criticism* (London: Methuen, 1932), 84.

17 Maurice Maeterlinck, "The Blind," *The Plays of Maurice Maeterlinck*, trans. Richard Hovey (Chicago and New York: Herbert S. Stone, 1905), 266–7.

18 As Moody finely describes it, "The 'We,' at once personal and inclusive, is a new voice, a new subject. The earlier parts of the poem call for a reading in different voices – perhaps four or five for the several distinct states of mind and feeling. But here, in a dramatised reading, the lines can no longer be distributed according to those characters or personae. One voice alone will not do either. All the voices are present; but changed out of themselves into an intensified common voice, as individual speaking voices can become one in song or incantation." A. David Moody, *Thomas Stearns Eliot: Poet*, 2nd ed. (Cambridge: Cambridge University Press, 1994), 97.

19 See, for instance, the cubo-futurist manifesto "A Slap in the Face of Public Taste," published in pre-war Russia. The quoted lines are from Anna M. Lawton, *Russian Futurist Manifestoes, 1912–1928*, ed. and trans. Anna M. Lawton and Herbert Eagle (first published by Cornell University Press, 1988, rpt. Washington DC: New Academia Publishing, 2005), 51–2.

20 Hugo Ball, "Karawane," in Jean-Jacques Thomas and Steven Winspur, *Poeticized Language: the Foundations of Contemporary French Poetry* (University Park: The Pennsylvania State University Press: 1999), 55.

21 Eliot, "The Lesson of Baudelaire," *The Tyro*, vol. I (Spring 1921): 4.

22 Jean Epstein, *La Poésie d'aujourd'hui: Un nouvel état d'intelligence* (Paris: Éditions de la Sirène, 1921). Eliot's response was that "The Epstein book is most interesting; I disagree with some important conclusions, but it is a formidable work to attack, and therefore very tonic. Also, he makes his texts – Aragon, Cendrars, Apollinaire etc., – a more serious affair, to be tackled in earnest." Eliot to Richard Aldington, September 8, 1921, *The Letters of T.S. Eliot, Volume I: 1898–1922*, ed. Valerie Eliot and Hugh Haughton, rev. ed. (New Haven, CT: Yale University Press, 2011), 580.

23 Eliot to James Joyce, May 21, 1921, in *The Letters, Volume I*, 560–1.

24 James Joyce, *Letters*, vol. 3, ed. Richard Ellmann (New York: Viking 1966), 22.

7

JEWEL SPEARS BROOKER

Dialectical Collaboration: Editing
The Waste Land

On October 23, 1922, less than two weeks after the publication of *The Waste Land* in the *Criterion*, T. S. Eliot mailed all manuscripts related to the poem to John Quinn, his benefactor and de facto lawyer in New York. The packet contained fifty-four leaves, divided into two sections. The first consisted of forty leaves of the main text and the second of fourteen leaves of related fragments and drafts.[1] Quinn accepted the gift "as a mark of friendship," adding that he would like to purchase "the MS. of the Early Poems" (*Facsimile* xxiv). At his death in 1924, Quinn's papers passed first to his sister Julia (Mrs. William Anderson), and at her death in 1934 to her daughter Mary (Mrs. Thomas Conroy), who put them in storage without looking at them. In the early 1950s, Mrs. Conroy discovered the Eliot manuscripts, and in 1958, she sold them to the New York Public Library. Neither Eliot nor Pound was informed (*Facsimile* xxix). Asked about the manuscripts in an interview shortly before he died, Eliot said: "We don't know, nobody knows, what became of them. Or who was responsible for their disappearance."[2] Three years after his death, the New York Public Library contacted Mrs. Eliot and gave her a copy of the manuscripts. She notified Ezra Pound, who assisted her in deciphering his comments, and in 1971, she published a scrupulously edited facsimile with a brief preface by Pound and an introduction that chronicles the preservation and recovery of the manuscripts.

As suggested by the grouping of the manuscripts that he sent to Quinn, Eliot wanted the materials to be considered in two different ways. On the one hand, he wanted to preserve the annotated main text as a tribute to Pound; on the other, he wanted the rejected parts to remain unpublished. He expressed both sentiments in a letter thanking Quinn for his assistance in securing the *Dial* award for *The Waste Land*.

> My only regret ... is that this award should come to me before it has been given to Pound.... In the manuscript of *The Waste Land* which I am sending

you, you will see the evidences of his work, and I think that this manuscript is worth preserving in its present form solely for the reason that it is the only evidence of the difference which his criticism has made.... I hope that the portions which I have suppressed will never appear in print and in sending them to you I am sending the only copies of these parts.[3]

This is the first of several expressions of appreciation for Pound's role in the final editing of *The Waste Land*. The recovered manuscripts corroborate Eliot's account of Pound's helpfulness; they also reveal that his first wife Vivien was involved in the genesis and shaping of the text.

The fact that Eliot welcomed the contributions of his wife and a fellow poet was not simply a case of friends helping friends. He and other modernists embraced collaboration as a positive principle, in part as a reaction against the celebration of the solitary genius in Romanticism. Eliot's interest in collaboration, explored in depth by Richard Badenhausen,[4] is consistent with his understanding of tradition as working with others – "No poet, no artist of any art, has his complete meaning alone"[5] – and with his appreciation of genres such as drama and epic that include multiple voices. Both poets insisted on the need for artists to work with other artists and on the special status of fellow poets as readers and critics. Pound, moreover, granted collaborator status to patrons, writing to Quinn that "if a patron buys from an artist who needs money ... the patron then makes himself equal to the artist."[6] Eliot, on the other hand, argues that the essential "other" in the creation of a work of art, was the audience, a position expressed in his essays on drama, the music hall, and ritual. "The working man who went to the music-hall and saw Marie Lloyd and joined in the chorus was himself performing part of the act; he was engaged in that collaboration of the audience with the artist which is necessary in all art."[7]

The Waste Land manuscripts and Eliot's contemporaneous correspondence make it possible to trace the work of the three parties – Eliot, his wife Vivien, and Pound – who were involved in shaping the final text. In a ditty sent to Eliot as the process was nearing completion, Pound describes his role in maieutic terms as that of the "sage homme" (wise man; pun on "sage femme," midwife) who "performed the caesarean Operation."[8] Pound saw Eliot's poem in progress for the first time on November 21, 1921 when, en route to Lausanne for medical treatment, Eliot passed through Paris, where the Pounds were then living; Pound saw the remaining materials in early January 1922 when Eliot stopped by on his way home. In an exchange of letters in late January, Eliot posed some follow-up queries, and Pound offered his final suggestions. Vivien Eliot, essential in the poem's gestation, was involved much earlier, first as muse and in 1921 as reader and sounding board. In May 1921, when she was away from London, she and Eliot mailed a draft of part II back and forth. In October, they were together in Margate, and after she left, he wrote to Sidney Schiff that he had composed lines for part III, but wanted to run them by Vivien before showing them to others.[9]

I. Life and Art in *The Waste Land*

The Waste Land as published is a result of negotiations between life and art as embodied in the tension between Vivien and Pound, with Eliot himself completing the dialectical movement. Vivien served as the advocate for life and Pound for art; Eliot clearly recognized the importance of both, valuing the authenticity emanating from Vivien and esteeming the authority issuing from Pound. Eliot underlined the distinction between life and art (the "what" and the "how") in his 1923 review of *Ulysses*. The central question about Joyce, he maintains, is: "how much living material does he deal with, and how does he deal with it ... as an artist?"[10] Indeed, in "Four Elizabethan Dramatists," published in 1924, Eliot argues that "actual life is always the material" of art.[11]

Eliot had an abundance of unmediated "living material." In January 1916, over a year into the war and six months into his marriage, he wrote to Conrad Aiken: "I have *lived* through material for a score of long poems, in the last six months."[12] His *"lived"* material included the death of his friend Jean Verdenal, his wife's adultery, their illnesses, her nervous breakdown followed by his own, financial burdens, overwork, uneasy relations with his parents, and war, "the one great tragedy" dwarfing all individual troubles.[13] Eliot emphasizes this "living material" in retrospective comments on *The Waste Land*, telling Theodore Spencer that "To me it was only the relief of a personal and wholly insignificant grouse against life; it is just a piece of rhythmical grumbling" (*Facsimile* 1). In a conversation with Donald Hall about the origin of the poem, he remarked, "One wants to get something off one's chest. One doesn't know quite what it is ... until one's got it off."[14]

Eliot's simultaneous commitment to the personal and the impersonal, to lived material (including, ironically, the "grouse against life") and to art put him in a catch-22: the situation that was so rich in material was physically and psychologically debilitating, making it almost impossible for him to master it as an artist. Most of the main text of the poem was written in 1921 – the first two parts between January and May, and the last three between October and the end of the year.[15] There was a hiatus over the summer, because of a ten-week visit by his mother, brother, and sister. The visit, which involved burdensome living arrangements, was exhausting, and soon after his family left, he collapsed. Vivien, who had suffered a breakdown in the spring, grumbled to Scofield Thayer: "I have not nearly finished my own nervous breakdown yet."[16] Eliot was granted a three-month medical leave from the bank and decided to consult Dr. Roger Vittoz in Lausanne. But first, on October 15, he and Vivien began his recuperation by going to Margate – she for two weeks and he for three. While there, he composed chunks of part III. On November 12, he returned to London, and on the 18th he and Vivien left for Paris, where they were to visit the Pounds and where she was to linger while he went to Lausanne. On the 21st, Eliot met with Pound and showed him some of *The Waste Land* manuscripts. This is the moment when Eliot, who had been drowning in "living material," refocused on craftsmanship. With Pound's suggestions in hand, he continued on to Switzerland where he revised what he had written and completed drafts of parts IV and V, the latter needing almost no revision.

Eliot discerned the value of Pound's detachment and expertise, so much so that he proposed publishing lines from Pound's "Sage Homme" along with *The Waste Land*: "Wish to use caesarian operation in italics in front."[17] Pound wisely advised against printing his doggerel, so Eliot decided to acknowledge his gratitude in another way. In the Boni and Liveright edition that he presented to Pound in 1923, he inscribed: "For Ezra Pound / *il miglior fabbro*." This dedication, "the better maker," is Dante's tribute in *Purgatorio* XXVI to his poetic predecessor Arnaut Daniel. When assembling his work for *Collected Poems 1909–1925*, Eliot added the dedication to the title page of *The Waste Land*, a position it has enjoyed in all subsequent printings. In 1938, at a time when it was fashionable to disparage Pound, Eliot found an occasion to praise him by explaining the dedication. In an essay in *Purpose*, G. W. Stonier had speculated that Eliot's dedication had contributed to an undeserved elevation of Pound's reputation;[18] in the following issue, Eliot responded, explaining that in using the phrase from Dante, he wished "to honour the technical mastery and critical ability manifest in [Pound's] own work, which had also done so much to turn *The Waste Land* from a jumble of good and bad passages into a poem."[19]

II. The Muse versus the Critic

The Waste Land had its debut on June 4, 1922 at a dinner party at the home of Virginia and Leonard Woolf. As recorded in Virginia's *Diary*, Eliot "sang it & chanted it rhythmed it. It has great beauty & force of phrase: symmetry; & tensity.... The Waste Land, it is called; & Mary Hutch[inson], who has heard it more quietly, interprets it to be Tom's autobiography" [sic].[20] Woolf's attention to art and Hutchinson's to life highlight two essential elements in the poem. At an earlier stage in the poem's existence, the tension can be seen in the editorial interventions of Vivien, representing "Tom's autobiography," and Pound, representing "beauty & ... symmetry." Vivien's mantra is emphasized in a letter to Eliot's brother at the conclusion of the family's summer visit in England. On August 23, 1921, she wrote begging forgiveness for behaving "just like a wild animal when [we] saw you off." She explained that "the emotionless condition" maintained during their visit had been such "a great strain" that she had been tempted to "burst out and scream and dance." After pouring out her feelings, she concluded "Good-bye Henry. And *be personal*, you must be personal, or else it's no good. Nothing's any good" (*Letters 1*, 577).

Vivien's italicized "*be personal*," reflected in her response to Eliot's drafts, was countered by Pound's frequent reminders to be impersonal. He recommended removing confessional elements, self-portraiture, personal pronouns, and other autobiographical markers. The contrast between Vivien's advice and Pound's is most evident in the typescript of "A Game of Chess." In May 1921, at a time when she was away from London, Eliot mailed her a draft. She scribbled her impressions, returning it with a note on the back of one of the sheets: "Make any of these alterations – or *none* if you prefer. Send me back this copy" (*Facsimile* 15). Her suggestions, significantly, were made some nine months before Pound saw Eliot's drafts.

Vivien was especially enthusiastic about the faux dialogue between the woman at her dressing table and her husband which begins, "'My nerves are bad tonight. Yes, bad. Stay with me'" (*Facsimile* 11, line 35). This section appears to be a transcript of a bedroom conversation between the Eliots. In the margin, Vivien wrote "W O N D E R F U L." When Pound saw the typescript, he wrote "photography" beside the very same lines. She had also written "wonderful" and "& wonderful" and "Yes" beside subsequent lines, including "Are you alive or not? Is there nothing in your head?" Pound countered, writing "photo" beside these mimetic lines. This instance of Eliot's accommodation of the antithesis between life and art illustrates the dialectical structure evident in the poem's composition.

As he had in the boudoir scene, Eliot in the pub scene honors Vivien's collaboration by accepting her suggestions. She considered "No, m'am, you needn't look old-fashioned at me" to be stilted, and recommended "If you don't like it you can get on with it." For "You want to keep him at home, I suppose," she substituted "*What you get married for if you don't want to have children*" (*Facsimile* 15). She added color by replacing "medicine" with "pills" in "It's that medicine I took, in order to bring it off" (*Facsimile* 13). Here, in the pub scene, Pound did not resist her realism, for unlike the dialogue in the boudoir scene, the gossipy chitchat does not echo the conversation of the Eliots themselves. As can be seen from her substitution of "Goo night" for "Good night" and her appreciation for the closing lines ("Splendid last lines"), her ear for pub talk, as her husband recognized, had a ring of authenticity (*Facsimile* 15).

Another window into the poles represented by Pound and Vivien can be seen in the revision of "The Fire Sermon," which originally opened with 72 lines in imitation of Alexander Pope's "The Rape of the Lock." In 1928, in an introduction for Pound's *Selected Poems*, Eliot referred to Pound's response to these lines. "Pound once induced me to destroy what I thought an excellent set of couplets; for, said he, 'Pope has done this so well that you cannot do it better; ... you cannot parody Pope unless you can write better verse than Pope – and you can't.'"[21] Most of "The Fire Sermon" was written in Margate after Vivien had returned to London. In his November 4 letter to Schiff, Eliot said, "I have done a rough draft of part of part III, but do not know whether it will do, and must wait for Vivien's opinion as to whether it is printable" (*Letters 1*, 601). Vivien must have considered the parody "printable," for under the pseudonym "F. M." (Fanny Marlow), she incorporated twenty lines (revised, improved) into "Letters of the Moment," one of her several contributions to the *Criterion*, and another indication of her collaborative efforts with Eliot.[22] Not only did he supply the couplets, but he also inserted two brief paragraphs, the second ending with an allusion to "The Love Song of J. Alfred Prufrock." "On my replying ... that I found Gilbert and Sullivan a bore, the same expression convulsed his features as ... if one had said, 'settling a pillow or throwing off a shawl;' No, I did not care for the *Boutique* at all, not at all" (361–2).

Pound disapproved of including echoes from the "Prufrock" period in *The Waste Land*. Especially noteworthy is his attempt to restrain Eliot's characteristic ambivalence, a trait that had hardened during his philosophical training. Impatient with intellectual waffling, Pound blue-penciled several examples in "The Fire Sermon." In the episode of the typist and clerk, beside the line "Perhaps his inclinations touch the stage," he circled the offending word and scribbled "Perhaps be damned" (*Facsimile* 45). Similarly, beside "And perhaps a weekend at the Metropole," he underlined "perhaps" twice and added "dam per'apsez" (*Facsimile* 31). Of Eliot's line about the typist "Across her brain one half-formed thought may pass," Pound circled and deleted "may" and chided, "make up / yr. mind / you Tiresias / if you know / know damn well / or / else you / dont" [sic] (*Facsimile* 47). Pound also frowned on including reminders of the autobiographically tinged characters and *mise-en-scène* of Eliot's early poems. In the Harvard poems, Eliot had masked his subjectivity by the use of drama and internal debate. But Pound had grown tired of this portrait of the artist as a young man. No more tea parties and erotically charged visits to older women. No more prudish, passive, thought-tormented, self-conscious intellectuals. No more Prufrocks, no more Hamlets, no more ambivalent and repressed gentleman callers.

A striking example of this sort of intervention can be seen in "The Death of the Duchess," a portion of *The Waste Land* manuscript with strong echoes of "Prufrock," "Portrait of a Lady," and "The Boston Evening Transcript." The characters are automatons in "silk hats," who

> On Sunday afternoon go out to tea
> On Saturday have tennis on the lawn, and tea
> On Monday to the city, and then tea.
> They know what they are to feel and what to think,
> They know it with the morning printer's ink....
> But what is there for you and me
> For me and you
> What is there for us to do?
>
>   (*Facsimile* 105, lines 2–12)

Pound recognized this speaker as the cousin of the self-possessed self-conscious young man in "Portrait of a Lady" who sips tea and observes himself in the mirror, "Not knowing what to feel or if I understand" (119).[23] In the muted music of these lines, he noticed the "cadence / reproduction / from Pr[ufrock] / or Port[trait / of a Lady]." In "Time to regain the door," he heard echoes of the Prufrockian "Time to turn back and descend the stair" (*Facsimile* 107). Then, in addition to resisting the music of 1909–11, Pound redlined confessional elements and first-person pronouns. In "The Fire Sermon," for example, Eliot initially wrote "Unreal City, I have seen and see / Under the brown fog of your winter noon" (*Facsimile* 31, lines 93–4). Pound brackets or circles "I have seen and see" and "your." Near the line "London, your people is bound upon the wheel!" he writes "vocative??" (*Facsimile* 43). In revisions such as these, Pound tempers Eliot's "personal grumbling," adjusting the balance between life and art and improving the tone of the final text.

III. Under the Knife: Pound's "Caesarean Operation"

In acknowledging Pound's improvement of *The Waste Land*, Eliot repeatedly refers to the importance of his excisions. "It was in 1922 that I placed before [Pound] in Paris the manuscript of a sprawling, chaotic poem called *The Waste Land* which left his hands, reduced to about half its size."[24] In his last interview, Eliot once again emphasizes the importance of Pound's cuts, recalling that he had expunged a great deal of "dead matter."[25] In this, the most important of his maieutic services, Pound had two kinds of recommendations – the first suggesting that entire sections be removed from the main text; the second recommending that "superfluities" (more or less independent fragments and poems) not be added to the main text.

Of the three major blocks excised from the manuscripts, two were suggested by Pound and accepted by Eliot, and one was initiated by Eliot and approved by Pound. Pound advised cutting 154 lines: 72 imitating Pope's "The Rape of the Lock" from "The Fire Sermon," and 82 inspired by Dante's Ulysses canto in the *Inferno* from "Death by Water." Eliot himself dropped the fifty-four lines that originally stood at the beginning of "The Burial of the Dead." Influenced by Joyce's *Ulysses*, the omitted section is an American variation of the "Circe" episode, which Eliot was reading in April and May 1921, and of which he wrote to Joyce: "I have nothing but admiration; in fact, I wish, for my own sake, that I had not read it."[26] The fifty-four deleted lines describe a night on the town in which the protagonists get drunk, go to a show, visit a brothel, and avoid arrest through the intervention of a policeman who joins the group. On the typescript that Pound would have seen in November and again in January, these lines preceded "April is the cruellest month" (1). Although he left no marks on this section of the manuscript, Pound did approve of dropping the Joycean prelude, for on January 24, 1922, he wrote to Eliot "The thing now runs from April ... to shantih without break" (*Letters I*, 626).

The first of Pound's block cuts, the imitation of Pope, originally stood at the beginning of "The Fire Sermon." Before recommending removing the entire section, Pound attempted to improve it, scribbling such notes as – "Too / loose;" "rhyme drags it / out to / diffuseness" (*Facsimile* 39). Pound perceived that the satire was both less amusing and less serious than Pope's. The other deletion he recommended – the shipwreck section loosely based on Dante's Ulysses canto – also strengthened the poem. It originally stood at the beginning of "Death by Water" and, at eighty-two lines, was the longest of the block cuts. Eliot composed this section while he was in Lausanne and showed it to Pound in Paris in January. These lines, like those describing the night out in Boston, are associated with America, specifically with Eliot's summers on Cape Ann by the north Atlantic.

> "Kingfisher weather, with a light fair breeze,
> Full canvas, and the eight sails drawing well.
> We beat around the cape and laid our course
> From the Dry Salvages to the eastern banks.
> (*Facsimile* 55, lines 13–16)

Pound first attempted to trim the section, condensing the above four lines to:

> with a light fair breeze,
> We beat around the cape
> From the Dry Salvages.
> (*Facsimile* 63, lines 13–15)

After some line-by-line tinkering, Pound advised expunging the entire narrative. At the same time, he recommended retaining the ten elegiac lines that now constitute the whole of "Death by Water." Evidently Eliot was not enthusiastic about discarding the sea voyage, for after returning to London, he sent Pound a question: "Perhaps better omit Phlebas also???"[27] Pound responded forcefully:

> I DO advise keeping Phlebas.... Phlebas is an integral part of the poem; the card pack introduces him, the drowned phoen. sailor, and he is needed ABSoloootly where he is [sic].[28]

The suggestion that the death of Phlebas fulfils the prophecy of Madame Sostrosis – "Fear death by water" (55) – suggests that Pound viewed the poem as unified by an unfolding narrative.

In addition to the main text, *The Waste Land* manuscripts include an assortment of poems and fragments written over a six- or seven-year period. Several brief pieces ("After the turning;" "So through the evening;" and "I am the Resurrection"), as both Lyndall Gordon and Lawrence Rainey have shown, were composed during Eliot's student days. Two poems – "The Death of St. Narcissus" and "The Death of the Duchess" – date from 1915 or 1916; most of the remaining drafts were composed in November and December 1921 as the poem was assuming its final shape. The Harvard fragments and the two independent poems, in an earlier style and confessional mood, were not included in the final poem, but several of the vignettes from 1921, especially those related to the City of London, were retained and integrated.

Eliot seems to have considered publishing three of the shorter pieces from 1921 – "Song" (fifteen lines), "Exequy" (thirty lines), and "Dirge" (eighteen lines) – with the final text of *The Waste Land*. Pound advised excluding these "remaining superfluities:" "I think you had better leave 'em, abolish 'em altogether.... One test is whether anything wd. be lacking if the last three were omitted. I don't think it wd."[29] Pound admired two lines in the "Song" – "When the surface of the blackened river / Is a face that sweats with tears?" (*Facsimile* 99, lines 10–11): "The song has only two lines which you can use in the body of the poem."[30] Eliot asked, "Would you advise working sweats with tears etc. into nerves monologue; only place where it can go?,"[31] to which Pound replied, "I dare say the sweats with tears will wait."[32] Eliot's momentary inclination to place the two lines in the boudoir scene of "A Game of Chess" suggests that they belong to the cluster of "living material" associated with Vivien. A few years later, in 1924, these lines were to appear, slightly varied, in drafts for "The Hollow Men," especially in the intensely personal poems, "Eyes that last I saw in tears" and "The wind sprang up at four o'clock."

Pound's "technical mastery" is not only evident in the cuts he recommended but also in his suggestions regarding style. In "The Fire Sermon," for example, part of Eliot's draft began:

> The typist home at teatime, who begins
> To clear ~~her broken breakfast~~ away her broken breakfast, lights
> Her stove, and lays out squalid food in tins,
> Prepares the ~~room~~ toast and sets the room to rights.
> Out of the window perilously spread
> Her drying combinations meet the sun's last rays,
> And on the divan piled, (at night her bed),
> Are stockings, dirty camisoles, and stays.
>
> (*Facsimile* 33, lines 129–36)

Pound condensed the first three lines to: "The typist home at teatime, who/ clears away her broken breakfast, lights / Her stove, and lays out squalid food" (*Facsimile* 45, lines 129–31). Beside the second quatrain, he inscribed "inversions / not warranted / by any real / exigence of / metre" and changed "on the divan piled" to "piled on the divan" (*Facsimile* 45, line 135). Pound disliked linguistic clutter, and throughout the manuscript, cut modifiers, participial phrases, and entire lines. He objected, furthermore, to syntactical inversions, consistently nudging Eliot toward a leaner sentence structure.

Pound also improved the tone of *The Waste Land*, especially in "The Fire Sermon." In addition to redlining the misogynistic description of Fresca's morning toilet, he marked several phrases belittling the typist and the clerk. In the draft, Tiresias "Perceived the scene, and foretold the rest, / Knowing the manner of these crawling bugs" (*Facsimile* 45, lines 142–3). Pound wisely wrote "Too / easy" in the margin. He struck out two quatrains on the clerk's tawdry boldness, and most important, he sanitized the passage in which the clerk, having coupled with the typist, takes his leave:

> And at the corner where the stable is,
> Delays only to urinate, and spit.
>
> (*Facsimile* 47, lines 179–80)

Pound scratched these lines, writing "probaly over the mark" (*Facsimile* 47). As his comment suggests, they are gratuitous and uncalled for by the vignette. In their crudeness, moreover, they tend to displace disgust from the clerk to the poet who is observing him.

Finally, Pound enhanced the quality of the verse in *The Waste Land*. He had a good auditory sense and pointed out numerous passages where the meter and rhyme needed attention. Beside the opening lines featuring the typist and clerk, quoted above, he wrote "verse not interesting / enough as verse / to warrant / so / much/ of it" (*Facsimile* 45). In "A Game of Chess," he marked the first three lines as "Too tum-pum / at a stretch" (*Facsimile* 11). Elsewhere, he chided, as I point out above, "rhyme drags it / out to / diffuseness" (*Facsimile* 39). Pound also sharpened Eliot's images, not only by eliminating modifiers, but by calling attention to the use of the pathetic fallacy, as in the "sullen river" (*Facsimile* 99).

IV. Eliot and Pound: Elucidation versus Weightiness

Pound's assistance in editing *The Waste Land* was invaluable, a fact acknowledged by Eliot and documented by the reappearance of the manuscripts. In spite of the congruence of some of their ideas about modern poetry, however, their attitudes toward the relationship between life and art were not the same. Eliot's focus was inductive, moving from life to art, from "*living material*" to form, from the "what" to the "how," from the existential to the theoretical. Pound's focus, on the other hand, was deductive, moving from art to life, from poetics to content, from the "how" to the "what," from movements and "isms" to poets and poems. Eliot projected the collapsing mind of Europe by focusing on his own mental breakdown, and Vivien's, whereas Pound thought of the modernist movement as Renaissance II. This contrast in focus – also a contrast in temperament – was useful in that it facilitated a process in which Eliot internalized polarities and then, in a dialectical loop, transcended them in the making of the poem.

The most revealing instance of the tension between Eliot's empiricism and Pound's aestheticism can be seen in their exchange regarding the epigraph. After Eliot conferred with Pound in Paris in January 1922, he returned to London and, based in part on their conversation, made a few more revisions. On or around January 20, he mailed Pound a packet to which he had added a new page containing the title and an epigraph from Joseph Conrad's *Heart of Darkness*.

> "Did he live his life again in every detail of desire, temptation, and surrender during that supreme moment of complete knowledge? He cried in a whisper at some image, at some vision, – he cried out twice, a cry that was no more than a breath
>
> – 'The horror! the horror!' "
>
> (*Facsimile* 2)

On January 24 Pound wrote: "I doubt if Conrad is weighty enough to stand the citation."[33] Eliot replied on the 26th: "Do you mean not use Conrad quot. or simply not put Conrad's name to it? It is much the most appropriate I can find, and somewhat elucidative."[34] On the 28th, Pound responded: "Do as you like about. ... Conrad; who am I to grudge him his laurel crown" (*Letters 1*, 630).

In this exchange, Eliot uses adjectives – "appropriate ... elucidative" – that point to content, to the living material of *The Waste Land*. He clearly felt that the great moral and political enigmas caught in *Heart of Darkness* were relevant to his poem, and that Marlow's memory of the whispered words of the dying Mr. Kurtz – "The horror! the horror!" – resonated with *The Waste Land* not in part but in whole, as epigraphs are designed to do. Kurtz is not simply an embodiment of evil or imperialism; as a poet, an artist, an orator, a philanthropist, an intellectual seeking forbidden knowledge, he is an objectification of the European mind in the process of breaking up. As Marlow notes, "All Europe contributed to the making of Kurtz."[35] The choice of this epigraph illustrates one of Eliot's strengths: in attending to his own "*living* material," he illuminates the living material of his moment in history (the mind of Europe collapsing in and after the Great War). Eliot's admiration of Conrad was not new. In 1911, in Paris, he had recommended Conrad's *Youth* and *Typhoon* to his French tutor, Alain-Fournier.[36] His fascination with Conrad is substantiated by the epigraph to "The Hollow Men" – "*Mistah Kurtz – he dead.*" – a poem in which Kurtz, like Brutus and Guy Fawkes, constitutes a link between idealism and apocalypse.

Pound, in stark contrast, ignored the content of the epigraph (and of *Heart of Darkness*), focusing instead on the author and whether or not he was "weighty enough" to be used in the epigraph. Eliot was nonplused and asked if Pound meant to suggest that he should omit "Conrad's name." Pound's retort that quoting *Heart of Darkness* would constitute a "laurel crown" for Conrad is astonishing. Eliot, after all, was in 1921 only an aspiring young American poet, whereas Conrad was the most distinguished living writer of his generation, with the possible exception of Thomas Hardy. Eliot brooded over Pound's disparaging remarks, and on March 12, without further comment, he notified Pound that he had "substituted for the J. Conrad" the passage from the *Satiricon* by Petronius,[37] in which Trimalchio recalls (in Latin) an incident in which the Sibyl tells him (in Greek) that she wants to die. As part of the Frazerian monomyth that Eliot drew on for structure and themes, the Sibyl, a figure of caged and desiccated divinity, is relevant to such motifs as the marginalization of God in the post-Nietzschean world. But as Eliot himself recognized, this epigraph generates a different poem, and as he confessed to his wife, he regretted making this concession to Pound (*Letters 1*, 630, note 4).

Eliot and Pound remained friends after 1922, but their collaboration, which ran from 1917 to 1922, was at an end. As Eliot explained, there came a point "at which difference of outlook and belief became too wide; or it may have been distance ... or both" (*Poetry* 335). Their collaboration in *The Waste Land* worked because it balanced "technical mastery" and "living material." The attenuation of their relationship was marked by a shift in terms in which life as lived was replaced by ideology. In Pound's case, the shift was toward economics and politics; in Eliot's, toward religion. In 1928, in a piece for *The Dial* called "Isolated Superiority," Eliot notes the paradox that "Pound has great influence but no disciples ... [for] influence can be exerted through form, whereas one makes disciples only among those who sympathize with the content."[38] Although Eliot clearly had qualms about Pound's emerging content, he admired him as a poet and critic and, in the 1946 essay in *Poetry*, defended him in the dark days following Pound's arrest for treason at the end of World War II. The collaboration with Vivien also dwindled to nothing in the mid-1920s, as their marriage darkened, their health worsened, and Eliot moved alone toward the baptismal font at Finstock Church. Henceforth, his collaborators would be primarily friends in the church, Emily Hale, and associates in the theater.[39]

NOTES

1. In preparing his article on the "lost" manuscripts, Donald Gallup moved the drafts of two fragments from the miscellaneous to the main text section, changing the balance to forty-two and twelve. See Donald Gallup, "The 'Lost' Manuscripts of T. S. Eliot," *The Times Literary Supplement* 3480 (November 7, 1968): 1238–40, and T. S. Eliot, *The Waste Land: A Facsimile and Transcript of the Original Drafts Including the Annotations of Ezra Pound*, ed. Valerie Eliot (New York: Harcourt, 1971), xxx.

2. Eliot, "A Conversation with T. S. Eliot." Interview with Leslie Paul. *Kenyon Review* (Winter 1964–5): 21 [11–21].

3. Eliot to John Quinn, September 21, 1922, *The Letters of T. S. Eliot: Volume 1: 1898–1922*, ed. Valerie Eliot and Hugh Haughton, rev. ed. (New Haven, CT: Yale University Press, 2011), 748.

4. See Richard Badenhausen, *T. S. Eliot and the Art of Collaboration* (Cambridge: Cambridge University Press, 2004).

5. Eliot, "Tradition and the Individual Talent" (1919), *The Complete Prose of T. S. Eliot: The Critical Edition: The Perfect Critic, 1919–1926*, 107 [105–14], ed. Anthony Cuda and Ronald Schuchard (Baltimore: The Johns Hopkins University Press, 2014. *Project MUSE.* https://muse.jhu.edu/).

6. Ezra Pound, *Selected Letters: 1907–1941*, ed. D. D. Paige (New York: New Directions, 1950), 53.

7. Eliot, "In Memoriam: Marie Lloyd" (1923), in *The Perfect Critic*, 420 [418–23].

8. Pound to Eliot, January 24, 1922, *Letters 1*, 626.

9. Eliot to Sydney Schiff, November 4?, 1921, *Letters 1*, 601.

10. Eliot, "*Ulysses*, Order, and Myth" (1923), in *The Perfect Critic*, 478 [476–81].

11. Eliot, "Four Elizabethan Dramatists" (1923), in *The Perfect Critic*, 505 [503–12].

12. Eliot to Conrad Aiken, January 10, 1916, *Letters 1*, 138.

13. Eliot to his Father, December 23, 1917, *Letters 1*, 242.

14 Eliot, "The Art of Poetry, I: T. S. Eliot." Interview with Donald Hall. *Paris Review* (Spring/Summer 1959): [47–70].

15 The chronology used in this essay is essentially that of Lyndall Gordon in *The Imperfect Life of T. S. Eliot*, rev. ed. (1998; London: Virago, 2012), and Lawrence Rainey in *Revisiting The Waste Land* (New Haven: Yale University Press, 2005).

16 Cited in Gordon, *The Imperfect Life*, 168.

17 Eliot to Pound, January 26?, 1922, *Letters 1*, 629.

18 Stonier, G. W., "The Mystery of Ezra Pound," *Purpose* 10 no. 1 (Jan/Mar 1938): 21–6.

19 Eliot, "On a Recent Piece of Criticism," *Purpose* 10 no. 2 (April/June): 93, [90–4].

20 Virginia Woolf, *The Diary of Virginia Woolf: Volume Two, 1920–1924*, ed. Anne Olivier Bell (New York: Harcourt, 1978), 178.

21 Eliot, "Introduction" to *Selected Poems*, by Ezra Pound (London: Faber, 1928), 18, [7–21].

22 Eliot, Vivien [F. M./Fanny Marlow], "Letters of the Moment," *Criterion* 2 no. 7 (April 1924): 360–4.

23 Eliot, "Portrait of a Lady," *The Complete Poems and Plays 1909–1950* (1952; New York: Harcourt, 1971).

24 Eliot, "Ezra Pound," *Poetry Magazine: A Magazine of Verse* 68 no. 6 (Sept. 1946): 330, [326–38].

25 Eliot, "A Conversation," 20.

26 Eliot to James Joyce, May 21, 1921, *Letters 1*, 562.

27 Eliot to Pound, January 26?, 1922, *Letters 1*, 629.

28 Pound to Eliot, January 28?, 1922, *Letters 1*, 630.

29 Pound to Eliot, January 24, 1922, *Letters 1*, 625.

30 Ibid.

31 Eliot to Pound, January 26?, 1922, *Letters 1*, 629.

32 Pound to Eliot, January28?, 1922, *Letters 1*, 630.

33 Pound to Eliot, January 24, 1922, *Letters 1*, 625.

34 Eliot to Pound, January 26?, 1922, *Letters 1*, 629.

35 Joseph Conrad, *Heart of Darkness*, 3rd edition, ed. Robert Kimbrough (1899; New York: W. W. Norton, 1988), 50.

36 Alain-Fournier to Eliot, July 25, 1911, *Letters 1*, 26.

37 Eliot to Pound, March 12, 1922, *Letters 1*, 641.

38 T. S. Eliot, "Isolated Superiority," A review of *Personae.*, *The Dial*, 84 no. 1 (Jan): 4, [4–7].

39 See also Jewel Spears Brooker, "Common Ground and Collaboration in T. S. Eliot," *Mastery and Escape: T. S. Eliot and the Dialectic of Modernism* (Amherst: University of Massachusetts Press, 1994), 65–80, and Ezra Pound, "Introduction," *Literary Essays of Ezra Pound*, 1935 (New York: New Directions, 1954).

8

MICHAEL COYLE

Doing Tradition in Different Voices: Pastiche in *The Waste Land*

Corresponding in 1919 with novelist Ramon Fernandez, Marcel Proust presented his idea that, far from being passive imitation, the writing of pastiche is "criticism in action."[1] Having launched his career earlier that summer with *Pastiches et mélanges*, this understanding of pastiche was for Proust a matter of some importance.[2] The writing of pastiche is, Proust affirms:

> a matter of hygiene; one must purge oneself of the all-too-natural vice of idolatry and imitation. And in place of underhandedly imitating Michelet or Goncourt by signing (here the names of this or that of our most amiable contemporaries), I did it openly through the form of pastiches, to sink back to being merely Marcel Proust when I write my novels.[3]

This gesture of being "merely" Marcel Proust has its corollary in T. S. Eliot's notion of "tradition:" the individual talent pales in significance to the tradition which potentially renders his or her voice as meaningful. So too does the vision of writing as a form of "hygiene." But although the idea that good writing should be hygienic marks a distinctly and broadly modernist (and particularly Futurist) preoccupation, informing the criticism of figures as diverse as Wyndham Lewis, Ezra Pound, Ernest Hemingway, and – of course – Eliot, Proust's connection of hygiene with the practice of pastiche in particular is something more unusual, more striking.[4] "Pastiche" designates writing that imitates the style of another artist or period. The word comes into English from the Italian "pasticcio" – a "hodge-podge of a pie containing both meat and pasta.... A pastiche uses recognizable ingredients but offers no new substance."[5] Our purpose in what follows is to understand how this "hodge-podge" can become something meaty. How is it that the imitation of style can, in the hands of modernist writers like Proust or Eliot, produce something at once "substantial" and "new" – a self-consciously modernist style stripped clean of history in the very process of apparently summoning history?

For Proust, pastiche is a kind of therapeutic exercise, a ritual cleansing, a purification achieved not by resisting but by submitting to stylistic influence. Or, to put it another way, Proust experienced the writing of pastiche as a kind of invocation of the muses, a summoning of spirit that enables poetic vision. Proust saw pastiche as being less a destination than a formal communion with tradition. Strikingly, his letter to Fernandez was written within months of the publication of Eliot's "Tradition and the Individual Talent" (1919). In this essay, explaining his notion of "the historical sense," Eliot proposes that "the most individual parts" of an artist's work "may be those in which the dead poets, his ancestors, assert their immortality most vigorously."[6] But here these two modernists part company. For Proust, such communion represents a point of departure; for Eliot it means a destination. What Proust wants to purge Eliot struggles to embrace.

Somewhat counterintuitively, Proust's position here proves the more conventional in that he regards historical style as something to be worked *through* in order to prepare the palette for something new. Consider the opening aphorism of Remy de Gourmont's "Tradition and Other Things," which appeared in the *Egoist* (July 15, 1914), in an authorized translation by imagist poet Richard Aldington: "We must not boast too much of tradition. It is no great merit to place our feet exactly in the tracks which the road indicates; it is a natural tendency. Though it is not very wrong to give way to this tendency, it is better to attempt a new path."[7] For de Gourmont, pastiche represents a natural but at last a retarding impulse, a kind of artistic indolence. The differences here are not so much cultural – two Frenchmen versus an Anglo-American – as they are historical. The five years (1914–19) that separate Gourmont's essay on "Tradition" from Eliot's, and from Proust's letter, were years of cataclysmic, global war in the aftermath of which the Western World struggled to discover what of its heritage still survived. What strength could the postwar world still draw from historical example? De Gourmont's and Eliot's essays might serve us, then, as milestones, the first marking the terminus of the Victorian era and the second the beginning of our own.

Few early twentieth-century critics, in either Paris or London, would have expected pastiche to be anything more than the kind of exercise apprentice artists undertake to achieve mastery of a tradition. For this reason Eliot's writing of pastiche in *The Waste Land* from the beginning prompted misunderstanding of what he was about. William Carlos Williams echoed the opinions of many readers when, in the pages of *Spring and All* (1923), he implicitly attacked Eliot as "the traditionalist of plagiarism."[8] Edmund Wilson initially called *The Waste Land* a "Rag-Bag of the Soul;" Louis Untermeyer regretted Eliot's "jumble" of "narratives, nursery rhymes, criticism, jazz-rhythms;" John Crowe Ransom found the poem only parodic and worried that the movement among different languages and styles would cause readers to experience "convulsions."[9] A century later, however, "postmodern" audiences are now long accustomed to seeing new works put together from features and fragments of older works.

Consider this example from the January 2014 issue of the jazz magazine *DownBeat*: David Zivan's review of Björkestra's *I Go Humble*. Björkestra is a jazz orchestra dedicated to reimagining the music of Icelandic singer-songwriter Björk. Midway through the review, Zivan focuses on "Hyperballad," a song from Björk's 1995 album, *Post*: "*Post*[] was a lovely pastiche of electronic sounds, laid under a plain, plaintive vocal. Here, the hi-hat renders the same clubby shuffle, but then come lush horn arrangements and warm piano chords. Only the vocal line, by Becca Stevens, is essentially the same."[10] Notice that Zivan describes Björk's original as a pastiche; he pointedly does not use that term to describe the new work that "covers" it. But he celebrates the Björkestra's reinvention of the original, and does so precisely by affirming that it is a genuinely new work, a work that marks its newness by alluding to (without reproducing exactly) stylistic features of the original (which is itself a pastiche). In other words, this record by Björkestra does not exist in a merely parasitical relation to the original. I note Zivan's review not because he is trying to forge theoretical principle but precisely because he isn't: this kind of short, two-paragraph review works by addressing interests common to both critics and to the broad audience for pop music. For Zivan, as for most twenty-first-century critics, pastiche is simply an ordinary aspect of artistic process. Style emerges in the context of earlier styles; new works are created out of old. What has happened, then, between Proust's moment and our own is what we today know as modernism, and in these events Eliot played a salient role.

This observation of historical change in our relation to the practice is now enshrined in critical tradition. Linda Hutcheon's early work marks a decisive moment in this process, particularly her *Theory of Parody* (1985) and her *Politics of Postmodernism* (1989). She regards parody as the distinctive postmodern mode and argues that postmodernism generally "takes the form of self-conscious, self-contradictory, self-undermining statement."[11] Hutcheon's work powerfully shaped not only the theorizing of the postmodern but also how scholars read modernist texts. Even where other voices drew different conclusions their arguments often bore traces of her strategies. Indeed, this associating of the postmodern with a particular mode (pastiche) is central to Fredric Jameson's *Postmodernism, or the Cultural Logic of Late Capitalism* (1991), even though Jameson implicitly suggests that Hutcheon identifies the wrong mode. Jameson opens by distinguishing pastiche – which he sees as a *postmodern* style – from parody – which he dismisses as modernist. For Jameson, as the Zivan review might suggest, pastiche has by our time become "well-nigh universal" (16):[12]

> Pastiche is, like parody, the imitation of a peculiar or unique, idiosyncratic style, the wearing of a linguistic mask, speech in a dead language. But it is a neutral practice of such mimicry, without any of parody's ulterior motives, amputated of the satiric impulse, devoid of laughter and of any conviction that alongside the abnormal tongue you have momentarily borrowed, some healthy linguistic normality still exists. (17)

In Jameson's account, pastiche means the deployment of a style freed from the historical forces wherein that style once marked the limits of technological possibility. Pastiche means style separated from history. In this way style proves less the expression of an individual author than techniques in a repertoire controlled by the author: style is no longer historically necessary – it is no longer the register of a particular historical moment. Style removed from history becomes something like a taxidermied specimen, removed from life and present in the text only as a sign of the author's mastery: "Faced with these ultimate objects – our social, historical, and existential present, and the past as 'referent' – the incompatibility of a postmodernist 'nostalgia' art language with genuine historicity becomes dramatically apparent. The contradiction propels this mode, however, into complex and interesting new formal inventiveness" (19). Pastiche is thus less an engagement of historical styles than a representation (re-presentation) of them. The subject of pastiche is, in Jameson's view, not then a past age but a validation of the present. Pastiche serves nothing more serious than nostalgia, offering a comforting view wherein historical struggle is made quaint, made safe, displayed precisely to show it no longer is alive.

As theorizers of the postmodern, it is to be expected that Jameson and Hutcheon would want to engage what seems most unsettling and most exciting about the purportedly new era. But I would argue that much of what they are calling "post" is simply the enduring and still unresolved challenges of modernist poetics. Or to put it another way, what Hutcheon and Jameson see as "postmodernist" is largely a function of their way of reading modernism. Both "self-contradictory, self-undermining statements" (Hutcheon 1) and pastiche are dynamically present in the single poem most often said to define *modernism* – Eliot's *The Waste Land*.

It is hard to see how lines like these from Eliot's "The Fire Sermon" serve to validate the present:

> Sweet Thames, run softly till I end my song,
> Sweet Thames, run softly, for I speak not loud or long.
> But at my back in a cold blast I hear
> The rattle of the bones, and chuckle spread from ear to ear.[13]

The first two lines here play with the music, even more than the meaning, of Edmund Spenser's "Prothalamion" (1596); the second two are a broken, disruptive allusion to Andrew Marvell's "To His Coy Mistress" (1681), where "Time's wingèd chariot hurrying near" (22) becomes "the rattle of the bones, and chuckle spread from ear to ear" (186). The Goldsmith and Marvell passages are both in tetrameters; this passage of Eliot's is irregular, unfolding in lines of five, six, five and seven feet, but uncharacteristically offering rhymed couplets as though nothing were out of the ordinary. Jameson maintains that "the incompatibility of a postmodernist 'nostalgia' art language with genuine historicity ... propels this mode [pastiche] ... into complex and interesting new formal inventiveness" (Jameson 1991, 19). Eliot's form here is certainly inventive, but the question remains what its inventions are *for*.

The apostrophe to the River Thames, a kind of spectral invocation of the muses, is wrong in tone for parody, but as pastiche Eliot's lines call attention to their modernity in every detail. Let us consider another passage from "The Fire Sermon":

> She turns and looks a moment in the glass,
> Hardly aware of her departed lover;
> Her brain allows one half-formed thought to pass:
> 'Well now that's done: and I'm glad it's over.'
> When lovely woman stoops to folly and
> Paces about her room again, alone,
> She smoothes her hair with automatic hand,
> And puts a record on the gramophone. (249–56)

A pastiche of eighteenth-century didactic poetry, these lines allude in particular to Oliver Goldsmith's, *The Vicar of Wakefield* (1766). In Goldsmith's novel, the famous lines appear as an air that a seduced but repentant daughter sings at her mother's request; the air is inset within prose narration:

"Do, my pretty Olivia," cried she, "let us have that little melancholy air your pappa was so fond of, your sister Sophy has already obliged us. Do child, it will please your old father." She complied in a manner so exquisitely pathetic as moved me.

When lovely woman stoops to folly, And finds too late that men betray, What charm can sooth her melancholy, What art can wash her guilt away?

The only art her guilt to cover, To hide her shame from every eye, To give repentance to her lover, And wring his bosom – is to die.

As she was concluding the last stanza, to which an interruption in her voice from sorrow gave peculiar softness, the appearance of Mr Thornhill's equipage at a distance alarmed us all, but particularly encreased the uneasiness of my eldest daughter, who, desirous of shunning her betrayer, returned to the house with her sister.[14]

Eliot's famously antinarrative poem nevertheless deploys numerous broken narratives, this allusion to Goldsmith among them. It is in fact a fragment that functions to close the previous narrative fragment, the twice-interrupted account of an assignation between "a small house agent's clerk" (232) and a typist that is, literally and figuratively, the heart of the poem. In Goldsmith, the short air, or song, represents a moment of lyrical reflection; in Eliot, the poetic lines show the typist resisting self-reflection, even as she glances "in the glass": "her brain allows one half-formed thought to pass" (251). Removing Olivia's "air" from Goldsmith's narrative frame, Eliot then transforms all but the first line; the typist, unlike Goldsmith's Olivia, experiences neither melancholy, guilt nor remorse. Instead, she proceeds mechanically onward, smoothing "her hair with automatic hand," and putting "a record on the gramophone" (255–6) – in other words even her music is mechanical and virtually automatic. She is neither abandoned, in Goldsmith's sense, nor given to abandon in the disapproving Victorian sense: simply alone, she is a machine – "a human engine" (216) – on autopilot. Eliot's lines neither parody nor imitate Goldsmith's. What happens here is neither satirical nor titillative. This passage is ordinarily recognized as a textual allusion, but it is more importantly pastiche in that Eliot's juxtapositions of historical styles deploys form to suggest the predictability of missing content. In *The Waste Land*, form is in this way content.

Pastiche in *The Waste Land*, albeit complex, is not always so heavy in tone. Its function is sometimes light, even comical, and the styles it reproduces can be modern as well as ancient. In "A Game of Chess," as the overwrought wife is on the verge of panic before her silent husband, she demands to know, "'Are you alive, or not? Is there nothing in your head?'" (126). The male voice does not answer her, but we hear the "nothing" that is in his own head – a popular song from Ziegfeld's follies of 1912 – "That Shakesperian Rag." The original lyric by Gene Buck and Herman Ruby is clever enough, full of self-satisfied, presentist swagger:

> Bill Shakespeare never knew of ragtime in his day,
> But the high browed rhymes of his syncopated lines,
> You'll admit, surely fit any song that's now a hit, so this rag I submit.
> That Shakespearian Rag – most intelligent, very elegant ...[15]

The implication is that Shakespeare was so good he could have made Broadway, even without knowing about ragtime. To hear the song, however, adds some irony to this joke, since David Stamper's music is essentially a march, a very white, Phillips Sousa-sounding march without the slightest trace of ragtime or, for that matter, of African-American syncopation of any kind. But, as David Chinitz has established, Eliot himself showed sustained interest in jazz, and that interest informs his allusion to this so-called "Rag."[16] There is, finally, more syncopation in Eliot's opening allusion to this "nothing" than can be heard in the entire original. "But" (127) hangs below the previous line ("'Is there nothing in your head?'") and liminally above Eliot's version of the first line of the chorus; as a line unto itself, it is stressed and followed by the slight pause of a line ending. Then comes his pastiche:

> O O O O that Shakespeherian Rag –
> It's so elegant
> So intelligent (128–30)

The repeated "O"s appear to mime the kind of repetition found in jazz (but not ragtime): "riffing," where a repeated note or pattern of notes becomes a motif more rhythmic than melodic. As distinct, single-syllable words, each "O" carries a stress. Consequently, this line opens with a kind of tonal and emotional stasis, more ponderous than jazzy. Five successive single-syllable words, five successive stresses, and then Eliot lets loose with one dazzling flourish. The extra syllable that transforms "Shakespearean" to "Shakespeherian" releases the tension built up by the first part of the line – five almost-static syllables followed by five that come rapidly, fluidly, lightheartedly. There is more jazz in this one word than in the whole of the 1912 "rag." The subsequent lines – "It's so elegant / So intelligent" – in the subsiding pulses of the multisyllabic adjectives, return us to the overwrought tone of the woman's questions. Jazz here makes for the briefest of interludes. The song makes no "difference" to the woman, who never felt its presence, and when next we hear the male voice, the "nothing" in his head has given way to a list of somethings that the couple will perhaps inevitably do to pass the time and keep themselves from feeling too keenly that time is passing.

The formal dynamics of Eliot's line, "O O O O that Shakespeherian Rag" (128), not only mark it as deftly accomplished pastiche but also suggest why attempts to read it "straight" as either a critique or a celebration of urban modernity so typically run into trouble. That the song in his head is the "nothing" charged to be there by his wife would suggest a negative view of modern culture; but at the same time this line represents the only playful moment in a fairly dreadful scene. The Waste Land does its best work in such passages as this, passages that deliberately generate ambiguity and resist attempts to "solve" its ambiguity. The tension of the poem requires both readings to be present – requires us to see the song as both "nothing" and as a little something special. Moreover, although the diagetic scene is dreadful, there is such life and invention in Eliot's language as to suggest, however implicitly, reason for hope. Pastiche is the modal key that unlocks this cage. Functioning as neither parody nor allusion, pastiche in *The Waste Land* summons historical difference and hermeneutic ambiguity without offering grounding for either.

Before the modernist era, pastiche typically functioned either as homage or as instruction. Proust, as we have seen, regarded it not as a goal in itself so much as a formal communion with tradition. But Eliot's poetry is decisively post-Baudelairean in that it typically looks not up to the clouds but down to the street for inspiration. The catalog of insignificant routines in "A Game of Chess" leads to a line break, after which the section resumes in a working-class pub. Formally, this segment is a dramatic monologue, one that out-Brownings Robert Browning in the energetic ugliness of its language: "When Lil's husband got demobbed, I said – / I didn't mince my words, I said to her myself" (139–40). But the speaker's emphatic reiteration of her own speech act, "I said ... I said," suggests a very particular, even demystifying relation to the Victorian conventions of the dramatic monologue. Where Browning or Tennyson represented speech in ways that endeavor to make us forget we are reading a poem, Eliot's speaker insistently reminds us that we reading represented speech. Just as the story of the sexual encounter in "The Fire Sermon" is framed and interrupted by the intrusive voice of Tiresias, the pub scene of "Game of Chess" is framed and interrupted by the publican's call of "HURRY UP PLEASE ITS TIME," what in the United States is known as last call, with the difference that in the UK patrons must leave the establishment. In effect, the situation tells us that the speaker knows she hasn't but a few moments to relate her heartless tale – she knows but can't resist getting into it. Her language is propelled every bit as relentlessly, desperately perhaps, as the overwrought speech in the upper-class boudoir of the previous scene. For all that this speaker is holding forth in a neighborhood pub where she seems to know the other patrons, calling out her goodnights on leaving, she too seems anxious for connection. Her speech, self-certain and aggressive, marking more absence than presence, is her only form of connection that the poem allows us to see.

Thinking of this scene in terms of pastiche helps foreground Eliot's challenges to nineteenth-century poetic tradition. Pastiche functions here to challenge readers to recognize themselves, offering a mirror to show what he would call in a poem of 1924 "the eyes but not the tears of tradition."[17] Jameson is right, in other words, to distinguish pastiche from parody, but his concomitant claim that pastiche is "a neutral practice of such mimicry, without any of parody's ulterior motives" needs qualification (17). What Eliot does here is not "mimicry" *per se*, but it is certainly critical, and doubtless critical in an "ulterior" fashion. Eliot's praxis extends the play of pastiche, producing interactions between historically alien styles and forms, so that style and form pull against one another, producing a dissonance wherein the elements of the poem seem incomplete, in need of resolution. This doesn't just mean the juxtaposition of different styles but the interaction of style with formal elements that destabilize them.

In no part of *The Waste Land* is this condition more apparent than in the notes that Eliot appended to the poem after its initial magazine publications. Ordinarily, such apparatus serves to limit semiotic play, to ground interpretation and suggest how the poem is to be read. Eliot's notes certainly do the latter, but they do so by example rather than by precept – by showing rather than by telling. Several times, as in the notes to lines 46, 199, or 360, he allows that he does not remember the exact source for his allusions, as though the poem were an oral performance and his commentary off-the-cuff. More importantly, the notes more often destabilize than secure readings of the poem. For starters, as Jo Ellen Green Kaiser has observed, although "at least one speaker of the poem knows only 'a heap of broken images,' the author of the notes knows that the poem has a 'purpose' and a 'plan.' "[18] Consider, then, Eliot's note to line 360: "The following lines were stimulated by the account of one of the Antarctic expeditions (I forget which, but I think one of Shackleton's): it was related that the party of explorers, at the extremity of their strength, had the constant delusion that there was *one more member* than could actually be counted." But Eliot's lines, which this note purportedly glosses, ordinarily summon not scientific associations but religious ones:

> Who is the third who walks always beside you?
> When I count, there are only you and I together
> But when I look ahead up the white road
> There is always another one walking beside you
> Gliding wrapt in a brown mantle, hooded (359–63)

As Jahan Ramazani's gloss in the *Norton Anthology of British Literature* puts it, "the experience is associated with Jesus' unrecognized presence on the way to Emmaus."[19] In other words, the common association here is with the Gospel of Luke 24:13–35:

> [13] And, behold, two of them went that same day to a village called Emmaus, which was from Jerusalem *about* threescore furlongs.

¹⁴ And they talked together of all these things which had happened.
¹⁵ And it came to pass, that, while they communed *together* and reasoned, Jesus himself drew near, and went with them.
¹⁶ But their eyes were holden that they should not know him.

Eliot's note does not so much cancel out this connection as problematize it; theoretically the poetic text is primary, the note supplementary – the poem inspirational and the gloss explanatory. But endnote though it might be, the note doesn't get "the last word" but instead moves perpetually in relation to the poem. The note, in other words, is itself textualized. Neither a parody of hermeneutics nor a hermeneutical parody, we might, in fact, consider it a pastiche of critical discourse written fully forty years before Vladimir Nabokov's *Pale Fire*.

There is, at last, no part of *The Waste Land* untouched by pastiche. In fact, "The Burial of the Dead" originally presented a fifty-four-line opening sequence that Eliot later cut, perhaps because it seemed to him too much an imitation of the "Night Town" section of Joyce's *Ulysses*. His decision was likely informed by Pound's critique of the "Fresca" section that originally opened "The Fire Sermon":

> Admonished by the sun's inclining ray,
> And swift approaches of the thievish day,
> The white-armed Fresca blinks, and yawns, and gapes,
> Aroused from dreams of love and pleasant rapes.
> Electric summons of the busy bell
> Bring[s] brisk Amanda to destroy the spell …²⁰

Valerie Eliot tells us that "This opening passage was written in imitation of *The Rape of the Lock*" and refers to it as a "pastiche;" Eliot himself wrote in 1928 that Pound had "induced me to destroy what I thought an excellent set of couplets; for, said he, 'Pope has done this so well that you cannot do it better; and if you mean this as a burlesque, you had better suppress it, for you cannot parody Pope unless you can write better verse than Pope – and you can't."²¹ Interestingly enough, Pound has to ask if the lines are intended as "burlesque," or parody. Uncharacteristically, he wasn't certain.

That Eliot took Pound's advice here suggests that he wasn't certain either, but as Mrs. Eliot notes, even after cutting this section Eliot remained fond enough of the material to republish much of it, pseudonymously, two years later. Removed from the textual dynamics of *The Waste Land* the lines do resolve into little more than burlesque, but it is possible to see that their original function was something rather different. To be sure, the figure of Fresca exemplifies the kind of mock dignity associated with burlesque in its older sense (vulgarizing lofty material or treating ordinary material with mock dignity). But in Popean satire there is no friction between form and content because his poetry invites readers to sit with the poet in judgment on human folly. In this deleted material from *The Waste Land* we are much less sure of ourselves, and Eliot's couplets metapoetically turn on the reader. After a passage imagining how different, how much healthier Fresca might have been in some other time or place – a "lowly weeping Magdalene" or a version of Dante Gabriel Rossetti's "lazy laughing Jenny" (*Facsimile*, 41, lines 43–5) – comes poetry that uncomfortably and unabashedly offers real wisdom – just as did the poetry of Pope:

> For varying forms, one definition's right:
> Unreal emotions, and real appetite....
> Fresca was baptised in a soapy sea
> Of Symonds – Walter Pater – Vernon Lee.
> The Scandinavians bemused her wits,
> The Russians thrilled her to hysteric fits.
> From such chaotic misch-masch potpourri
> What are we to expect but poetry? (*Facsimile*, 41, lines 52–61)

At this moment in the poem, Fresca is luxuriating in her bath, and these lines liken her reading of *fin-de-siècle* aesthetes (Symonds, Pater, Lee) to being baptized in her own bathwater. As an indiscriminate "chaotic misch-masch potpourri," her reading suggests the apparently random juxtapositions of *The Waste Land* (as well as the original meaning of "pastiche" – a "hodge-podge"). Rather like the hostess of Pound's "Portrait d'une Femme" (1913) and her "sea-hoard of deciduous things" (25), or even like Eliot's own "Portrait of a Lady" (1915) with her "velleities" (15) and "things that other people have desired" (82), Fresca is "a sort of can-can-saloniere."[22] But how are we to understand that last rhetorical question? Do we comfort ourselves by assuming Eliot means a poetry of "unreal emotions," very different from his own? Assume a kind of irony, since this dismissal of poetry comes in the context of a very ambitious poem? Take the dismissal of poetry seriously and consider its role in the self-interfering dynamics of the poem? Or, of course, some combination of all of the above?

If this material were merely parody, simply satire, readers would not face such calls for their own activity. As pastiche, in the modernist sense we have been developing, Eliot's question about "expect[ing] ... poetry" is unanswerable except in relation to a reading of the entire poem. Meanwhile, the turn to Popean couplets serves no *nostalgic* purpose, as Jameson suggests occurs with "a postmodernist ... art language;" the author of the "Essay on Man" would not have understood Eliot's misanthropic (not just misogynist) vision, where the deepest sign of our modern spiritual failure is our relentless self-exaltation ("Bill Shakespeare never knew of ragtime in his day," etc). Neither do these couplets appear as Jameson's "style separated from history:" the Fresca passage closes with the grotesquely transformed quotation from Marvell's "To His Coy Mistress" that, as we've seen, survives in lines 185–6 of the published poem:

> But at my back in a cold blast I hear
> The rattle of the bones, and chuckle spread from ear to ear.

In *The Waste Land* as published, these lines end a verse paragraph; in Eliot's draft they close the business with Fresca. In the draft, the comparative order and dignified music of the Popean pastiche crashes here into the jagged irregularities of the modern: "A rat crept softly through the vegetation / Dragging its slimy belly on the bank" (*Facsimile*, 41, lines 73–4). The Marvell material suggests history and time are aggressive forces that have already laid hands upon us. This is no escape from history. It is more than "the random cannibalization of all the styles of the past, the play of random stylistic allusion."[23] Eliot's allusion is not pastiche but an intense modeling of the ways that tradition might redeem history, or not. The question is whether history has anything to teach us.

Pastiche in *The Waste Land* is not then slavish imitation any more than it is primarily parody. It represents the very active pursuit of the tradition that Eliot proposes we seek in "Tradition and the Individual Talent." One of Jameson's great strengths is his further development of that Marxist insight into how styles emerge not as the expression of personal voice but rather of history, of what is technically and historically possible. Removed from historical necessity, style becomes merely another "referent" – a signifier that has become a decorative signified. In 1919 Charles Sanders Peirce's or Ferdinand de Saussure's founding works on semiotics were not widely known, and Eliot did not think in these terms. But he had nevertheless a profound understanding of the embeddedness of style in history: "Someone said: 'The dead writers are remote from us because we *know* so much more than they did.' Precisely, and they are that which we know" ("Tradition," 16). Eliot refers here to writers themselves, but his interest isn't in their biographies: his interest is in their technical and stylistic discoveries. Eliot's pastiches function to engage a cultural and artistic wholeness whose presence is never to be assumed. Anecdotes about individuals, allusions to ideas and quotations of phrases are but the smallest part of this engagement. More important is the horizon of expectations (another theoretical phrase that Eliot never used), the vision of the world physically embodied in poetic style and form.[24] *That* and not the sentiments or ideas of quoted lines, or even the music of earlier styles, is the signified pursued by Eliot's pastiches. It is in that formal embodiment of history that Eliot produces something new and models how "the past should be altered by the present as much as the present is directed by the past" ("Tradition," 15). Not clean, marked by "the broken fingernails of dirty hands" (303), pastiche is one of Eliot's most powerful ways of showing how the past is always already complete and yet always subject to change.

NOTES

1 *Correspondance de Marcel Proust*, ed. Philip Kolb, 21 vols. (Paris: Plon, 1970–93); Tome XVIII, 380.

2 *Pastiches et mélanges* appeared in June. See http://www.proust-ink.com/proust/chronology.html

3 *Correspondance de Marcel Proust*; Tome XVIII, 380. With thanks to Gabrielle McIntire for her translation of this passage which improves so well on what I had offered; quoted with permission.

4 For discussion of the importance of hygiene to Eliot's writing see Amanda Jeremin Harris, "T. S. Eliot's Mental Hygiene," *Journal of Modern Literature*, 29 no.4 (2006).

5 C. Bowen, "Pastiche." *The Princeton Encyclopedia of Poetry and Poetics*, ed. Roland Greene and Stephen Cushman, 4th edition (Princeton, NJ: Princeton University Press, 2012), 1005.

6 T. S. Eliot, *Selected Essays* (New York: Harcourt, 1964), 4.

7 Remy de Gourmont, "Tradition and Other Things," *The Egoist* 1, no. 14, trans. Richard Aldington (July 15, 1914), 261. Reproduced at http://archive.org/stream/TheEgoistVol.1No.14/Egoist_1_14_djvu.txt.

8 William Carlos Williams, *Spring and All* (1923), republished in *Imaginations* (New York: New Directions, 1970), 94–5.

9 Reviews quoted from Jewel Spears Brooker, ed., *T. S. Eliot: The Contemporary Reviews* (London: Cambridge University Press, 2004). Wilson's review appears on 77; Untermeyer's on 93; Ransom's on 107.

10 David Zivan, *DownBeat* (January 2014), 77.

11 Linda Hutcheon, *The Politics of Postmodernism* (New York: Routledge, 1989), 1.

12 Fredric Jameson, *Postmodernism, or, The Cultural Logic of Late Capitalism* (Durham: Duke University Press, 1991), 16.

13 Eliot, *The Waste Land*, in *The Complete Poems and Plays* (London: Faber and Faber, 1969), 183–6. Subsequent references to *The Waste Land* will be cited parenthetically by line number.

14 Oliver Goldsmith, *The Vicar of Wakefield: A Tale. Supposed to Be Written by Himself* (London: R. Collins, 1776), chapter 24; quoted from the online Project Gutenberg edition: http://www.gutenberg.org/files/2667/2667-h/2667-h.htm.

15 "That Shakesperian Rag," lyrics by Gene Buck and Herman Ruby, music by Dave Stamper (New York: Joseph W. Stern & Co, 1912).

16 David Chinitz, *T. S. Eliot and the Cultural Divide* (Chicago: University of Chicago Press, 1993); see especially chapter 1, "The Jazz Banjorine," 19–52.

17 From "Doris' Dream Songs," published in *Chapbook*, 39 (Nov. 1924), 36–7; Eliot later broke up this sequence, excerpting this part and including it in *Collected Poems: 1909–1962* as "Eyes that last I saw in tears" (New York: Harcourt, 1991), 90.

18 Jo Ellen Green Kaiser, "Disciplining *The Waste Land*, or How to Lead Critics into Temptation," *Twentieth-Century Literature* 44 (1998): 87.

19 Jahan Ramazani, *The Norton Anthology of Modern and Contemporary Poetry*, Vol. 2 (New York: Norton, 2003), 485.

20 Eliot, *The Waste Land: A Facsimile and Transcript of the Original Drafts Including the Annotations of Ezra Pound*, ed. Valerie Eliot (New York: Harcourt, 1971), 39, lines 1–6.

21 Quoted by Valerie Eliot, 127, note 1 of *The Waste Land: A Facsimile*, taken from Eliot, from his Introduction to *Ezra Pound: Selected Poems* (London: Faber & Gwyer, 1928) (rpt. 1949), xxi.

22 Ezra Pound, "Portrait d'une Femme," *Pound: Poems & Translations*, ed. Richard Sieburth (New York: Library of America, 2003), 234. The phrase "a sort of can-can-saloniere" appears in line 70 of Eliot's draft of "The Fire Sermon" (*The Waste Land: A Facsimile*, 41).

23 Jameson, 18.

24 Hans Robert Jauss develops his idea of "horizons of expectation" in "Literary History as a Challenge to Literary Theory," *New Literary History* 2 no.1 (Autumn, 1970), 7–37; redacted from chapters V–XII of *Toward an Aesthetic of Reception* (Minneapolis: University of Minnesota Press, 1982).

PART III

Critical and Theoretical Approaches

9

RACHEL POTTER

Gender and Obscenity in
The Waste Land

There is no question that the nature of gender difference is a central preoccupation of T. S. Eliot's *The Waste Land*. After all, Eliot tells us in the "Notes" to the poem that the insight of the "important" and unifying figure of Tiresias – who knows what it is to be a woman and a man – is fundamental to the poem's "substance."[1] "Substance" is a word whose origins lie in the Greek "hypostasis," meaning "standing under," and Eliot does imply structural as well as visionary cohesion here. In a connected but different claim within his notes, Eliot also insists that femaleness produces a significant unity of being in the poem. The women – Marie, Madame Sosostris, the implied Cleopatra, Philomel, Lil and her friend, Mrs. Porter, the typist, Queen Elizabeth, and the various anonymous women – are all "one" woman (Ibid.). The suggestion that these fragments of myth, history and imagination are unified by their gender forms part of Eliot's desire to enforce poetic unity in *The Waste Land*. But does it tell us anything about his understanding either of gender difference or being?

Readers have long disagreed about how seriously to take Eliot's notes and their claims to poetic synthesis. Critics including I. A. Richards, F. R. Leavis, and James Longenbach accept Eliot's suggestion that Tiresias embodies the poem's unity.[2] But most readers have seen no such cohesion. Instead, the poem's power has been seen to lie in the energy of its disordered parts, a force that constitutes Eliot's engagement with the irreconcilable historical and political divisions of the time,[3] making the poem a product of the play of linguistic signifiers and proliferation of desire and meaning in language,[4] or a philosophical engagement with the irreducible particulars of positivist interpretations of the world.[5] As Michael North puts it, Tiresias embodies "the failure of reconciliation"; he is the "mere juxtaposition of part and whole that dramatizes the gulf between them" (100). Or, as Michael Coyle states: "there is no consistent speaker for this poem."[6] But, most readers have agreed with North's suggestion that "reconciliation" is a horizon of meaning for the poem's disordered parts. As North puts it: "Eliot could only approach peace through conflict, as if he could only grasp linguistic unity as an implication of linguistic disorder, and, finally, as if he could imagine social solidarity only by extension of social chaos. Disorder thus becomes not a fault to be overcome, but a necessary moment in the process of arriving at order" (104). The terms of the opposition between disorder and order, and the means with which such oppositions might be bridged – something that North helpfully describes as an incomplete movement toward or a grasping – troubled Eliot as a writer and was a central preoccupation of the philosophers he admired including Henry Adams, Irving Babbitt, and George Santayana.

This relation between disorder and implied unity is also significant when we consider the more specific question of Eliot's writing of sexuality and gender difference in *The Waste Land*. A scattered number of readers have emphasized women's reconciling roles in the poem.[7] Most critics, however, have argued that Eliot's women enforce – or, actually are the key sites for – the poem's depiction of political, linguistic, and subjective disorder. Women have been seen as sites of unmanageable physicality[8] or as the cause and expression of historical forces Eliot found threatening, which included mass culture, low culture, and mass democracy.[9]

Other readings have seen Eliot's constructions of women less as a product of history and politics, and more as something that played out at the level of Eliot's own subjectivity. Tony Pinkney, in a psychoanalytic reading of the poem, sees misogyny and murderous violence in Eliot's depictions of women. Quoting from Eliot's "Sweeney Agonistes" he states that "any Eliotic text has to, needs to, wants to, in one way or another, do a girl in; and if it fails to achieve that goal, it is itself murderously threatened by the girl."[10] Pinkney's claim that Eliot attempts, but fails, to impose masculine forms of order on female bodily chaos has been reiterated in a range of feminist and historical readings. As Cassandra Laity puts it in the introduction to the influential collection of essays *Gender, Desire, and Sexuality in T. S. Eliot*, in addition to the parts of Eliot's writing which are "blatantly misogynist and homophobic," recent criticism has been keen to understand the more "intricate engagements with multiple forms and degrees of desire, contemporary feminism, the feminine, and homoeroticism."[11]

The last of these terms has been a particularly significant one for arguments that Eliot's poems express his own unacknowledged drives. In 1952 Eliot successfully suppressed an essay by John Peter claiming that *The Waste Land* depicts the poet's love for Jean Verdenal, whom Peters described as "a young man who soon afterwards met his death, it would seem by drowning."[12] After Eliot himself had passed away in 1965 Peter decided to reprint his essay, only with a contradictory caveat attached, explaining that "at Eliot's insistence all copies of the issue on hand after publication were destroyed, and when the run of volumes I-XVI was subsequently re-issued ... he refused to sanction the reprinting of my essay" (165). But Peter also insisted that he had never imputed homosexuality or carnal knowledge to Eliot's poetry and had sought Eliot's forgiveness for the mistake. Eliot's offended and aggressive silencing of Peter's essay, and Peter's own recoil from this offence, seemed, in turn, to stifle others on the subject of Eliot's homoeroticism. It was not until 1977, when James E. Miller brought out *T. S. Eliot's Personal Waste Land*, that anyone mentioned it again.[13]

But as with most attempts to control what people say, Eliot's silencing of Peter merely stimulated curiosity, even if this did not find expression until much later. Since the early 1990s, a number of important studies have analyzed the homoeroticism of Eliot's poetry. Colleen Lamos mounts a dual project in her 1998 book, *Deviant Modernism: Sexual and Textual Errancy in T. S. Eliot, James Joyce, and Marcel Proust*. She attempts to move beyond what she calls the "exhausted impasse of the unity versus fragmentation debate" to a more nuanced consideration of those moments in *The Waste Land* when the writing "strays" from its intentions, a process she describes as a perversion from masculine heterosexual norms: Eliot "struggle[s] against identifications and desires that he considered perverse yet that found symptomatic expression within his own texts."[14]

In a poem, then, defined by the collapse of unified certainties in gender binaries, nationality, belief, and voice, is it worth taking seriously Eliot's claim that the women in the poem aesthetically unite through their gender? If these figures are unified by their femaleness, but disconnected by history, nationality, class, and age, what comprises this unity apart from sheer physical sameness? And what would constitute this physicality? Further, can this category of being override the more obvious ways in which these female figures are defined by their psychological isolation, and are thereby expressive of the disconnections Eliot believed had been unleashed through liberal humanist philosophy and its parallel political ideologies? This essay seeks an answer to these questions by trying to open up and reexamine the language Eliot uses to describe women's disordered physicality. I argue that Eliot tethers female physicality to the obscene, a category that bridges aesthetic and cultural forms of disorder. This bridging means that Eliot's female bodies are both expressive of the cultural and political conflicts Eliot found troubling and a challenge to that cultural and political context. The "one" woman of *The Waste Land* has more of a critical edge, I want to suggest, than it might seem.

The word "obscene" is from the Latin *obscenus*, meaning "adverse, inauspicious, ill-omened;" also "abominable, disgusting, filthy and indecent."[15] The origins of the word incorporate the idea that the obscene thing or word threatens communal unity, and the ideas of contamination and threat were carried through into the word's modern legal and aesthetic meanings. But the word also came to signify that which was offstage, so that the obscene thing or word was seen as that which should not, or could not, be brought on stage, put into writing or brought to consciousness.[16]

Despite the Latin origins of the word and a long and robust history of European writing of sex and sexuality, the production and dissemination of "obscene" writing in Britain and the United States was not significantly policed until the mid- to late-nineteenth century. The UK Obscene Publications Act of 1857 established a new legal basis for the prohibition of obscene literature both in the United Kingdom and the United States. Lord Campbell, the instigator of the act, left it to the courts at common law to devise a definition of literary obscenity. The result was the notoriously vague "Hicklin Ruling" of 1868, which stipulated that a work was illegal if an isolated passage revealed a "tendency" to "corrupt those whose minds are open to such immoral influences and into whose hands a publication of this sort may fall."[17] The authorities were particularly concerned about the impact of obscene words on the minds of women and the young person. Further, it was the depiction of sex and the use of sexualized, or "dirty" words, that were considered to be the main threats to "open" minds in the late-nineteenth and early twentieth centuries. Most works of fiction, and even the Bible, could be (and were) considered obscene under such criteria, and the result was a legal assault on the dissemination of writing in the late-nineteenth and early twentieth centuries. This was partly because powerful pressure groups interested in book control – including the notorious Society for the Suppression of Vice, run by Anthony Comstock in New York, and the National Vigilance Association based in London – were tenacious in their attempts to track down books that they considered to be sexually obscene.

The representation of female and male physicality, then, was a source of moral and literary crisis for Eliot and his generation. Many writers in the 1910s and 1920s, including James Joyce, Djuna Barnes, Mina Loy, Wyndham Lewis, Ezra Pound, D. H. Lawrence, and others, were asked to cut out sexual and excremental references from poems and novels, either because of fears of legal censorship or due to aesthetic concerns about the proper parameters of literature. Eliot, along with his contemporaries, excised physical references from the early drafts of poems. *The Waste Land* was much more obviously scatological and sexual in its original form. Base bodily functions – Fresca's "needful stool," the typist's young man who "Delays only to urinate, and spit," prostitution at Myrtle's place – were edited out of the final version of *The Waste Land*.[18] Some of these excisions were prompted by Pound's red pen; others occurred because Eliot changed his mind about including them. These excisions meant that the poem's "unruliness," as Harriet Davidson puts it, was more pronounced in its early drafts: "the textual history of the poem, from draft, to edited version, to published version with endnotes, tends to tame some of the unruliness of the poem," although she leaves it open whether the taming was the result of aesthetic decisions or something external to that – a kind of legalistic pressure.[19]

Censorship, however, did not simply result in the removal of references to prostitution, sex, and excrement in novels and poems. The censorship of literature was also seen by writers of this period as a sinister form of modern bureaucratized power. The censorship of books was controlled by a number of different kinds of people: it was administered by government employees such as customs officials and postmen who policed national borders and internal communication systems; it was controlled by an unofficial network of individuals involved in the production and dissemination of books, which included editors, publishers, publishers' readers, printers and typists; and it was monitored by a general context of cultural reception, which included the published views of reviewers, journalists, and religious leaders. Modernist writers saw the publishing climate of these years as powerfully censorious because of the decentered nature of this network of agents, a fragmentation that made the logic, terms, and agency of censorship uncertain.

Prohibition and threats of prohibition did not deter Eliot and his contemporaries from writing about the body or from incorporating obscene words into their texts; in fact, for some of them the charge of illegality seemed to spur them on to write more explicitly about sex and the body. The intellectual and artistic consequences of this were significant. Many writers, including Eliot, were encouraged to engage with and challenge what were seen as the ridiculous book censorship laws in the United States and United Kingdom. In the process they became champions of authorial free speech. Despite silencing John Peter's essay in the 1950s imputing homoeroticism, Eliot had been critical of literary censorship throughout his life, both when it came to his own work and to that of his contemporaries. He complained when *Poetry* editor Harriet Monroe removed the word "foetus" from his 1917 poem "Mr. Appolinax" without asking his permission, insisting that this represented an instance of misplaced puritanism. When copies of *The Little Review* were seized by the postmaster general because of the obscenity of Wyndham Lewis's short story "Cattleman's Spring Mate," Eliot supported the editors of the journal in an essay he penned for *The Egoist* in 1918.[20] He signed petitions and wrote a number of essays in support of

Ulysses in the 1920s and argued the case for publishing Radclyffe Hall's *The Well of Loneliness* in *Criterion* editorials during 1928.[21] He also protested against the censorship of D. H. Lawrence's paintings in 1929 and offered to appear as an expert witness in the *Lady Chatterley's Lover* trial in 1960, although in the end he was not called into the witness box.[22]

Eliot was undoubtedly critical of the way that censorship functioned to stifle literary freedom. There were also ways in which the idea of a hypocritical censorious culture made its mark on his writing. He believed that the fragmented structure of the censorship networks controlling the dissemination of texts and the singling out of sexualized obscene words and images as sites of moral corruption were a product of the political and institutional divisions of modern culture. This was significant for his poetry and not least because such divisions were central to his literary criticism, his critique of humanism, and his political skepticism about modern democracy – even while he celebrated aesthetic fragmentation in his poems. At the same time, the pressure of a censorious culture was not simply a negative, prohibitive force that curtailed expression; it also functioned to stimulate the testing of aesthetic limits. Sexual and excremental obscenities could both signify contemporaneity and act as forms of cultural disruption.

Eliot had a lifelong fascination with sexually and racially obscene language and imagery. Loretta Johnson, Gabrielle McIntire, and David Chinitz have argued that Eliot's obscene bawdy poems, of which his Bolo and Lulu poems are the key examples – several of which were first published in *The Letters of T. S. Eliot: Volume One* in 1988, with more appearing in Christopher Ricks's *Inventions of the March Hare* in 1996 – should be considered as significant parts of his oeuvre. Johnson situates these poems in a long literary genealogy of bawdy, in which spirituality and fleshiness define each other: Eliot's bawdy poems reveal "the flip side of his spiritual poetry."[23] McIntire concludes that these poems "necessarily change the ways we read" Eliot, partly because they reveal his "ongoing obsessions with sex, race, and history – concerns that recur in more moderate incarnations through his canonical writings,"[24] and partly because they "play recklessly on prohibitions while offering a satirical poetics of desire and memory" (13).

Rather than being part of a bawdy aesthetic, the obscene bodies in *The Waste Land* have a different flavor, partly because the satirical and Rabelaisian elements central to his Bolo poems are absent. Instead, these bodies stand as sites of degradation, animalistic violence and noncommunication. In this they are more akin to the sprawling and menacing bodies that appear in "Burbank with a Baedeker: Bleistein with a Cigar," "Sweeney Erect" and "Whispers of Immortality," which situate such explorations in a literary genealogy. In "Whispers of Immortality," for instance, Grishkin's contemporary "feline smell" (27) is identified with a literary heritage originating in John Webster and John Donne, both of whom opened up writing to the "skull beneath the skin" (2). Despite the similarities with the ugly physicality and sexuality of the "Sweeney" poems, however, I want to suggest that the female bodies in *The Waste Land* form part of a meditation on the obscene, partly because satire and irony make way for a more sustained focus on gender difference and images in which obscene bodies enforce human isolation and miscommunication. McIntire is right to insist that Eliot's obscenities are energized by the prohibitions that define them as obscene. The obscenities in *The Waste Land* also gesture beyond themselves, to the absence of unifying categories of being that might make such bodies meaningful.

In the first draft version of *The Waste Land* Eliot describes Fresca's "hearty female stench"[25] – a phrase that uses foul smell to make the female sexual body disgusting. While Eliot edited this phrase out of the final version of the poem, its powerful evocation of a repellent sensuality that inheres in the female body has wider resonance for *The Waste Land*, where cloying synthetic odors and clothing barely mask the bodies they conceal. Just as Lil's imagined false set of teeth fail to obscure her decaying mouth, so the confusing synthetic odors of Cleopatra's lush perfumes or the typist's "drying combinations" (225) do not screen the degraded physicality of their sexualized bodies. The effects of this are twofold. While there is a radical disjunction between the body's unpleasant substance and the ostensibly charming accoutrements of feminine masquerade, Eliot also presents the body's processes and impulses as being beyond the individual's control. Both of these disconnections – between the body and its garb, and sheer corporeality and desire – are grounded in a sense of women's shared physicality. The physical stir of sexual desire is thus as inescapable as bodily odor and decay. As well as constituting a particular perspective on the body, this imagery also advocates a theory of history and time since Eliot figures desire as the inescapable starting point for a mythical cycle of decay. The kinds of masquerade used by women may change through the ages, and be a particularly potent focus and form of modernity, but the body beneath has always been both a reproductive prison and a substance subject to decay. As such, bodies, in Eliot's poetry, carry the seeds and the shape of their future deterioration, and even mythical figures do not escape the fateful, physical ravages of time. The Greek figure of Tiresias has always been figured as an old man in poems and plays. But in Eliot's hands his age is visualized through the details of his female physical disintegration – "Old man with wrinkled female breasts" (219). In place of what Johnson describes as the mutually defining relationship of fleshiness and spirituality in Eliot's bawdy poems, then, *The Waste*

Land erects a different dialectic: physical decay is informed by and pulls against artifice. Keeping in mind the meaning of the obscene cited earlier, we can see how Eliot, by focusing on both the degraded body and its masking, plays with or reflects upon the nature of the obscene. The writing of these physical details exposes what it is that human culture wants to keep hidden about women's bodies. In terms of *The Waste Land* as a whole, the "strange synthetic perfumes" (87) and "glitter" (84) of Cleopatra's jewels mask – but also fail to mask – the "hearty female stench" that lies beneath. The poem dramatizes the mutually defining dynamic of human physicality and the "glitter" of human artifice. But it also exposes their separation.

Disconnection – of the body from the words or objects that mask it – also informs the images of art in the poem. Physical decay defines and curtails human agency and freedom, and art is connected to images of freedom or escape from the body. Sexualized bodies both imprison women – Lil, after all "nearly died of young George" (160) – and are forms of decay. They are also the foundations for violence and failed communication. Sexual desire is both the "little life" (7) that will make something out of the "nothing" that haunts male-female dialogue (120–3), and a form of mythical and modern violence. Both desire and violence constitute forms of life with uncertain destinations. In "A Game of Chess" and "The Fire Sermon" sexual interaction constitutes a supreme instance of psychic isolation, mired as it is in male violence and female fear. While the story of Philomel's "change" allows her to escape into animalistic form, however, Eliot describes the enduring fixity of her fate in myth and art – "And still she cried, and still the world pursues" (102). In Greek and Roman myth, after she is raped by Tereus, Philomel has her tongue cut out and is hidden in a fortress, before being turned into a swallow (in Greek versions) or a nightingale (according to Latin authors) and escaping. This is a moment in which sexual violence instigates a myth of human turning animal. Of course, Greek myths abound in such crossovers. But in Eliot's hands the animalistic flight away from human confinement has aesthetic resonance. Ideas of freedom in *The Waste Land* tend to involve images of momentary flight or movement frozen in artistic time. Pictorially Philomel will always be flying away from her human mutilation and toward that window, just as Marie's ephemeral feeling of freedom as she descends the mountain will poetically endure.

Again, this dialectic of sexual violence and desire and freedom partly centers on time. Female bodies in *The Waste Land*, controlled as they are by their physical subjection to time express what is unconscious and blinded. The ability to transcend this subjection to violence and decay involves creating an art or song or language that communicates across time. But this transposition of meaning is thwarted by modern life. Art can only resonate in the present if its beauty can be heard or understood. Eliot had long been preoccupied poetically with the idea of misdirected or indecipherable beauty. Prufrock, for instance, knows that the mermaids are singing but does not think that they will sing to him: "I have heard the mermaids singing, each to each. // I do not think that they will sing to me" (124–5). In "Sweeney Among the Nightingales," meanwhile, the mythical "hornèd gate" (8) that leads up from Hades is guarded by the apelike Sweeney, and the stars are "veiled" (10) from the poem's various characters. Rather than gazing upward at the stars or listening to the nightingales singing, these inebriated characters look at each other through windows and doors. These barriers enforce the poem's suggestion that human proximity produces silence, suspicion, withdrawal, and isolation.

This modern experience of being shut off from the wonder and transcendent beauty of song is one that Eliot makes explicitly physical in *The Waste Land*. Even though the nightingale "Filled all the desert with inviolable voice" (101) this song is translated into its imitative representation: "'Jug Jug'" (103). But Eliot also connects this translation of voice into language with blocked hearing: the voice is "'Jug Jug' to dirty ears" (103). Here, Eliot implies that the body, by being clogged up by dirt and waste, is a barrier to beauty and meaning. Song also fails to signify in "The Fire Sermon" when its tones are drowned out by the "rattle of the bones" (186), chuckles, and sexualized "horns and motors" of men pursuing prostitutes (197). At other moments in the poem, Eliot attends to linguistic, rather than acoustic, barriers, but the focus is still on obscured or failing body parts. The poet's eyes fail, as does his voice and mind, when confronted by the hyacinth girl (38–9). A similar set of failures occurs in his interactions with the woman whose "nerves are bad:" "'Do / You know nothing? / Do you see nothing? Do you remember / Nothing?'" (121–3). The verbal and psychological barriers between men and women are here concentrated on deficiencies of sight and voice. In a different part of the poem absence and disconnection are expressed by way of sordid physical images. In one instance, the "nothing" is likened to "The broken fingernails of dirty hands" (303).

Eliot was not alone among his peers in writing about the physically degraded and physical limitations of the human form, as well as about the details of dirty or decomposing bodies. In James Joyce's and Franz Kafka's hands such failures are part of their meditations on urban poverty and bureaucratic structures. Stephen's decaying teeth and unwashed body form part of Joyce's descriptions both of Dublin's colonial status and its urban poverty, while in Kafka's narratives the filthy and confining offices of the bureaucrats enforce the enervating fact of urban crowding and industrial overproduction.

In *The Waste Land* dirty bodies form part of Eliot's more general focus on the ubiquity of modern waste, while his malodorous and unseemly bodies and clogged ears and eyes make communication difficult. The body, in Eliot's hands, is its own corruption. Bodily functions, odors, and dirt thereby constitute a shared human physicality. At the same time, however, the body secures the barriers separating individuals. Ezra Pound picked up on both the shared, animalistic nature of Eliot's sexualized bodies and their isolating force – what he labels as their absence of attraction – when he observed of *The Waste Land*: "Breedings of animals, / Humans and canibals [*sic*], / But above all else of smells / Without attraction."[26] Not only are the female bodies in *The Waste Land* obscene in the semantic, rather than strictly legal, sense of the word – disgusting, filthy, and indecent – they also embody a key contradiction. At once the substance of a shared humanity, they also serve to isolate.

The obscene female body, then, connects to Eliot's wider philosophical and political reflections on the contradictions of modern culture. The problem of isolation was central to Eliot's philosophical and political arguments. Richard Shusterman discusses the impact of Eliot's doctoral thesis on the work of F. H. Bradley, in which Eliot includes an entire chapter on solipsism, what Bradley referred to as the "finite centre" of individual consciousness.[27] This philosophical meditation formed part of Eliot's more general interest in the clear distinctions between private truths and external authority. In later critical essays and poems Eliot focuses more attention on the problematic subjectivism of Romantic and humanist philosophy and poetry. As Shusterman suggests, such distinctions pose a problem both for human communication and community, and this idea plays out fruitfully in Eliot's early poems such as "The Love Song of J. Alfred Prufrock" and "Portrait of a Lady" which focus on human misunderstanding and isolation. The ironized social failures of these early poems echo only faintly in the brutalized interactions of *The Waste Land*, though, where the woman whose "nerves are bad" (111) bullies her interlocutor with unanswerable questions and the typist indifferently turns away from her lover to seek her own image in the mirror. If dialogues often seem at cross-purposes in the early poems, the failure of communication has become even more pronounced in *The Waste Land*. Here sexual interaction prompts disconnected self-reflection rather than emotional intimacy. The "nothing" that resonates through the poem more generally signifies an absence of knowledge and connection between men and women. If Madame Sosostris "Is known to be the wisest woman in Europe" (45) then the language of the poem implies that this is because her knowledge and wisdom are debased categories.

If women are "one" in their shared physical substance, then, this oneness exposes the absence of meaningful connections in *The Waste Land*. The failed dialogues and psychological isolation of the poem are the foundation for Eliot's explorations into what makes humans connect. He argues that meaningful kinds of unity have been replaced by false and empty forms of order – linked to democratic process, law, and bureaucracy. His depictions of women in *The Waste Land* form part of this reflection. I have argued here that women in *The Waste Land* are held together by nothing other than the oneness of their shared and obscene physicality, a construction of the physical that connects to Eliot's more general theory of human substance and humanism. Eliot's critique of humanism resides partly in his skepticism about how, in the absence of moral or religious hierarchies of meaning, the physical stuff of the human body can be a route to political or moral freedom. Freedom, for Eliot, entails class and national belonging. T. E. Hulme, in one of his last published essays on humanism, echoes Pound's focus on the animalistic substance of Eliot's bodies in *The Waste Land* when he claims that the human "*is the only exit from the animal world.*"[28] For both Hulme and Eliot this human exit requires the meaningful divisions of moral order and authority. For Eliot, however, the cultural and class dissociations of modern life have destabilized these divisions. His critique of humanism was partly connected to the idea that liberal culture had produced a fragmented and legalistic moral sphere empty of significance, a series of connections which defined his defense of classicism, monarchism, tradition and religion. He also, as we see above, viewed the modern literary censorship of obscene words and images as an important form of empty moralism and cultural fragmentation, and a threat to the freedom of poets and novelists. The obscene bodies of *The Waste Land* capture the conflicts of cultural fragmentation and moral emptiness; they are both fleshy symbols of the barriers separating individuals and represent a challenge to the moralism of modern censoriousness which wants nothing but to hide the body.

The focus on the obscene body as the ground of a shared human substance also features in Eliot's essayistic critiques of social and cultural fragmentation. He produces a vivid picture of the moral consequences of disintegrating class divisions in 1923, for instance, when he argues that "the middle classes are morally corrupt" and in "England as elsewhere, under democracy, are morally dependent upon the aristocracy," which in turn are "subordinate" to the middle classes.[29] The lower classes, meanwhile, are dropping "into the same state of protoplasm as the bourgeoisie" (Ibid.). This vision of class breakdown – in another context he states that "there will soon be only one class" – echoes the imagery of moral collapse and degraded physicality that marks *The Waste Land*.[30] Class homogenization, for Eliot, creates not meaningful unity but the sameness of meaningless protoplasmic life, just as the merging of Cleopatra into Madame Sosostris or the typist produces a unity of being empty of significance.

But the obscene protoplasmic life that constitutes the ground of female being in *The Waste Land* is also, as North puts it in the quotation at the beginning of this chapter, a "necessary moment" (104) in the process of arriving at a new kind of significance or order. And this imagined order might be seen less as a gendered binary imposed by Eliot on his women and men, and more as the beauty or poetic language which arises out of human substance – in *The Waste Land* this unity is described as artifice, as well as meaningful song, art, or language. By signifying through time, poetry connects humans to the past and to each other and also transcends the divisions of protoplasmic life. My contention in this essay has been that this meaningful poetic language is also linked to a freedom from the empty constraint of a modern bureaucratized censorship that hounds down the obscene words of literary texts. The shared physicality of Eliot's poetic women constitutes a poetic challenge to this constraint.

NOTES

1 T. S. Eliot, *The Waste Land, T. S. Eliot: The Complete Poems and Plays* (1969; London: Faber and Faber, 1987), footnote to line 218. Subsequent references to Eliot's poems will be made parenthetically by line number.

2 F. R. Leavis, *New Bearings in English Poetry: A Study of the Contemporary Situation* (Middlesex: Penguin, 1972), 73. James Longenbach argues that Tiresias embodies a mystic unifying vision in *Modernist Poetics of History* (Princeton, NJ: Princeton University Press, 1987), 203.

3 Political readings of the poem's fragmentation include Raymond Williams, *Culture and Society: 1780–1950* (1958; New York: Columbia University Press, 1983); Terry Eagleton, *Exiles and Émigrés* (New York: Schocken, 1970); Sanford Schwartz, *The Matrix of Modernism* (Princeton, NJ: Princeton University Press, 1985); Michael Levenson, *A Genealogy of Modernism: A Study of English Literary Doctrine 1908–1922* (Cambridge: Cambridge University Press, 1984); Michael North, *The Political Aesthetic of Yeats, Eliot, and Pound* (Cambridge: Cambridge University Press, 1991); Stan Smith, *The Origins of Modernism: Eliot, Pound, Yeats and the Rhetorics of Renewal* (London: Harvester Wheatsheaf, 1994).

4 For important arguments along these lines see Maud Ellmann, *The Poetics of Impersonality: T. S. Eliot and Ezra Pound* (Brighton: Harvester, 1987), and Christine Froula, *Modernism's Body: Sex, Culture and Joyce* (New York: Columbia University Press, 1996).

5 See Richard Shusterman, *T. S. Eliot and the Philosophy of Literary Criticism* (London: Duckworth, 1988); Manju Jain, *T. S. Eliot and American Philosophy: The Harvard Years* (Cambridge: Cambridge University Press, 1992); Jeffrey Perl, *Skepticism and Modern Enmity: Before and After Eliot* (Baltimore: Johns Hopkins University Press, 1989); M. A. R. Habib, *The*

Early T. S. Eliot and Western Philosophy (Cambridge: Cambridge University Press, 1999).

6 Michael Coyle, "'Fishing, with the arid plain behind me:' Difficulty, Deferral, and Form in *The Waste Land*," *A Companion to T. S. Eliot*, ed. David Chinitz (Chichester: Wiley-Blackwell, 2009), 158.

7 Influential readings of this kind include Marja Palmer, *Men and Women in T. S. Eliot's Early Poetry* (Lund: Lund University Press, 1996); Lyndall Gordon, *T. S. Eliot: An Imperfect Life* (London: Vintage, 1998); and Ronald Schuchard, *Eliot's Dark Angel: Intersections of Life and Art* (Oxford: Oxford University Press, 1999).

8 Foremost among these critics are Susan Gilbert and Sandra Gubar. See *No Man's Land: The Place of the Woman Writer in the Twentieth Century* (New Haven, CT: Yale University Press, 1994), and Rachel Blau DuPlessis, *Genders, Races, and Religious Cultures in Modern American Poetry, 1908–1934* (Cambridge: Cambridge University Press, 2001).

9 Michael Tratner, *Modernism and Mass Politics: Joyce, Woolf, Eliot, Yeats* (Stanford, CA: Stanford University Press, 1995); Peter Nicholls, *Modernisms: A Literary Guide* (Basingstoke: Macmillan, 1995).

10 Tony Pinkney, *Women in the Poetry of T. S. Eliot: A Psychoanalytic Approach* (London: Macmillan, 1984), 18.

11 Cassandra Laity, "Introduction: Eliot, gender, and modernity," *Gender, Desire, and Sexuality in T. S. Eliot*, ed. Cassandra Laity and Nancy K. Gish (Cambridge: Cambridge University Press, 2004), 3.

12 John Peter, "A New Interpretation of *The Waste Land* (1952)," *Essays in Criticism* 19 (1969): 143.

13 James Miller, *T. S. Eliot's Personal Waste Land: Exorcism of the Demons* (London: Pennsylvania State University Press, 1977).

14 Colleen Lamos, *Deviant Modernism: Sexual and Textual Errancy in T. S. Eliot, James Joyce, and Marcel Proust* (Cambridge: Cambridge University Press, 1998), 110, 1.

15 *The Compact Edition of the OED*, vol. 1 (Oxford: Oxford University Press, 1971), 1966.

16 See Felice Flanery Lewis, *Literature, Obscenity and the Law* (Carbondale: Southern Illinois University Press, 1976).

17 Quoted in Donald Thomas, *A Long Time Burning: The History of Literary Censorship in England* (London: Routledge & Kegan Paul, 1969), 264.

18 *The Waste Land: A Facsimile and Transcript of the Original Drafts Including the Annotations of Ezra Pound*, ed. Valerie Eliot (New York: Harcourt, 1971), 23, line 12; 35, line 180; 5, lines 19 and ff.

19 Harriet Davidson, "Improper desire: reading *The Waste Land*," *The Cambridge Companion to T. S. Eliot*, ed. A. David Moody (Cambridge: Cambridge University Press, 1994), 124.

20 "Mr. Appolinax" was originally published in *Poetry* 8 no.6 (September 1916), 292–5. For details of the excision see T. S. Eliot to John Quinn, March 4, 1918, in *The Letters of T. S. Eliot, Volume One, 1898–1922*, ed. Valerie Eliot (London: Harcourt Brace Jovanovich, 1988), 223.

21 Eliot, "Literature and the American Courts," *The Egoist* 3 no.5 (March 1918): 39.

22 See Peter Ackroyd, *T. S. Eliot* (Harmondsworth: Penguin Books, 1993), 331.
23 Loretta Johnson, "T. S. Eliot's Bawdy Verse: Lulu, Bolo and More Ties," *Journal of Modern Literature* 27 no. 1/2 (Fall 2003): 24 [14–25].
24 Gabrielle McIntire, *Modernism, Memory, and Desire* (Cambridge: Cambridge University Press, 2008), 38.
25 *The Waste Land: A Facsimile*, 39, line 41.
26 Ezra Pound to T. S. Eliot, December 24, 1921, in *The Letters of T. S. Eliot, Volume One*, 498–9.
27 See Richard Shusterman, "Eliot as Philosopher," in A. David Moody, ed., *The Cambridge Companion to T. S. Eliot* (Cambridge: Cambridge University Press, 1994), 35.
28 T. E. Hulme, "A Notebook," *Further Speculations*, ed. Sam Hynes (Lincoln: University of Nebraska Press, 1962), 182.
29 Eliot, *Selected Essays*, 3rd ed. (1932; London: Faber and Faber, 1976), 458.
30 Eliot, "Prolegomena to Poetry," *Dial* 70 (1921): 451.

IO

RICHARD BADENHAUSEN

Trauma and Violence in *The Waste Land*

One would be hard-pressed to locate a modernist poem more animated by trauma and violence than *The Waste Land*. Wounded bodies and fractured minds face readers at every turn in the form of rape victims such as Philomela and the typist, war veterans struggling desperately in their relationships, and powerless women like Lil, a mother of five who flounders under crushing circumstances that have aged her prematurely and nearly caused her death. Cadavers, as material embodiments of the effects of violence, also litter the poem's landscape: the "crowd" of the "undone" dead flowing over London Bridge (62–3), the "corpse" planted a year ago in Stetson's garden (71), the "dead men [who] lost their bones" (116) in "rats' alley" (115), Lil's aborted fetus (159), and Phlebas the Phoenician, whose bones are being "Picked" over by the currents of the sea (316), are just a few examples.[1] The prophet Tiresias lingers over these horrible events as witness, trying to manage and process them; yet he ends up only highlighting his own impotence and perpetual suffering by identifying with the anguish of *The Waste Land's* victims but not possessing the capability of relieving their misery.

The poem self-consciously evokes the catastrophic First World War that had ended a few years earlier, yet it does not engage those events directly, instead choosing to contemplate the devastating effects of the conflict on individual bodies and minds and the deadened landscape they inhabit. The many allusions in the poem – themselves a product of violent action, cut off from their original textual bodies and repositioned to serve Eliot's aims – also educe a consistent narrative of extratextual trauma and violence. Those references center on works by Jessie Weston, Gérard de Nerval, Dante, Shakespeare, and Thomas Kyd that turn on tales of loss, violence, trauma, and mourning. Even the poem's original title, "He Do the Police in Different Voices" from Charles Dickens's *Our Mutual Friend*, and its initial epigraph, Kurtz's culminating cry, "the horror, the horror," from Joseph Conrad's *Heart of Darkness*, suggest that a state of emergency and trauma hangs over *The Waste Land*. In these ways the poem stands as one of the monumental edifices to the brutal effects of modernity. Such violence, though, is difficult to process in *The Waste Land* because Eliot often elides the causes of his speakers' psychological damage. Only in rare cases are the actual perpetrators of violence even named.[2] Instead, the poem concentrates on the victims and their struggles, but the accompanying originary wounding narratives seem frustratingly out of reach. That is, the poem's emphasis is on suffering itself – "I Tiresias have foresuffered all" (243) – rather than on the origins of that anguish in violent encounters.

The most compelling discussion of violence in modernist literature happens to be one of the most recent: Sara Cole's brilliant examination of the manner in which violence offers an occasion for literary triumph through its ability to propel and animate texts, though that process is also freighted with the horror and shame that accompanies acknowledgment of the modern world's brutality. In *At the Violet Hour: Modernism and Violence in England and Ireland* – a title that borrows the phrase "At the violet hour" directly from *The Waste Land* – Cole reveals how modernist "literary works created intricate, often exquisite formal solutions to the challenges posed by violence," and she traces "how violent events enhanced as well as deformed their structures and surfaces."[3] She locates modernism's attempts to formalize violence in its art and argues that the resultant tensions of that project can best be understood through the competing terms of "enchantment" and "disenchantment" (39). The latter notion grows out of Friedrich Schiller's and Max Weber's critique of a modern world overly determined by technology, capitalism, mass culture, and rationalism – conditions that led to the "large-scale diminishment of sacredness" (40). A literature of enchantment thus emerges in the early twentieth century "to provide beauty and imaginative release where there is brutality and suffering" (40). These works operate by "[h]ealing, enriching, [and] creating memorable visual forms to capture terrible realities" (40). Central to Cole's argument is *The Waste Land*, a poem that reflects "on the troubling relationship between art, with its core commitment to beautiful forms, and the violence that has wrecked human life throughout history" (80). Cole believes *The Waste Land* does not resolve this contradiction but rather recognizes that art "trades on" the power of violence, "at times appropriating its force and creating something especially brilliant, at other times succumbing to the sheer ruin that violence leaves in its wake" (81). Ultimately, Cole sees violence as crucially important to modernist art because it possesses the capability of enacting "magical transformation" (39) of the sort most powerfully memorialized in the Christian crucifixion and resurrection narrative, where horrific violence brings about redemption.

Cole's reading is a true tour de force. It offers a bold, imaginative paradigm for understanding the manner in which modernism was both repulsed and fascinated by violence and for appreciating the ways in which the architectonics of its works were built on the foundations of this tension. Yet I would like to push a bit against this model by putting a thumb on one side of the scale, so to speak, to propose that Eliot's poem is tipped far more toward disenchantment than enchantment. I see a poem distressed by violence but not redeemed by the artistic project that underlies it. My reading suggests a work that is intensely preoccupied with the various blockages that occur when victims struggle to recover from wounding experiences, a work that emphatically displays how trauma represents a stark dead end. Three key facets of the poem demonstrate Eliot insistently turning away from the ostensible enchantment of violence and the consolations that can stem from such magical transformations in favor of underscoring the many ways that recovery from trauma is maddeningly impeded. First, Tiresias hovers over the various traumatic histories of other characters as a fellow sufferer, yet he is unable to make anything happen due to his status as a secondary witness – one who overly identifies with the wounding narratives of other victims – and his position as a prophet: while he can envision traumatic events in the future, he is unable to halt them when they occur in the present. Second, Eliot constructs part IV of the poem, "Death by Water," as a failed elegy – a self-conscious occasion to highlight the nature of disrupted mourning and turn away from the consolation typically generated by the genre. Finally, the poem offers a stark examination of post-war traumatic shock and its destructive effects upon intimate relationships in the frustrating dialogue between what seems to be husband and wife that sits at the middle of part II, "A Game of Chess." Although I agree with Cole that *The Waste Land* aspires to find a way out of the disruptions associated with violence, particularly in its final section focused on recovery, I envision a much more vexed outcome and a poem that struggles to endorse the larger redemptive project alluded to in the preface to Eliot's notes or in the poem's final lines.

Tiresias as Impotent Witness

Tiresias's own history turns on a series of wounding events. Blinded by Juno for offering a displeasing answer to her question about whether men or women experience more pleasure during sex, the prophet's hermaphroditic past is tied to a punitive transfiguration that resulted from his having struck two snakes copulating. He carries the marks of those traumas in Eliot's poem via both his "wrinkled dugs" (228), which signify his transformation into a woman, and his ability to foresee the future – the latter capability a gift from Jupiter to counter Juno's punishment. Tiresias thus exists as a displaced character, one incapable of grounding himself in home, relationships, or a comforting history. He is not only "throbbing between two lives" (218), a reference to his own confusing history, but he is stuck mediating the many traumas of those who populate the poem, including the typist, Philomela, and Lil. When Eliot suggests that what Tiresias "*sees*, in fact, is the substance of the poem" (note 218), he is proposing that the prophet acts as a kind of trauma clearinghouse in which are stored many different traumatic histories of individual victims. Tiresias's central experience is the witnessing of death, sexual violence, and devastation on an immense scale, which is why he remarks that he has "foresuffered all / Enacted on this same divan or bed" (243–4) – his witnessing is tied directly to suffering. In other words, he has been subjected to earlier traumatizing events and now reexperiences the pain of those moments as other injured parties either dramatize their wounding or retell their stories. Additionally, because Tiresias possesses, like all prophets, foreknowledge of the poem's events, he carries the immense burden of perceiving injuries that are yet to come. The prophet hovers both within and outside the poem's wounding events, observing, listening, and identifying with the civic and social anguish taking place. Tiresias is able to unite "all the rest" (note 218) not through speaking the words of victims, but by becoming the central site of emotional wounding in the poem.

Tiresias embodies a situation described by trauma theorist Dori Laub, who explains that "the listener to trauma comes to be a participant and co-owner of the traumatic event: through his very listening, he comes to partially experience trauma in himself."[4] This so-called secondary witnessing represents the danger faced by analysts who cannot help but be affected by the power of traumatic narratives; such listening, explains Laub, "leaves ... no hiding place intact" (72). One becomes a fellow possessor of the event who thus runs the risk of partially experiencing it and even identifying with that trauma. Dominick LaCapra has also written extensively about the hazards of secondary witnessing, highlighting the great difficulty that emerges "when the virtual experience involved in empathy gives way to vicarious victimhood, and empathy with the victim seems to become an identity."[5] Later, LaCapra points out how it "is dubious to identify with the victim to the point of making oneself a surrogate victim who has a right to the victim's voice or subject position" (78). Tiresias possesses a unique problem in this regard: as a prophet who has privileged access to the traumatic knowledge of his fellow victims that no other analyst would have, he has a much more difficult time respecting the subject boundaries delineated by Laub and LaCapra. As LaCapra notes, the analyst must acknowledge himself as a separate individual who "possesses his own separate place, position and perspective" (58). Eliot's insistence that Tiresias is implicated and even involved in the trauma experienced by the typist at the hands of the "young man carbuncular" (231) when the prophet intrudes to note "I too awaited the expected guest" (230) and parenthetically interrupts the moment of violation by signaling his own suffering, thus blurs identities and literally drives Tiresias into occupying the subject positions of the poem's other victims. This move thereby demonstrates the danger of becoming a co-owner of the wounding event, offering a paradigmatic example for how Tiresias envisions his implication in the lives of others.

Prophets like Tiresias bear the burden of knowledge, but they typically are powerless to act on that knowledge, as is the case in *Oedipus Rex*. They are curiously paralyzed figures, and in *The Waste Land*, Tiresias alludes to the long scope of the heavy weight of his co-suffering when he reminds the reader that these trials have been taking place for over three millennia: "I who have sat by Thebes below the wall / And walked among the lowest of the dead" (245–6) – a reference to his role in Book 11 of *The Odyssey* when he helps Odysseus understand in the Underworld what awaits him upon rejoining the living when he returns home to Ithaca. This timeless feature of Tiresias's relationship to trauma ensures that he will remain stuck in that position. As LaCapra has pointed out, one of the key components of working through trauma is for the victim to find a way in which she can distinguish between past and present and say to herself that it may not be possible to escape entirely from earlier events, but to be able to affirm, "I'm existing here and now, and this is different from back then" (144). Yet given that Tiresias has "foresuffered all" and knows that in the future similar woundings will take place, there is no way he can make those distinctions between past and present that are crucial to recovery. As LaCapra observes, gaining critical distance from a trauma ultimately entails "distinguish[ing] between past, present, and future" (143), which are distinctions that Tiresias fails to make in his compulsive reenactment of trauma as he "does" the different voices in an intense identification with the many wounding events he has witnessed.

Elegy, Mourning, and the Refusal of Consolation

The Waste Land can be read on one level as a poem about mourning, particularly due to its publication on the heels of the devastation that had taken place during World War I, and the fighting that continued to rage on in other conflicts like the Greco-Turkish war. Jay Winter has pointed out that the First World War "brought the search for an appropriate language of loss to the centre of cultural and political life," and I agree with other critics that Eliot is explicitly participating in this conversation.[6] Eliot is interested in the challenges associated with acknowledging death and processing the difficult emotions that accompany it, especially when the location of the corpse is remote or unknown. Such emotional reckoning with death has been managed in many cultures via elegiac forms, and in his important study of the modern elegy, Jahan Ramazani proposes that *The Waste Land* be read as a "covert elegy,"[7] though he does not settle decisively on the specific loss the poem is attempting to overcome, proposing a variety of possibilities that include Jean Verdenal, Eliot's father, the collective dead of the First World War, or even Western civilization itself. In the three paragraphs he devotes to Eliot's poem, Ramazani argues that Eliot disguises his elegiac purposes as a way of avoiding a too-close association with "his mournful personae" (26) while still undergirding the effort with strong debts to Whitman's elegy for Abraham Lincoln and John Milton's elegy for Edward King. Yet I see the poem taking up the elegiac project much more directly in "Death by Water" by asking how individuals process loss – in this case, the death of Phlebas the Phoenician – and, more importantly, by interrogating the problems inherent in that grieving project. In this respect, the whole poem can be understood as a "site of mourning" – to use Winter's suggestive phrase about the various devices (linguistic and otherwise) that helped mediate bereavement after the war – one that provides a structure for responses to trauma. Such a reading also views *The Waste Land* as anticipating Peter Sacks's valuable exploration of elegiac conventions as "literary versions of specific social and psychological practices."[8] For the purposes of my argument, though, what is most important about Eliot's manipulation of elegy is that he is refusing the redemptive possibilities embedded in a poetic form whose overt goal is to trade on the power of art to transform suffering into solace.

While Jahan Ramazani has identified a number of echoes of well-known elegies in *The Waste Land*, and other critics have provided some suggestive readings that locate elegiac strains in the poem, I view "Death by Water" as a corrupted elegy, an elegy gone bad, one that collapses due to the psychological deficiencies of its speaker and Eliot's refusal to attach any possibility of transcendence or consolation to this death due to his interest in the nature of disrupted mourning.[9] Here it is in full:

> Phlebas the Phoenician, a fortnight dead,
> Forgot the cry of gulls, and the deep sea swell
> And the profit and loss.
>   A current under sea
> Picked his bones in whispers. As he rose and fell
> He passed the stages of his age and youth
> Entering the whirlpool.
>   Gentile or Jew

> O you who turn the wheel and look to windward,
> Consider Phlebas, who was once handsome and tall as you.
>
> (312–21)

Like many elegies, this section of *The Waste Land* makes much of the name of the deceased, though in this case the speaker dispenses with the typical invocation of some outside inspiration, such as a divine being or force of nature, and gets right to the point by keying in on "Phlebas the Phoenician, a fortnight dead" (312). That line echoes in a number of ways Milton's "For Lycidas is dead, dead ere his prime,"[10] including the similar sounding name, the emphasis on "dead" – through repetition in Milton's case and its position at the end of a line in Eliot's case – a like number of syllables, and even a parallel placement of a medial caesura. But aside from their central subjects both sharing the same fate of drowning, the poems could not be more dissimilar. Whereas traditional elegies are sustained over an extended number of lines so as to allow for the emotional buildup on which the genre depends (and which it exploits), Eliot offers a brutally succinct treatment that is cut off after ten lines.

This abruptness – as it relates to the aborted nature of this particular case of mourning – is yet another success achieved by Ezra Pound's editing of this section. He encouraged Eliot to eradicate the drawn-out maritime narrative, which, in an early draft, had concentrated the elegiac focus of the final lines that originally served as a response or coda to the sailor's call to "Remember me" – surely an explicit allusion to the command of the Ghost of Hamlet's father at the end of act I of *Hamlet*.[11] Whereas most classic elegies adopt a formal diction and tone, Eliot's version employs a direct, colloquial vocabulary and informal attitude. The subjects of most elegies are also treated with great reverence – this is expressed often in a laudatory review of the deceased's accomplishments – but Eliot's speaker offers no praise and instead indicts Phlebas: he "Forgot the cry of gulls" (313). Edward King's role in his own death is excused by Milton due to the unreliability of the ship in which he sailed, yet Phlebas's passing is simply accepted. Instead of idealizing the dead body as Milton does ("flote upon his watry bear," 12), Eliot treats his corpse with a lack of discretion: "A current under sea / Picked his bones in whispers" (315–6).

While the universe of Milton's poem is inhabited by a comforting mix of classical deities and a Christian afterlife that ensures a secure place in eternity for the fallen soul, Phlebas exists in a world of materiality that makes no promises about life after death beyond the fact of a decaying body. Nor does Eliot's speaker express any anger about the death or toward any unfeeling gods or forces of nature that might have brought it about; instead, the event is gazed on with a flat, affectless eye. In fact, there is a kind of detached impassivity running through the entire account. As Sacks points out, the "movement from loss to consolation ... requires a deflection of desire" (7); but one of the recurring features of *The Waste Land* is how often potentially charged emotional moments are accompanied by "indifference" (242), to use a word associated with the typist during her sexual encounter with the young man carbuncular. Such impairment impedes the consolatory project from getting under way. While conventional elegies tend to progress toward the discovery of a universal truth, Eliot's lament not only parodies that convention in its last three lines, but it cautions the audience ("Consider Phlebas ...") rather than offering the consolation that is the ultimate objective of the form. Instead of peaceful, soothing closure, the poem and its abrupt conclusion seem to have facilitated a kind of melancholic paralysis in which loss cannot be processed properly. This positions the poem, then, as a type of anti-elegy, a representation of trauma that elucidates the devastation of being blocked emotionally. Not only is Eliot demonstrating his poetic skill in transfiguring the genre, but he is also turning its conventions against themselves as a way of revealing the dislocations so often caused by trauma. He locates his speaker in the position of elegist, but then repeatedly obstructs the usual pathways to successful consolation. This resituates the focus of the poem away from the potential redemptive qualities of aesthetic responses to violence and more squarely on the suffering of victims subject to that violence.[12]

War and the Domestication of Trauma

The Waste Land shares with much Great War literature a concern with the psychological effects of modern combat. In particular, Eliot's poem is interested in exploring the damage wrought upon male-female relationships as a result of the war, fixating on the absence of intimacy between partners whose physical and psychological experiences have diverged so radically that they find themselves faced with a debilitating emotional distance. Vera Brittain, the early twentieth-century writer and pacifist, worried that the war might provoke just such a loss of emotional connection with her fiancé, Roland, who eventually died in battle. In her memoir, *Testament of Youth* (1933), she recounts a "fear that the War would come between us – as indeed, with time, the War always did, putting a barrier of indescribable experience between men and the women whom they loved, thrusting horror deeper and deeper inward."[13]

Eliot received quite a bit of firsthand information about the horrors of combat from Maurice Haigh-Wood, Vivien Eliot's brother, who spoke frankly about his service in the infantry with the Manchester Regiment. Eliot's brother-in-law sought to explain in a letter from June 1917 the apparent "complete indifference" of those who had fought at the front as an "attitude, a screen" that resulted from the moral impossibility of relating "unspeakable tragedies" to those "uninitiated" civilians at home who had not experienced them.[14] Haigh-Wood then continues to give the reader a taste of why veterans might avoid such accounts, noting the grimness of the subject matter: the "swollen and blackening corpses of hundreds of young men," the "appalling stench of rotting carrion," fellow soldiers "with bowels dropping out, lungs shot away, with blinded, smashed faces, or limbs blown into space," and "Wounded men hanging in agony on the barbed wire, until a friendly spout of liquid fire shrivels them up like a fly in a candle" (Ibid., 205). Eliot was taken enough by the letter that he forwarded it to the editor of *The Nation* two weeks after its receipt, believing it would interest readers by helping to explain why soldiers were reluctant to talk about their experiences. Published a few days later, Haigh-Wood's account served as a challenge to official restrictions that sought to sanitize the home front by removing any trace of wounded and destroyed bodies, a condition critic Allyson Booth identifies as "the problem of corpselessness."[15] This gesture also anticipates Eliot's move in *The Waste Land* to restore the presence of corpses by making them more visible against the various settings of the poem, whether they take the form of Stetson's corpse (71), the dead men from "rats' alley" (115), "bones cast in a little low dry garret" (194), the remains of Phlebas's body in the "current under sea" (315), or most explicitly, "the little light dead people,"[16] which was an excised line from "A Game of Chess." Eliot is interrogating the difficulty for veterans of returning home to an environment unprepared to deal with their problems. Of particular interest to him is the manner in which domestic spaces are inhospitable to traumatized soldiers struggling to reconcile their wartime experiences with the very different demands of civilian life.

Eliot's poem, of course, contains an explicit reference to a married couple whose relationship is under pressure as a consequence of the war. In the final scene of "A Game of Chess," we overhear an anonymous female speaker relating the story of her friend Lil, whose husband Albert has just been demobilized after his wartime service. Lil is physically ravaged as a result of the burdens of motherhood and other domestic pressures: she's had five children, of which the last almost killed her; she has had an abortion; she has some serious dental problems; and at age thirty-one she already appears so "antique" (156) that her spouse "can't bear to look" at her (146). In spite of those liabilities, Albert still "wants a good time" (148) with Lil, though other women are apparently ready to satisfy him sexually if his wife does not. An apt portrayal of the havoc wreaked upon marriages by the recent war, Eliot's scene ends with an evocation of Ophelia's penultimate departing words in act IV, scene 5 of *Hamlet*, which grounds the preceding marital portrait within the tradition of tragic love relationships that have collapsed due to miscommunication, misunderstanding, and a lack of intimacy. It will not be long, the allusion hints, before Lil will be compelled to destroy herself in perhaps the same fashion as Ophelia, and the poem's incessant reminder of "Death by Water" only reinforces the likelihood of that fate. Indeed, the tale about Lil is interrupted ominously – overtaken by the pub keeper's repeated cry of last call, "HURRY UP PLEASE ITS TIME" – its denouement swallowed up because "A Game of Chess" is ending, and all we are left with is a blank white space before the start of the next section of the poem.

Lil and Albert's story, though, is not the only examination of post war relationship struggles in the poem. Viewing the exchange that precedes the pub scene (beginning "'My nerves are bad to-night,'" 111) through the subsequent information revealed by Lil's friend allows one to surmise that this conversation takes place between a male-female couple – albeit a more genteel version – that is also experiencing serious problems as a result of the husband's war service. Although this moment in the poem has typically been read as a series of questions framed by quotation marks that go unanswered by the male companion and are instead merely constructed as silent responses in his head (because no quotation marks appear around his lines), I offer a reading that imagines both sides of this tête-à-tête being verbalized. While my interpretation can be sustained even if the male speaker's lines are merely thought rather than articulated – he becomes, then, simply a numbed, unresponsive veteran, a silent victim lost on his own island of suffering – it suggests a male speaker who is a more active agent actually interested in reaching out and making progress. The fact that his wife fails to recognize his desires to communicate and connect makes this deteriorating marriage even more dysfunctional and tragic, though this schism between marital partners demonstrates that successful homecomings were often almost impossible for traumatized soldiers.

The dramatic dialogue in part II gets underway when an unnamed female confesses to having bad "nerves" (111), code at the time for a hysterical condition. She uses the excuse to demand that her male partner remain at her side. The complaint quickly turns, however, to a condemnation of the companion's inability to speak and share his thoughts: "'What are you thinking of? What thinking? What? / I never know what you are thinking. Think'" (113–4). This might initially seem like a petty grievance that occasionally surfaces in most marriages, but this male character has shut down emotionally and is failing to communicate as a result of some significant trauma.

His reply only confirms that sense: "I think we are in rats' alley / Where the dead men lost their bones" (115–6). The apparent non sequitur, even though he picks up on the earlier word "think," actually fits when understood as surfacing out of the dislocation often experienced by traumatized veterans. In addition, the reference to "rats' alley" is consistent with such a background, since that expression was a common wartime name for a trench, where corpses sat at the mercy of rats picking away at limbs.[17] In using such slang, the male speaker is also falling back on language that further highlights the gulf between veterans and civilians, between male combatants and women. Helping to reinforce that chasm, rather than responding to this rather remarkable vision, the female speaker returns to her own anxieties, asking a series of questions about noises she hears, which are dismissed by her companion as "nothing" (120). Once again, the wife goes on the attack: "'Do / You know nothing? Do you see nothing? Do you remember / Nothing?'" (121–3).

Ironically, the distressed wife criticizes her partner's inability to recollect experience immediately following his memory of fallen colleagues, though this again demonstrates the severe miscommunication taking place. She is honing in on a central feature of returning veterans' impairment, namely their inability to share with civilians the details of their experience. War veterans often felt that those remaining at home could never understand the horrors of their fighting. Language itself often seemed inadequate in capturing the essence of their suffering, and they themselves actually *did not* remember due to the various dislocations experienced by trauma victims. As one character in Henri Barbusse's war memoir *Under Fire* explains, we are "machines of forgetting," an acknowledgment that arrives as a result of another character asserting, "everything we've seen is too much. We're not built to take all this in."[18] Once again, picking up on the key word in his partner's accusation, "remember," Eliot's speaker acknowledges, "I remember / Those are pearls that were his eyes" (124–5), as if revisiting corpses on the battlefield via Shakespeare's *The Tempest*. He uses the present tense, as if he has just drifted off to that space of death and remembrance, while the allusion to Ariel's song for the second time in the poem evokes yet another drowned body, in this case Ferdinand's supposed "drowned father," the King of Naples,[19] lying on the ocean floor much like Phlebas the Phoenician, his bones being picked at by the currents of the sea.

At this point, perhaps recognizing the faraway look in the eyes of her companion, the female speaker asks: "'Are you alive, or not? Is there nothing in your head?'" (126). This explicitly aligns the male individual with the many characters in the poem who are "neither / Living nor dead" (39–40): that middle ground of tortured existence that I have associated with the traumatic state and which was one of the most common analogues for the condition of the shell-shocked veteran. As Wyatt Bonikowski notes in his book on shell shock, the soldier-victim "was not dead, but he was not quite alive either since he seemed to be inhabited by some alien force encountered at war and brought home with him … it is as if these men are the living dead, as if somehow *death* and not life animates them."[20] Like those whom "death had undone" (63), Eliot's figure has been "undone" psychologically by his traumatic experience and spends his days like the crowds of wounded shades flowing over London Bridge in the "Unreal City" (60). In "A Game of Chess," Eliot is domesticating trauma, showing the reader what the poem's earlier images of mass trauma look like distilled to the personal and private, as a clash between two individuals who are vying for the primacy of their respective victimhoods. Just such a struggle occurred in Eliot's own tortured first marriage to Vivien Haigh-Wood. In one of her letters that begins by referencing her husband's 1921 breakdown, Vivien states with some exasperation, "I have not nearly finished my own nervous breakdown yet."[21] The curious phrasing in "A Game of Chess" of death having "undone" these people suggests not that they have died like Dante's condemned shades, but that their encounters with death around them (as on the battlefield) have unraveled their psyches to the point that they might as well be ghosts wandering the city.

The fair answer, then, to the question of whether he is "alive, or not" is "neither." And the query about whether his head contains "nothing" is particularly painful given the previous evidence suggesting that part of the problem is that there are *too many* horrible memories rattling around in his mind, including appalling recollections of decomposing corpses, which he has now mentioned twice. But instead of going to that battlefield well for yet a third time, the speaker's disposition takes a manic turn as he quotes, or more likely sings, lines from the 1912 ragtime tune "that Shakespeherian Rag" (128). Here we have a speaker who has closed down emotionally as a result of the pain of the previous unsuccessful attempts at communication. From this point onward, the husband will offer no more revelations, and the exchange winds down with one final set of self-absorbed questions from the wife about how to fill up the time in her day and a set of abrupt, unexciting proposals by the husband delivered in a monotone.

This exchange is much more fractured and difficult to follow than the subsequent straightforward narrative accounting of the overhead conversation in the pub. Unlike that final discussion that is unfolded in a long, single, coherent stanza, the repartee between husband and wife starts and stops haltingly in broken-off lines and stanzas. Filled with fatuous questions of the sort a child might ask, and seemingly nonsensical answers that provide little relief to the increasingly tense debate, the set piece serves to demonstrate Booth's contention that "the dislocations of war often figure centrally in modernist form, even when war itself seems peripheral to modernist content" (4). In fact, in the case of Eliot's treatment in *The Waste Land* of the traumatic consequences of combat experience, I see a poem that is attempting to drag the various ruptures caused by the Great War from the edges of "modernist content" right into its center via the trope of trauma, even though most portrayals of Eliot tend to emphasize his reticence about the war.[22]

While Cole emphasizes the formalization of *violence* in modernist literature, my reading suggests Eliot is interrogating *suffering*, which positions *The Waste Land* in a different light. Due to the obfuscation of initial wounding events in the poem and the position of characters seemingly stuck in posttraumatic paralysis, Eliot has backed himself into a corner regarding the question of recovery, even though the various myths overlaid onto the poem seem to hold out redemption as a possibility. Eliot invokes the Grail legend in his "Notes" to *The Waste Land*, thus gesturing to the manner in which a supernatural outside source may restore a wounded king and his ravaged land, and the gathering thunder clouds towards the end of the poem suggest an imminent cleansing rain that will help "set my lands in order" (425). Yet recovering from trauma entails bringing the origins of an injury into the light of the present day where they can be identified, acknowledged, and processed. Because *The Waste Land* so insistently conceals the roots of trauma, its characters are left trapped in their suffering without knowing how to turn to the healing aspects of the past. The poem as such foregrounds the *effects* of violence upon human beings who seem to possess a hopeless future. Where Cole uncovers solutions to the challenges of violence via the mechanism of aesthetic triumph that provides "imaginative release," I see mostly dead ends. This reorientation is especially important because it repositions Eliot from a writer who sees salvation in art to one looking for answers beyond that arena; ultimately, it offers one possible explanation for Eliot's turn in the 1920s toward education, religion, and community as potential solutions to some of the profound moral problems of his age.

NOTES

1 T. S. Eliot, *The Complete Poems and Plays* (1969; London: Faber and Faber, 1985). Further references to this text will be cited parenthetically.

2 A notable exception in part II of the poem is Tereus, the legendary king of Athens who brutally raped and cut out the tongue of his wife's sister, Philomel.

3 Sarah Cole, *At the Violet Hour: Modernism and Violence in England and Ireland* (Oxford: Oxford University Press, 2012), 5. Further references to this

text will be cited parenthetically. Peter Sheehan's *Modernism and the Aesthetics of Violence* (Cambridge: Cambridge University Press, 2013) also examines the modernism-violence nexus, but he does not engage Cole's arguments.

4 Dori Laub, "Bearing Witness or the Vicissitudes of Listening," *Testimony: Crises of Witnessing in Literature, Psychoanalysis, and History*, ed. Shoshana Felman and Dori Laub (New York: Routledge, 1992), 57. Further references to this text will be cited parenthetically.

5 Dominick LaCapra, *Writing History, Writing Trauma* (Baltimore: The Johns Hopkins University Press, 2001), 47. Further references to this text will be cited parenthetically.

6 Jay Winter, *Sites of Memory, Sites of Mourning* (1996; Cambridge: Cambridge University Press, 2007), 5.

7 Jahan Ramazani, *Poetry of Mourning: The Modern Elegy from Hardy to Heaney* (Chicago: University of Chicago Press, 1994), 26.

8 Peter M. Sacks, *The English Elegy: Studies in the Genre from Spenser to Yeats* (Baltimore: The Johns Hopkins University Press, 1985), 2. Like Ramazani and others, Sacks sees *The Waste Land* functioning as a site where Verdenal's death is being mourned (261). Further references to this text will be cited parenthetically.

9 See, for example, Colleen Lamos's "The Love Song of T. S. Eliot: Elegiac Homoeroticism in the Early Poetry," *Gender, Desire, and Sexuality in T. S. Eliot*, ed. Nancy Gish and Cassandra Laity (Cambridge: Cambridge University Press, 2004), which sees the elegiac mode in Eliot's work as a means for him "*simultaneously* to affirm and to repudiate same-sex affection" (24). Sandra M. Gilbert and Susan Gubar read the poem "as a dirge for Verdenal" that "becomes a kind of fragmented and surrealistic pastoral elegy" in *No Man's Land: The Place of the Woman Writer in the Twentieth Century*, vol. 2: *Sexchanges* (New Haven, CT: Yale University Press, 1989), 311; David Spurr explores the poem's struggle to mourn successfully due to a postmodern awareness of the speaking subject's continual dismantling even when continuing to seek out the catharsis typically found in elegies in "*The Waste Land*: Mourning, Writing, Disappearance," *Yeats Eliot Review* 9 no. 4 (1988): 161–4; and Gregory Jay examines the way in which *The Waste Land* engages in a dialogue with some of its notable elegiac forebears in *T. S. Eliot and the Poetics of Literary History* (Baton Rouge: Louisiana State University Press, 1983), 156–71.

10 John Milton, *The Complete Works of John Milton*, ed. John T. Shawcross (Garden City, New York: Anchor, 1971), 8.

11 Eliot, *The Waste Land: A Facsimile and Transcript of the Original Drafts Including the Annotations of Ezra Pound*, ed. Valerie Eliot (New York: Harcourt, 1971), 61, line 81.

12 Cole sees "Death by Water" as the "ideal of an enchanting transformation of violence and bodily harm to wonder and beauty" and thus a "paradigm for poetic consolation" (68), which is the exact opposite of how I view the lines functioning.

13 Vera Brittain, *Testament of Youth* (1933; New York: Penguin, 1994), 143.

14 Eliot, *The Letters of T. S. Eliot, Volume 1: 1898–1922*, ed. Valerie Eliot and Hugh Haughton, rev. ed., (London: Faber and Faber, 2009), 204, 205.

15 Allyson Booth, *Postcards from the Trenches: Negotiating the Space between Modernism and the First World War* (New York: Oxford University Press, 1996), 11. Further references to this text will be cited parenthetically.

16 Eliot, *The Waste Land: A Facsimile,* 13, line 46.

17 For an exhaustive study of trench slang names, see Peter Chasseaud, *Rats Alley: Trench Names of the Western Front, 1914–1918* (Stonehouse, UK: Spellmount, 2006). "Alley" is slang for a British communication trench, while the ubiquity of rats at the front caused many a trench name to evoke that omnipresence, including Rat Lane, Rat Farm, Rat Pit, and many a Rats' Alley (Chasseaud 2006, 13, 118–19, 373).

18 Henri Barbusse, *Under Fire*, trans. Robin Buss (New York: Penguin, 2004), 305, 304.

19 William Shakespeare, *The Tempest*, ed. Robert Langbaum (New York: Signet, 1987).

20 Wyatt Bonikowski, *Shell Shock and the Modernist Imagination: The Death Drive in Post-World War I British Fiction* (Burlington, VT: Ashgate, 2013), 2, 18.

21 Vivien Eliot to Scofield Thayer, October 13, 1921, *Letters,* 1, 592.

22 In "'Where are the Eagles and the Trumpets?': Imperial Decline and Eliot's Development," *A Companion to T. S. Eliot,* ed. David Chinitz (Oxford: Wiley-Blackwell, 2009), Vincent Sherry espouses this position when he notes that "the record the war leaves in Eliot's poetry of the late teens is not nearly so explicit a history as may be found in other civilian poets" (95).

II

EVE SORUM

Psychology, Psychoanalysis, and New Subjectivities

From the opening stanza with its shifting pronouns, *The Waste Land* presents speaking voices that challenge the autonomy of the individual subject. Over the course of the past century, this challenge has spurred two conflicting critical stances: on the one hand, that *The Waste Land* provides a method to unify its many voices and subjects; on the other, that the poem records and even promotes the inevitable fragmentation of the modern subject. Early New Critical readings influentially championed the first perspective; in 1932 F. R. Leavis asserts that Eliot's note about Tiresias "provides the clue" to the poem's project to "focus an inclusive human consciousness," while in 1937 Cleanth Brooks argues that the poem functions as a "unified whole" emerging from a central "protagonist."[1] A later line of critics disagreed, citing fragmentation rather than unity as the defining state of the modern subject and of the poem; we might look to Maud Ellmann, who claims that "the poem violates the very notion of a private self," or Michael Levenson, whose reading of the first line shows how "the boundaries of the self begin to waver."[2] Either way, the debate makes clear that whether the poem is described as a triumph of a unified consciousness or as a "tragedy of unreconciled voices,"[3] *The Waste Land* is terrifying and exhilarating in part because it is simultaneously deeply atomizing and replete with voices urging connection. The variation in scholarly responses suggests that examining the issue of subjectivity and the role of psychology in *The Waste Land* means confronting contradictory critical impulses and interpretive pathways. In this essay I will argue that we see Eliot expressing a theory of subjectivity in the poem that, while reflecting several of Sigmund Freud's contemporaneous theories, ultimately places a far greater emphasis on the material world as central to determining the boundaries and the content of subjectivity. The polyphony in *The Waste Land* becomes connected, in my reading, to attempts to reach outside the individual subject – to engage in acts of empathy – even while acknowledging the painful and dangerous nature of such perspective shifting.

Published just two years after Freud's *Beyond the Pleasure Principal* (1920), *The Waste Land* was read by critics like Leavis as a manifestation of the importance of psychoanalytic interpretation, with Eliot's Tiresias as "the appropriate impersonation" of the modern figure in "an age of psychoanalysis."[4] Yet Eliot's relationship to Freudian thought is complicated and often dismissive. In one of his 1922 "London Letters" to the *Dial*, for example, he remarks that the ideas coming out of Vienna are "a dubious and contentious branch of science."[5] Thus, while an examination of Freud's concepts of "unpleasure" and the unyielding presence of the "repetition compulsion"[6] is illuminating and even needed when discussing subjectivity in *The Waste Land*, more defining for Eliot were other circulating theories of the unconscious and of the boundaries of human subjectivity.

In claiming this, I follow Paul Stasi's recent argument that reading Eliot's dissertation on the philosopher F. H. Bradley alongside *The Waste Land* reveals how "Eliot constructs a theory of inter-subjectivity, which emphasizes the role of culture in the creation of subjects, objects, and the historical ground on which subjects meet."[7] The link between Eliot's poetry and his research on Bradley, a British Idealist philosopher at Oxford, has been extensively explored by critics including William Skaff and Michael Levenson, among others, but it is worth quoting Eliot's claim, from a June 1919 letter to Lytton Strachey, that "Anything *I* have picked up about writing is due to having spent (as I once thought, wasted) a year absorbing the style of F. H. Bradley – the finest philosopher in English."[8] Yet we cannot stop with Bradley's philosophy; we must go beyond Eliot's formulation of the unconscious in his dissertation and early essays and examine his own therapeutic experience with the Swiss psychologist Dr. Roger Vittoz. Eliot had read Vittoz's book on *The Treatment of Neurasthenia by Means of Brain Control* in 1921, just before going to Lausanne to be treated by the psychologist in person. While in Lausanne Eliot continued work on *The Waste Land* and produced, according to Lawrence Rainey's meticulous research on the various manuscripts, the handwritten fair copies of parts IV and V, as well as some other lines of poetry meant to link the different elements of part III more firmly together.[9] The versions of subjectivity that emerge in *The Waste Land* present a fusion of a Bradley-inspired understanding of the porous boundaries of the subject and a Vittozian emphasis on the centrality of process – of repetition and conditioning – in order to create a functioning subject. We will see that rather than simply an outward manifestation of repressed trauma, the repetitions of the poem indicate attempts to *reconstruct* subjectivity in a world in flux.

Eliot articulates his own theory of the subject while discussing Bradley's argument from *Appearance and Reality* (1893) that reality is founded upon "immediate experiences"[10] – the perceptual events in which the boundaries between the self and the surrounding world are no longer visible. These experiences are then resolved, for Bradley, into a unified, unknowable whole called the "Absolute."[11] While Eliot dismisses Bradley's idea of the Absolute as an imaginary resolution,[12] he does take up enthusiastically the idea of immediate experience and, centrally, the ultimate *relativity* of the relationship between self and world: the existence of the subject depends on the object, and vice versa. Thus, Eliot writes, "reality as we may know it, the ultimate criterion which gives meaning to our judgments of existence, is so far as it appears at all, our experience, yet an experience which only to a certain extent – from a certain necessary but untenable point of view – is 'ours.'"[13] These flickering borders between subject and object, subject and subject, mean that there is always a line of connection between seemingly alienated perspectives, for "[a]nother person, and in its degree another *thing*, is not for us simply an object; there is always, I believe, a felt continuity between the object and oneself" (Ibid., 81). Examining this reading of Bradley thus presents an Eliot more concerned with the possibilities and even the *inevitabilities* of connection than we often realize, and reveals his vision of a fragmented but coherent modern subject. It also shows how subjectivity is necessarily defined through interactions with and perceptions of the material and interpersonal world. While *The Waste Land* presents a cosmos in which subjects are profoundly alienated from both themselves and from others, as well as one in which the idea of the coherent subject is fundamentally questioned, the poem simultaneously suggests that "subjects can reconnect through the construction of a common world built, in part, out of the 'unreal' objects of language and culture" (Stasi 43). All of the "objects of language and culture" provide the building blocks of the individual subject, even as they also reveal the composite and social nature of that subject. The route to this connection is through perception, as Eliot describes in his essay on "The Perfect Critic:" "Not only all knowledge, but all feeling, is in perception."[14] By grounding knowledge and feeling in acts of perception, Eliot posits individual identity as not simply affected by external stimuli, but as composed by them – knowledge and feeling are "*in* perception" (my emphasis).

We can begin to see connections between the psychological and the material when examining the theories and, particularly, the therapeutic practices of Dr. Roger Vittoz. During Eliot's 1921 breakdown and while undergoing an unsuccessful rest treatment in Margate, Eliot appealed to Julian Huxley for information about Vittoz, whom Huxley had seen and who, according to Eliot's letter, was compelling because he was a "specialist in psychological troubles," and neither a "nerve" doctor nor, as he wrote in a later letter to

Sydney Waterlow, "a psychoanalyst."[15] Vittoz's theory of the subject and of treatments of psychological disorders differs from Freud's, in part, because he argues that the will can and should be used to control the "unconscious" brain – the repository of what Vittoz terms "subjective" experience.[16] Vittoz posits that the core of the subject is defined by the regulation of the relationship between the subconscious and the "conscious" brain – the latter of which engages in "objective" acts of judgment and reason (1–2).[17] Psychological problems result, Vittoz argues, from an imbalance between these two parts of the brain. A return to what he calls "normal" brain control is when "every idea, impression or sensation is controlled by reason, judgment and will, that is to say, that these can be judged, modified, or set aside as required" (3). Vittoz's therapeutic practices, which Eliot underwent, involved working toward this control through a series of physical and mental repetitive exercises – exercises that ranged from focusing on basic physical actions (like bending one's limbs) to meditating on calming images and symbols.[18] Vittoz roots psychological unity in both physical and mental practices while also emphasizing that repetition can be therapeutic, rather than a sign of repressed neuroses or the working through of a traumatic event.

Eliot's study of both Bradley's porous and conditional subject and Vittoz's practical vision of mental and physical unity suggests that the speaking voice/s of The Waste Land could be read in light of such constructive visions of a divided subjectivity. Of course, this focus begs the question of what or, rather, who might be the subject of The Waste Land. If, as Michael Levenson has argued, this poem can be seen as "a doctrinal act, the poem as a critical gesture,"[19] then probing of the limits of the subject involves questioning its own subject. The first part of the poem, "The Burial of the Dead," erupts with latent forces both poetically and thematically, and the need to bury these forces provides tension throughout this section. The cruelty of April is not simply in its imposed growth, but also in its "stirring" up of dormant memories, a stirring that unleashes that proliferation of the voices that define and haunt the poem.[20] The boundaries of the subject are thereby called into question before we have even figured out who is speaking; by the fifth line – "Winter kept us warm" – the authoritative impersonal voice of the first lines claims a kind of community that is embodied grammatically, even if not corporeally, in the space of the poem. But this unexpected underground authority then engages in a shift that – despite its claim of an "us" – indicates that the "us" of the poem is multiple, rather than united; suddenly the "us" is in the realm of memories about the pre-war world of the "Hofgarten" (10) and sledding in northern mountains. The second half of the stanza hints at a more historically and socially embedded set of perspectives with its specifications of place ("the Starnbergersee" and "Hofgarten," 8, 10), of nationality ("Litauen, echt deutsch," 12), and even of individual identity ("Marie," 15), but the shifting pronouns and the movements between past and present suggest that the subject of this poem is not so easily parsed. Indeed, the stanza ends with winter, bringing us from the promise of regeneration and growth of April, back to the stasis of that season of "forgetful snow" (6).

Yet here is where we have to begin to distinguish the difference between the pathological and the normal subject – the difference between a "felt continuity between the object and oneself" (Eliot *Knowledge and Experience*, 81) that Eliot describes in his dissertation, and a subject for whom there is no continuity, only an onslaught of objects and others. This is the trauma voiced in the first lines of the second stanza:

> What are the roots that clutch, what branches grow
> Out of this stony rubbish? Son of man,
> You cannot say, or guess, for you know only
> A heap of broken images, where the sun beats,
> And the dead tree gives no shelter, the cricket no relief,
> And the dry stone no sound of water. (19–24)

The terror of this scene for the "Son of man" is that he can connect nothing – repeated later and more explicitly in "The Fire Sermon['s]" "I can connect / Nothing with nothing" (301–2) – and can see no generative potential in this apocalyptic view, which seems to present only that which has been destroyed or made barren. This same scene reappears in the fifth part, "What the Thunder Said," and generates a voice there that, as we will later see, defines and delimits the nature of intersubjective interaction. At this earlier moment, however, the speaking voice points to various attempts to know and feel, and then to the failures of those attempts. Momentarily omniscient and distanced, the speaker tells the "Son of man,"

> (Come in under the shadow of this red rock),
> And I will show you something different from either
> Your shadow at morning striding behind you
> Or your shadow at evening rising to meet you;
> I will show you fear in a handful of dust. (26–30)

With the evocation of both the following and the preceding shadows, the speaker suggests that at stake are the very *means* by which we acknowledge both identity and temporality. In one sense, we know when and where we are through these shadows – they are signifiers of our ability to step outside of ourselves and, even if only distortedly and passingly, to get a glimpse of how we might appear. And the shadows also hint at those shades, those shadows of the dead that haunt the poem, from the first lines until the figure of the "third who walks always walks beside" (359) found in the final section. Yet this is a profoundly self-centered vision in this arid and empty world populated only by the I, the you, the shadows, and the "fear in a handful of dust" (30). The dust, like the shadows, already carries a double valence: on the one hand, it is the physical marker of the dead, who have gone back to the dust. On the other, it is suggestive of an utter absence of a consolatory, productive, or self-reflective element in nature – an example of nature resisting its traditional role as an enabler of poetic meaning-making.

This self-centeredness is even more apparent in light of the textual history of the poem. The facsimile of *The Waste Land* manuscripts shows us that these first lines of this section ("Come in under the shadow of this red rock," 26) originate in an earlier poem, "The Death of Saint Narcissus," which was probably written in 1915. In this early poem, Eliot describes the life of a saint who goes into the desert to escape both his own male body and the teeming cities too full of "faces, convulsive thighs and knees."[21] Out in this desert landscape Narcissus imagines that he has become first a tree, then a fish, and then a girl, losing his body in these hallucinations until he finally succumbs to an actual death by burning arrows. Instead of the "red rock" of *The Waste Land*, here the poet asks the reader to "Come under the shadow of this grey rock"[22], and then reveals that we will see a shadow that does not resolve into the abstracted "fear in a handful of dust" (*The Waste Land* 30) we get in "The Burial of the Dead," but into the figure of Saint Narcissus: "I will show you his bloody cloth and limbs" (*Facsimile,* 95, line 6). The poem goes on to describe the saint as reaching a state of profound and almost unbearable self-awareness, for the movements of the air and his body create such sensitivity ("His eyes were aware of the pointed corners of his eyes," 95, line 14) that he can no longer live among other men, becoming a "dancer before God" (95, line 17). In this new role Saint Narcissus takes on the experiences of other life forms, first assuming the state of a tree, "twisting its branches among each other" (97, line 22), then a fish "With slippery white belly held tight in his own fingers" (97, line 25), and finally a young girl raped by a drunken old man, "Knowing at the end the taste of her own whiteness" (97, line 30). Each of these assumed forms and knowledge are accompanied by a kind of violence that is perpetrated by someone who is both himself and an other (he feels drunken and old, for example, after "knowing" the rape of his own body, 97, lines 30–2). Saint Narcissus therefore returns to his own body and welcomes giving it in self-sacrifice:

> Until the arrows came.
> As he embraced them his white skin surrendered
>   itself to the redness of blood, and satisfied him. (97, lines 36–8)

With this palimpsest of the first stanza from the "The Death of Saint Narcissus," we can connect *The Waste Land* shadows with a vision of a world where, behind the shadows, lurks the knowledge of the tortures produced by a self-immolating empathy. Echoing Freud's definition of narcissism as describing "the attitude of a person who treats his own body in the same way in which the body of a sexual object is ordinarily treated,"[23] the metamorphoses in the poem ostensibly bring the saint closer to God through a layered experience of simultaneous martyrdom and aggression. The poem, in fact, portrays a figure who seems to embody an absolute rescinding of the self in order to know the horror attendant on other forms of life – a rescinding of self that involves the complete adoption of another person's perspective, even when it is one that harms the self. There is a masochistic impulse in this empathetic stretching, therefore; self-sacrifice is the ultimate and the logical outcome of the saint's surrender to death. In this way, Saint Narcissus is figured as the simultaneously beautiful and terrifying example of one whose yearning to take on another perspective is, at the same time, the desire for self-destruction. The act of perspective-taking threatens to lead to the end of the self and points to the possible dangers to the individual subject who tries to occupy other experiences. The boundaries of the subject are thus not simply porous, but also liable to distortions that may destroy the self.

Indeed, even in that final stanza, in which Saint Narcissus seems to have finally returned to his own body, a further metamorphosis occurs – this one on the textual level. We see Saint Narcissus pierced by arrows, but this image is drawn from the life of a different saint, St. Sebastian, about whom Eliot had written an earlier poem, "The Love Song of St. Sebastian," in 1914. This poem had emerged from Eliot's 1911 trip to Italy, where he saw his favorite image of St. Sebastian, though his St. Sebastian poem does not include any description about the saint's life or death; it is only in the Saint Narcissus poem that we get the arrows and the martyred death. Thus not only does "The Death of Saint Narcissus" return us to the combined corporeal pleasures and dangers of assuming another perspective, but it also leads us into a series of textual shifts in subject: the St. Sebastian of the early poem is resurrected in the death of Saint Narcissus, who in turn reappears in the unmoored speaking voice of *The Waste Land*.

In this exploration of the "shadows" within *The Waste Land*, therefore, we begin to understand the shadows cast by its textual history – a kind of textual unconscious in the poem. Indeed, the question seems not whether we can locate the materials of the unconscious in *The Waste Land*, but whether there is anything *but* those materials in the poem. Skaff makes the most thorough case for how to read Eliot's own layered understanding of the unconscious, arguing that it emerges from his studies in philosophy, scientific psychology, and anthropology at Harvard. From this blend of sources, though with particular reference to Bradley, Eliot developed a theory of the unconscious as involving metaphysical, psychological, and physiological levels that blend and create a "composite unconscious" (Skaff, 47). Eliot's metaphysical consciousness, which is connected to the immediate experience that operates as Bradley's foundational structure, is communal and (because it changes over time) historical, providing the closest approximation to an ideal, "objective" reality and understanding because it involves the "integration of all those points of view that provide us with our world" (Skaff, 60). The physiological basis of the unconscious emerges in the workings of the body and those processes – a pumping heart, breathing lungs – that are continuously occurring without our awareness. The psychological consists of all of those experiences and perceptions contained in our memory and those impulses that may be unrecognized but that still influence our actions and belief. The psychological unconscious is the one most closely linked to Freud's version of the unconscious: that repository of memories, experiences, hopes, and fears that percolate within and influence our actions and personality, even though we may be unaware of them. If, then, Freud's focus was on the unconscious of the individual, while Carl Gustav Jung stressed the collective unconscious, Eliot merged the individual and the collective into one (Skaff, 47). According to Skaff, therefore, Eliot's unconscious is not only composite because of the three layers but also because he views the psychological as always participating in and emerging from collective memory.

This composite nature of the poetic unconscious in *The Waste Land* develops from those very first lines of the poem with the voices, the multiple perspectives, and the underlying personal and historical memories. While bodies certainly are present in the poem, often in ways that remind us of their distressing half-lives (recall that corpse of Phlebas the Phoenician, floating while "A current under sea / Picked his bones in whispers," 315–16), it is the body of the poem itself that most evocatively manifests the forces of a collective unconscious, with shifting poetic voices that point to the cumulative and changing nature of both personal and general experience. Both Eliot's "Notes" – however much of an afterthought they may have been for the poem – and the myriad references, quotations, and gestures point to the historical and cultural memories that infuse the conscious life of the poem and emerge in sometimes disturbing, sometime exhilarating, ways. For example, the final line of "The Burial of the Dead" – "'You! Hypocrite lecteur! – mon semblable, – mon frère!'" (76) – enacts both an intersubjective and an intertextual movement. When the speaker suddenly addresses the reader, the poem not only showcases its own porous boundaries between its voice and the voice of dead poets, but also exposes the fissures between its present moment of reading and various past moments of composition.

In moments of intertextuality like this one – as well as in the images that have haunted the whole of "The Burial of the Dead" – the question of repetition and its relationship to the composite unconscious emerge. The final stanza of "The Burial of the Dead" foregrounds the terrifying potential and the structuring nature of the repetitive impulse. The scene of this "Unreal City" (60) is defined by, first of all, the return of the dead – the form of repetition that this poem explores in its opening lines and then manifests on a grand scale in this stanza: "A crowd flowed over London Bridge, so many / I had not thought death had undone so many" (62–3). The rhythmic repetition of phrases ("so many ... so many") points to the exhaustion engendered by the repetitive act, an exhaustion that resolves to the horror of returning to a past moment of trauma – an incident that is strong enough, to use Freud's explanation, to breach the "shield against stimula" that usually protects the mind from the influx of signals from the external world (Freud *BPP*, 70). In this scene, the traumatic experience involves the return of the supposedly buried dead, and is triggered, in this case, by the sight of a figure from an ancient battle ("'Stetson!,'" 69) in the ghostly crowd who "flowed over London Bridge" (62). In the case of Stetson, not only does he signify the return of the battle dead, but he also leads the speaker into a frenzy of anxiety about the potential unearthing and generation of more dead: "'That corpse you planted last year in your garden, / Has it begun to sprout? Will it bloom this year?'" (71–2). While this grisly repetition manifests itself as unsought and unpleasurable, it also, as Freud explains, functions as a method of psychological ordering and gaining control: through repetition of "an unpleasurable experience," one can "achieve a far more solid mastery of the powerful impression than was possible through mere passive experience" (*BPP*, 74–5). Indeed, we see in the reference to the battle at Mylae a connection between the dead of World War I and the ancient dead, while Eliot also gives us a literary framework when he directs us to John Webster's 1612 play *The White Devil* for his reference to the "Dog" (75) who might also unearth the corpse.

To suggest that we see some sort of connective, ordering, and extending version of subjectivity in the fragments of the first section does not mean that we can conclude that this is the poem's final word on how to imagine the boundaries of the subject. In part II, in fact, Eliot explores further the pathology of the subject and the boundaries that remain in place and forestall any meaningful intersubjective connection or communication. The dynamics of the conversations we overhear in "A Game of Chess" are defined by the title: chess is both a form of interaction prescribed by the constraints of the formal, adversarial relationship of the chess game, and a game that involves trying to enter into the head of the opposing player, anticipating the opponent's moves in order to counteract them. The game presents a space of interaction in which strategy depends on imagining other perspectives. The text of what follows suggests that such strategic thinking is impossible in this relationship and that attempts to understand another point of view hinder, rather than facilitate connection. The strange and richly ornamented scene in which the woman sits, a kind of carved queen in a "Chair ... like a burnished throne" (77), provides the setting for a breakdown in communication between the thinking voice of the poem, and the nervous woman:

> 'My nerves are bad to-night. Yes, bad. Stay with me.
> Speak to me. Why do you never speak. Speak.
>   What are you thinking of? What thinking? What?
> I never know what you are thinking. Think.'
>
> I think we are in rats' alley
> Where the dead men lost their bones.
>
> 'What is that noise?' (111–17)

The frantic voicing of the woman, who desires and asks for both outward and inward connection – though perhaps in a counterintuitive order, for speech comes before thought in this formulation – meets a thought, either unvoiced or unheard, that suggests the man's mind is occupied with things that verge on the unspeakable. Eliot reinforces this disconnect through the excisions he made for the published version, trimming away some of the responses to the woman's questions so that she (and we) have even less access into the man's mind. The dialogue goes so horribly awry here because the man's mind is with the lost dead of World War I: in the earlier drafts, he responds to her question of "What is the wind doing?" (*Facsimile* 11, line 44) with "Carrying / Away the little light dead people" (13, 45–6), which is then changed in the published version to the decidedly more oblique "Nothing again nothing" (120). The "little light dead" are transformed into words that present a loss of language rather than a loss of life. Along with the dead people, meaning-making and communication become casualties of the war.

At this point we might think that *The Waste Land* posits a post war apocalyptic social landscape in which intersubjective understanding is impossible. Yet we turn at the beginning of the next section, "The Fire Sermon," to a poetic I who, even as it predicts the end of song, returns through textual illusions to earlier moments of the Spenserian lyric, tracing a long continuum of verse. While the deathly "rattle of the bones" (186) and the blaring sounds of "horns and motors" (197) provide, on the one hand, a disillusioning backdrop to the attempted song, they also point to the historical and literary nature of this poetic unconscious. The sounds create a temporal tapestry on the Thames that connects to Freud's psychoanalytic framework in *Beyond the Pleasure Principle* describing the structure of perception and consciousness. There Freud presents the human subject – the conscious subject – as acted upon by the stimuli that are filtered and allowed through by the sense organs and that are necessarily a "random sampling of the external world" (68). This idea of the filtering subject, what Freud calls a "living vesicle with its cortical layer for the reception of stimuli" (68), resonates with Bradley's theory of a "finite centre," which, Eliot writes, "so far as I can pretend to understand it, is immediate experience,"[24] and is comparable, though not identical, to the idea of the soul. Yet the difference between Freud's living vesicle and Bradley's "finite centre" – a difference that helps explain why Bradley's version might ultimately make more sense in Eliot's framework – is that Freud's theory emphasizes the success of the "shield against stimuli from the external world," versus the absence of shield for the stimuli coming from within, thereby assigning more influence to the internal stimuli (*BPP*, 69). Eliot emphasizes in his analysis of Bradley, however, that the subject is the site at which, through interactions with the external world, the "real" world comes into being.[25]

In this reading, therefore, the palimpsests of lives and detritus that appear in the London scene are as constructive as they are symptomatic of the historical layering of the poetic subject and of the varying perspectives that emerge from one geographical place. Indeed, this may be why many critics read Tiresias as giving insight into the "subject" (in all meanings of the word!) of the poem. Tiresias is not simply important because he unifies the experiences of the modern subject, understanding both the male and female and embodying – like the "taxi throbbing" (217) – the mechanized nature of modern psychology, which is always subject to desires that seem both transactional and out of its control. Rather Tiresias presents a consciousness that, in its unique ability to understand multiple perspectives, reveals a "real" world coming into being. In this way, the version of subjectivity that we get through Tiresias involves a vision of the self as multivalenced and polyphonous, having "foresuffered all" (243). Thus Rochelle Rives's description of Eliot's theory of emotion – "neither subjective nor personal" but "concentrated and amenable to order because of its role in uniting a cacophony of experiences" – applies as well to Eliot's theory of the subject.[26] The subject acts as a filter and a focalizer of experiences, thereby creating a kind of unification, but only through collation, and not integration and reconciliation.

If we turn to the final section, "What the Thunder Said," we begin to see how a more productive result of perspective shifting may emerge from such experiences of disorientation. We revisit the scene of "red rock" and barren desert first presented in "The Burial of the Dead," this time enlarged into a world in the aftermath of social, political, and cultural cataclysms:

> After the agony in stony places
> The shouting and the crying
> Prison and palace and reverberation
> Of thunder of spring over distant mountains (324–8)

Into this apocalyptic world comes the voice of the thunder, presenting sounds that the speaker transforms into a Sanskrit-based moral and ethical structure: the Sanskrit *"Datta," "Dayadhvam," "Damyata,"* which Eliot translates as "Give, sympathise, control" (note 401). When thinking about the composite and interconnected subjects and the merging of the metaphysical and the psychological unconscious within Eliot's poem, the middle term, *"Dayadhvam"* (412), stands out, for it suggests that some ability to step outside the self is still necessary in order to make it through this waste land. In a note to that middle term, however, Eliot quotes from Bradley's *Appearance and Reality*: "my experience falls within my own circle, a circle closed on the outside ... the whole world for each is peculiar and private to that soul" (note 411). This note seems to suggest the *impossibility* of intersubjective connections – of empathetic imagining – in this new world.

Of course, we know from Eliot himself that his endnotes have led "so many enquirers off on a wild goose chase," encouraging, as he wrote in a 1956 essay, "the wrong kind of interest among seekers of sources."[27] In his study of Eliot, Stephen Spender cited his friend Richard Wollheim's claim that the note on Bradley was deliberately misleading about Bradley's position, because Bradley ultimately argued that "everything that occurs within what we think of as individual minds is really an aspect of a single comprehensive consciousness."[28] Yet, such knowledge should make us consider *how* to read this quotation, not simply make us dismiss it out of hand. For there does turn out to be a bit of a twist here, if not of the same order as the made-up Tarot cards and the Jessie Weston references. A number of years ago Michael Levenson reminded us that this note should not be taken as indicative of Eliot's own view of shifting perspectives because in his dissertation Eliot was positing a "new theory of meaning" in his response to Bradley's position, a theory in which the experience of the world "is the product of multiple perspectives."[29] We can see this in Eliot's own words perhaps most clearly in an essay he wrote about Leibniz and Bradley (published in *The Monist* in 1916, the period during which he was finishing up his dissertation): "If we insist upon thinking of the soul as something *wholly* isolated, as *merely* a substance of states," he writes, "then it is hopeless to attempt to arrive at the conception of other souls."[30] Eliot then goes on to say, "what we do know is that we are able to pass from one point of view to another, that we are compelled to do so, and that the different aspects more or less hang together" (Ibid., 207). "[C]ompelled to": this phrase resonates with our experience of those first lines of *The Waste Land*, for there is something both compulsive and coerced about the restless shifts in perspective. And yet I think that this sense of compulsion also points to Eliot's emphasis on the necessity of perspective-taking; it is only through these shifts that we might be able to find something that hangs together, some move outside of the solipsistic "I." Eliot's quotation of Bradley thereby points to the haunting possibility of such isolation, but also to the need to move beyond it.

This does not mean, however, that we can ignore the sense of loss and disruption that seems to be at the heart of these shifts in point of view – that self-alienation that art historian Wilhelm Worringer emphasized as central to the empathetic act.[31] In fact it is, I think, through *highlighting* this loss that Eliot transforms the act of moving between subjective viewpoints from something that could be ethically dubious (the attempt to project yourself onto and into another perspective, thereby subsuming it and claiming it for your own) into one that is ethically subtle (the recognition of the violence done to both self and to the other with every perspective shift, even though we must inhabit other perspectives, as he puts it in the essay, in order to have "the conception of other souls").[32] In other words, the act of seeing through another's eyes is painful and disorienting because it involves a breaking down of boundaries between self and other. This boundary-breaking leaves one, like Eliot's Tiresias, "throbbing between two lives" (218) with a painful knowledge equivalent to "hav[ing] foresuffered all" (243). Yet it is only through such difficult acts of perspective-taking, as well as through the realization that one is always in the process of being composed and recomposed, that one can hope to inhabit the modern, post war world.

NOTES

1   F. R. Leavis, "*The Waste Land*," reprinted in *T. S. Eliot: A Collection of Critical Essays*, ed. Hugh Kenner (1932; Englewood Cliffs, NJ: Prentice-Hall, 1962), 92; and Cleanth Brooks, "*The Waste Land*: A Critique of the Myth," *Modern Poetry and the Tradition* (Chapel Hill: University of North Carolina Press, 1939), 136, 139.

2   Maud Ellmann, *The Poetics of Impersonality* (Cambridge, MA: Harvard University Press, 1987), 15; Michael Levenson, *A Genealogy of Modernism: A Study of English Literary Doctrine 1908–1922* (New York: Cambridge University Press, 1984), 171.

3   Matthew Hart, "Visible Poet: T. S. Eliot and Modernist Studies," *American Literary History* 19 no. 1 (2007): 184.

4   Leavis "*The Waste Land*," 92.

5   Quoted in William Skaff, *The Philosophy of T. S. Eliot: From Skepticism to a Surrealist Poetic* (Philadelphia: University of Pennsylvania Press, 1986), 74. Further references to Skaff will be cited parenthetically. Many friends of Eliot were influenced by Freudian thought and even underwent analysis with Freud. There are only two possible oblique references to Freud in Eliot's letters up to 1922; both simply refer to Vienna. The first is in a 1921 letter to Mary Hutchinson, asking whether Alix and James Strachey's London apartment is free while they are off in Vienna (he may have been unaware, of course, of their reasons for visiting Vienna, which was to undergo analysis with Freud). Eliot to Mary Hutchinson, June 16, 1921, in T. S. Eliot, *The Letters of T. S. Eliot, Volume 1: 1898–1922*, ed. Valerie Eliot and Hugh Haughton, rev. ed., (New Haven, CT: Yale University Press, 2011), 566. The second is from the same year in which Eliot made the comment about Freud in his "London Letter" (1922); in this letter he writes to Scofield Thayer, the owner of the *Dial*, concluding with the vague "I trust you [are] gaining spiritual and physical benefit from Vienna," where Thayer was in analysis with Freud (Eliot to Scofield Thayer, January 20, 1922, *Letters, 1*, 623).

6   Freud describes the repetition compulsion as one in which an unpleasurable action or event is repeated and, in its repetition, allows the subject an active control over the event (Sigmund Freud, *Beyond the Pleasure Principle*, ed. Todd Dufresne, trans. Gregory C. Richter (New York: Broadview, 2011), 74–5).

7   Paul Stasi, *Modernism, Imperialism, and the Historical Sense* (New York: Cambridge University Press, 2012), 43. Further references to this text will be cited parenthetically. We can also look at Louis Menand's claim that we must see Eliot's emphasis on the "public" nature of experience in relation to both his dissertation and to his article on "Leibniz's Monads and Bradley's Finite Centers" (1916). See Louis Menand, *Discovering Modernism: T. S. Eliot and His Context*, 2nd edition (1987; New York: Oxford University Press, 2007), 48.

8   Eliot to Lytton Strachey, June 1, 1919, *Letters, 1*, 357.

9   Lawrence Rainey, *Revisiting The Waste Land* (New Haven, CT: Yale University Press, 2005), 35.

10 F. H. Bradley, *Appearance and Reality: A Metaphysical Essay* (New York: Macmillan & Co, 1893), 223. Bradley also calls the "immediate experiences of the felt" the "this-mines," to emphasize the way in which immediate experience

first seems specific to the individual. This specificity is what his turn to the Absolute will try to avoid.

11 Ibid. 242. Bradley writes in his "Recapitulation" chapter of the books that the Absolute is a "whole superior to and embracing all incomplete forms of life," and is thus "perfect" (242).

12 See Levenson, 180–1, for a clear discussion of Eliot's response to Bradley's position.

13 Eliot, *Knowledge and Experience in the Philosophy of F. H. Bradley* (London: Faber and Faber, 1964), 32. Further references to this text will be cited parenthetically.

14 Eliot, *Selected Prose of T. S. Eliot*, ed. Frank Kermode (New York: Harcourt Brace Jovanovich, 1975), 55.

15 Eliot to Julian Huxley, October 26, 1921, *Letters, 1*, 594; Eliot to Sydney Waterlow, December 19, 1921, 617.

16 Roger Vittoz, *Treatment of Neurasthenia by Teaching of Brain Control*, trans. H. B. Brooke (New York: Longmans, Green, and Co., 1911), 1. Further references to this text will be cited parenthetically.

17 The only recent article to discuss Vittoz and Eliot is Matthew K. Gold's "The Expert Hand and the Obedient Heart: Dr. Vittoz, T. S. Eliot, and the Therapeutic Possibilities of *The Waste Land*," *Journal of Modern Literature* 23 no. 3–4 (2000): 519–33, in which he argues that we can read *The Waste Land* as a "record of Eliot's sickness and his cure" (519) and that we need to think of this cure through the lens of Vittoz's theories. While I am not making this argument about the poem, Gold gives valuable details about both Eliot's reading of Vittoz's book and the practices and theories of the psychologist.

18 Gold, 525.

19 Levenson, 168.

20 Eliot, *Collected Poems 1909–1962* (London: Faber and Faber, 1974), line 3. All quotations to *The Waste Land* refer to line numbers from this edition of the poem, except when noted that they are from the facsimile and manuscript text.

21 Eliot, *The Waste Land: A Facsimile and Transcript of the Original Drafts Including the Annotations of Ezra Pound*, ed. Valerie Eliot (New York: Harcourt, 1971), 95, line 19. Further references to quotations from this text will be cited parenthetically by both page and line number.

22 *The Waste Land: A Facsimile*, "The death of Saint Narcissus" 95, line 1.

23 Freud, "On Narcissism: An Introduction," *The Freud Reader*, ed. Peter Gay (New York: W. W. Norton, 1989), 545.

24 Eliot, "Leibniz's Monads and Bradley's Finite Centres," *Knowledge and Experience in the Philosophy of F. H. Bradley* (1916; London: Faber and Faber, 1964), 205.

25 See Gold, 44–5.

26 Rochelle Rives, *Modernist Impersonalities: Affect, Authority, and the Subject* (New York: Palgrave Macmillan, 2012), 13.

27 Eliot, "The Frontiers of Criticism," *On Poetry and Poets* (1956; New York: Farrar, Straus, and Cudahy, 1957), 122, 121.

28 Quoted in Stephen Spender, *T. S. Eliot* (New York: The Viking Press, 1975), 25.

29 Levenson, 184.
30 Eliot, 1964, "Leibniz's Monads and Bradley's Finite Centres," 206.
31 Worringer emphasized this counterintuitive aspect of aesthetic empathy in his treatise, arguing that "in empathising this will to activity into another object ... we *are* in the other object.... In this self-objectification lies a self-alienation." Wilhelm Worringer, *Abstraction and Empathy: A Contribution to the Psychology of Style* (1908; Chicago: Ivan R. Dee, 1997), 24.
32 Eliot, "Leibniz's Monads and Bradley's Finite Centres," 206.

12

GABRIELLE MCINTIRE

The Waste Land as Ecocritique

I

Let us start with the pollution and the waste. These are defining features of the early twentieth-century landscapes and cityscapes that T. S. Eliot turns to through his oeuvre, with his poetry repeatedly registering ecosystems that are out of balance. From "The yellow fog that rubs its back upon the window-panes" (15) in "The Love Song of J. Alfred Prufrock" (1915) to "the smoke and fog of a December afternoon" (1) in "Portrait of a Lady" (1915), the "river" that "sweats / Oil and tar" (266–7) in *The Waste Land* (1922), the "vapour in the fetid air" (99) in *Ash-Wednesday* (1930), the recurring attention to "waste" in *Choruses from the Rock* (1934), and the "parched eviscerate soil" (67) of his last major poem, *Little Gidding* (1942), to name only a few examples among many, Eliot consistently shows sensitivities to fragile or degraded environments. In *The Waste Land* he simultaneously renders the postwar world as quasi-apocalyptic and replete with personal, political, spiritual, and cultural problems that threaten to unravel all meaning. In suggesting that ecological crises accompany these other problems of early twentieth-century modernity, Eliot pushes us to consider the analogies between compromised environmental exteriors and a complex range of similarly polluted interior states.

In reading *The Waste Land* we should take the title of the poem literally as well as figuratively. With Eliot's keen eye for surroundings and landscapes, he is both writing about a barren, postwar *land* that is marked by pollutants, vulnerable to smog, littered with trash, and, in a sense, dying, while he is inviting us to understand this bleak setting and ecology as offering symbolic and metaphorical commentary on our own wasted (and wasteful) existences. Lawrence Buell suggests that *The Waste Land* is "one of the first canonical works of modern Anglo-American literature to envision a dying society in the aftermath of world war,"[1] and one of the ways Eliot achieves this is by rendering a fallen post-pastoral world where nature is no longer available or able to restore us. The Biblical desertscape near the start of the poem is filled with "stony rubbish" (20), and the post-Dickensian, post-Baudelairean London cityscape is marked by degradation and decay: the "brown fog of a winter dawn" (61) hangs over pedestrian commuters as they cross London Bridge into the City center, and this smog lingers through the day to reappear later as "the brown fog of a winter noon" (208).[2] The commuters themselves exhale "Sighs, short and infrequent" (64), as if perhaps trying to expunge despair as well as pollution.[3] Indeed, like the wasted landscapes that surround them, the poem's denizens are unwell, diseased, barely alive, or even dead: from the line also borrowed from Dante, "I had not thought death had undone so many" (63), to Stetson's ghost (69), "rats' alley / Where the dead men lost their bones" (115–16), the blunt question, "'Are you alive, or not?'" (127), talk of abortion, the undead Tiresias who haunts the poem, and Phlebas's drifting bones, we can see why Eliot's close friend and sometime editor, John Davy Hayward, once observed that the key "theme" of the poem is "death in life."[4] Eliot writes toward the close of *The Waste Land*, "We who were living are now dying" (329).

The land is similarly under threat of death. In this case it is a double threat, involving both the inevitable annual destruction brought by winter – a seasonal cycle that may be linked to origins of ritual and religious practices which Eliot foregrounds in acknowledging his debt to Sir James Frazer's *The Golden Bough* in his "Notes on the Waste Land" [*sic*] – as well as the more irreversible damages left in the wake of human warfare and pollution. The poem, as such, unfolds in sites of crisis that are themselves *in extremis*. Place in this way becomes all at once a subject and object of scrutiny as Eliot offers us meditations on the very meaning of locale, spatiality, and topography, and the ways in which environments both permeate and reflect human existence.

In the first lines of part III, "The Fire Sermon," the speaker begins with a lament for a legendary pastoral past: "The nymphs are departed" is repeated twice (175 and 179). And although part of the riverscape is "broken" (173), and the rustle of the natural is lost to human senses – "The wind / Crosses the brown land, unheard" (174–5) – this first-person speaker still appeals to nature for solace, as if insisting that the healing powers associated with ancient bucolic, literary, and ritualistic traditions could still be active amidst a desolate modernity. Locating this pastoral turn in the very the heart of London, the speaker addresses the personified Thames with a repeated, gentle apostrophe: "Sweet Thames, run softly, till I end my song. // ... Sweet Thames, run softly till I end my song, / Sweet Thames, run softly, for I speak not loud or long" (176, 183–4). Eliot borrows the refrain directly from Edmund Spenser's late sixteenth-century *Prothalamion*, where

Spenser explicitly writes of seeking "to ease my payne" by walking by the "shoare of silver streaming *Themmes*" (10–11).⁵ In Eliot's context, the Thames appears for a brief moment as it once might have – as relatively pure and unlittered – although such cleanliness is reported only through negation:

> The river bears no empty bottles, sandwich papers,
> Silk handkerchiefs, cardboard boxes, cigarette ends
> Or other testimony of summer nights. (177–9)

It is a surprise that the river is temporarily free of the signs of human detritus, and Eliot's portrait of the river remains marred by the garbage that is missing. The momentary condition of the Thames' relative purity also stands in contrast to the same river later in the poem, paradoxically in its location beyond the City center, that "sweats / Oil and tar" (266–7) and is filled with markers of trade, consumption, and deforestation: "The barges wash / Drifting logs/ Down Greenwich reach/ Past the Isle of Dogs" (273–6). Again, Eliot personifies the river, as if, like the human inhabitants of the waste land, it must labor – "sweat[]" – to excrete impurities. And when the apostrophic gesture to the natural so quickly fails, instead of solace we find coldness, death's remains, and mockery, as Eliot moves from Spenser to Andrew Marvell's "To His Coy Mistress" – a love poem filled with urgency and longing – with a bleak revision incorporating echoes from Ezekiel to suggest that even the elements are against us: "But at my back in a cold blast I hear / The rattle of the bones, and chuckle spread from ear to ear" (185–6).

This section of the poem, "The Fire Sermon," takes its title from one of the Buddha's sermons about abstaining from desire, and surely this includes desires that lead to overconsumption, excess waste, and pollution. After "The rattle of the bones" we read,

> A rat crept softly through the vegetation
> Dragging its slimy belly on the bank
> While I was fishing in the dull canal
> On a winter evening round behind the gashouse
> Musing upon the king my brother's wreck (187–91)

This dirty, degraded rat is one of the many animals that appear in *The Waste Land*, captive to its (mostly) troubled settings. We find also a "cricket" (23), a "Dog" (74), a "nightingale" (100), other rats (115, 195; perhaps Eliot's favorite animal after the cat), "gulls" (313), "cicada" (353), a "hermit-thrush" (356), "bats" (379), a "cock" (391), a "spider" (407), and a "swallow" (428) – a diverse array of mostly undomesticated animals, each of which carries intense or mythic significance for the human imagination. In his attention to this creaturely biodiversity that is, by necessity, linked to the polluted and waste-filled sites of the poem – the cityscape and the desertscape – Eliot is also, in part, registering that the wild is, in fact, not so wild any more. The wild is too intricately bound up with culture, symbol, and with environmental fallout to be really "free" any longer.

The environment of the London canal that Eliot depicts is as desolate as the end of traditions, shipwrecks, and the death of kings. With resonances of the Old Testament's symbolics of the spiritual and physiological nourishment provided by "loaves and fishes," Eliot offers another version of the Fisher King legend where the person fishing is evidently looking in the wrong place for nourishment, redemption, or healing of the land. Seeking sustenance in a place constructed for industrial and commercial transit, near to a "gas-house" – a site of manufacturing for modern petroleum fuel – will only lead the speaker to find polluted fare. And the canal itself is merely a tributary of "the natural," branching out from the River Thames, almost rhizomatic, but not organically so: the canal *abuts* the natural, coursing into and from the natural, but it is a place where human-made filth, disorder, sterility, and decay literally flow. As Richard Lehan argues, *The Waste Land* "suggests that as the city lost touch with the land, with the rhythms and the psychic nourishment of nature, a spiritual meaning was lost."[6] Indeed, Eliot seemed well aware that cities have "ecosystems" too: urban spaces are not bubbles that are immune from climate, weather, air, water, or food pollution. Part of what the poem proposes is thus that physical and spiritual nourishment linked to the natural world is not guaranteed even though we depend on it for our very survival.

~

Whether he knew it or not, Eliot was writing a version of what we would now call ecopoetics, or ecocriticism. Ecocriticism delineates forms of critical, literary, artistic, or cultural engagements with the natural environments in which we live, breathe, and exist. Emerging as a distinct approach within the humanities over the last few decades, influenced by environmental studies and ecology, ecocriticism pays attention to the ways in which sensitivities and awarenesses of our environmental milieus make their way into aesthetic expression. One path-breaking ecocritic, Jonathan Bate, defines ecology as "a holistic science, concerned in the largest sense with the relationship between living beings and their environment.... From an early stage ... the term served to denominate both a biological science and an environmental attitude."[7] Literary ecocriticism is inspired by these investigative tools yoked to literary studies, involving, as Timothy Clark suggests, "*a study of the relationship between literature and the physical environment, usually considered from out of the current global environmental crisis and its revisionist challenge to modes of thought and practice."⁸* In *The Waste Land*, worries about fragile and deteriorating ecologies are embedded in its mythos and preoccupations, with its attention to polluted states working in addition – as a supplement – to Eliot's other, more explicit anxieties about the state of a postwar, ruined world where so much about human experience has become "Unreal" (60, 207, 376).

The Waste Land depicts a culture and a society in which we are no longer able even to think "the natural" as undefiled. Eliot, in this sense, seems already aware of the terrifying breaches that a "post-natural" world signifies between "nature" and "the human," where "nature" is profoundly unbalanced by the effects of the human on a global scale even as we spectacularly fail to bear adequate witness to the massiveness and irreversibility of these changes. *The Waste Land*, in other words, comments on the cultural, personal, and ecological consequences of modern industrialization that we feel increasingly today. Nature in his poetry, just as the human, is ill. In "Rhapsody on a Windy Night" Eliot personifies another figure of nature, this time by signaling that even the moon "her"-self is (sexually) diseased and amnesiac: "The moon has lost her memory. / A washed-out smallpox cracks her face" (55–6).

II

Going back to some of Eliot's earliest poems, unpublished during his lifetime and written shortly after he began his master's degree at Harvard in 1909, we already find fascinations with urban pollution and refuse. In "First Caprice in North Cambridge" Eliot writes of "The yellow evening flung against the panes / Of dirty windows" (2–3), while "a crowd of tattered sparrows / Delve in the gutter with sordid patience" (8–9).⁹ In "Second Caprice in North Cambridge" he delineates a certain "charm" in "The helpless fields that lie / Sinister, sterile and blind – / Entreat the eye and rack the mind, / Demand your pity... // the débris of a city" (1–8). In his published work, as early as "The Love Song of J. Alfred Prufrock" (1915), Eliot renders the city air as a cat-like smog that is at once pet-like, domesticated, sexualized, and repulsive:

> The yellow fog that rubs its back upon the window-panes,
> The yellow smoke that rubs its muzzle on the window-panes,
> Licked its tongue into the corners of the evening,
> Lingered upon the pools that stand in drains,
> Let fall upon its back the soot that falls from chimneys (15–19)

The "yellow fog" and "yellow smoke" each "rubs" and "licks," touching "the corners of the evening," as if putting "its tongue" into a fragment of time itself – a reading we should be open to since immediately after Eliot completes his descriptions of the "yellow smoke" he begins a lengthy protest against the lack of time that echoes Ecclesiastes: "There will be time, there will be time / To prepare a face to meet the faces that you meet; / There will be time to murder and create...." (26–8). As with *The Waste Land*, internal psychic environments and the external cityscape are, again, crucially analogous. The "streets" themselves have "insidious intent" (9), while the human figures in "Prufrock" are caught in a cityscape replete with desperation, sordidity, and destitution, and fail in their efforts at intimacy and (be)longing, unable to communicate: "'That is not what I meant at all./ That is not it, at all'" (97–8).

"Portrait of a Lady," first published just a few months after "Prufrock," similarly begins by setting the scene atmospherically in smoke-filled air: "Among the smoke and fog of a December afternoon" (1). Eliot is still paying close attention to the very *air* of the city and its diminished quality, an air that marks a fluid exchange between an uncannily porous and proximate interior and exterior – between self and what is Other. Eliot's speakers must repeatedly take in the pollution around them, though how they metabolize it is left in question and we can only surmise that the results are not healthful. In the last verse paragraph of "Portrait of a Lady" we find another scene of smoky outside air in which the speaker anticipates a failed romantic connection, likely with Emily Hale, with whom Eliot maintained a strong, quasi-romantic connection until his second marriage:

> and what if she should die some afternoon,
> Afternoon grey and smoky, evening yellow and rose;
> Should die and leave me sitting pen in hand
> With the smoke coming down above the housetops (114–17).[10]

The "smoke" here is *descending*, not ascending, as if Eliot is suggesting that polluted air does not simply go away, disappear, or evaporate, but that its pernicious effects recirculate, coming "down" again to linger and pervade the places that we live.

"Preludes," the next poem in the *Prufrock* volume, describes a "winter evening" by way of smoke and discarded garbage:

> The burnt-out ends of smoky days.
> And now a gusty shower wraps
> The grimy scraps
> Of withered leaves about your feet
> And newspapers from vacant lots (4–8)

In the first line here we are reminded of the question in "Prufrock," "Then how should I begin / To spit out all the butt-ends of my days and ways?" (59–60), as if the modes by which we internally process time also produce waste: "burnt-out ends" and "butt-ends." The natural "leaves" (albeit from the cultivated trees of urban planning), are "withered" and appear in "grimy scraps" – filthy, torn, and fragmented, as if beaten by more than the weather. While William Wordsworth had famously insisted on a correspondence between the inner soul and the outer world in terms of beauty and sublimity more than 100 years before Eliot was writing, Eliot's poetry repeatedly follows the same formula of correspondence between inner and outer, but finds both interiority and exteriority fallen and vulnerable to wasting away. In "Preludes" Eliot writes further of the resonances between the degraded external environment – whether natural or otherwise – and the polluted "soul": "You dozed, and watched the night revealing / The thousand sordid images / Of which your soul was constituted" (26–8).

III

We also need to look carefully at desertscapes in *The Waste Land* since through Eliot's oeuvre he pays astute attention to two primary ecosystems in crisis: the desert and the city.[11] As he will write in his later verse-drama, *Choruses from the Rock* (1934), the desert is not "remote," not far away, but *here*, within one's own corporeal frame as it finds itself caught within the transit networks of the city's infrastructure:

> The desert is not remote in southern tropics,
> The desert is not only around the corner,
> The desert is squeezed in the tube-train next to you,
> The desert is in the heart of your brother. (70–3)

The desert, that is, exists as both place and idea, lodged in the very "heart" of one's "brother," whom, we recall, Eliot indicates in the closing line of "The Burial of the Dead" in *The Waste Land* is our very likeness: "'You! hypocrite lecteur! – mon semblable, – mon frère!'" (76).

Thus, as with Eliot's attention to the ecological settings of his speakers elsewhere, his external landscapes metaphorically and symbolically function as versions of Eliot's "objective correlative," offering sometimes nearly mimetic counterparts to personal interior states. In his 1920 essay, "Hamlet and His Problems," Eliot argues that "The only way of expressing emotion in the form of art is by finding an 'objective correlative'; in other words, a set of objects, a situation, a chain of events which shall be the formula of that *particular* emotion; such that when the external facts, which must terminate in sensory experience, are given, the emotion is immediately evoked."[12]

As the contemporary ecocritical writer, Barry Lopez, proposes, we are in a constant process of dialogue and exchange between our inner and outer worlds: our interior landscapes are a "projection within a person of a part of the exterior landscape," and our very way of thinking is "influenced by ... the intricate history of one's life in the land, even a life in the city, where wind, the chirp of birds, the line of a falling leaf, are known.... The interior landscape responds to the character and subtlety of an exterior landscape; the shape of the individual mind is affected by land as it is by genes."[13] Ancient pastoral traditions posit much the same idea. As Terry Gifford points out, "real transferable learning about inner nature [can come] from dealing with and observing outer nature."[14] Sigmund Freud in *Civilization and Its Discontents* proposes something similar when he briefly suggests a radical coextensiveness with the urban geography of Rome and the human psyche. For Freud, the mind is like a palimpsest that always contains traces of indelible memories, experiences, and ruins: as in the "Eternal City," where layers upon layers of architecture exist, in our psyches "nothing that has once come into existence will have passed away and all the earlier phases of development continue to exist alongside the latest one."[15]

In *The Waste Land*, Eliot's desert is a place of brokenness and trial, and it appears first through that question posed near the beginning of the poem that I mention above: "What are the roots that clutch, what branches grow / Out of this stony rubbish?" (19–20). The speaker is echoing here, intra-textually already, the enigmatic statement of the poem's first lines where "April" is "stirring / Dull roots with spring rain" (3–4). Within the space of about a sonnet length, then, instead of "roots" that promise the regenerative new growth of springtime, these roots pull at one from garbage in a desiccated land. As elsewhere in the poem, there is no speakable or even guessable answer to questions posed, and this desert offers not solace to the "Son of man" (20), but overbearing natural intensities alongside aesthetic and semantic disintegration – "A heap of broken images" (22). This wasted land of sweltering heat is a place where one might be tested, physically and psychologically, to the limits of one's strength. In fact, in his "Notes" to these lines that he includes at the end of the poem Eliot directs us to verses from Ezekiel and Ecclesiastes, establishing explicit resonances with Old Testament terrains of deserts, temptations, droughts, and scourges. Eliot has thus already displaced us temporally *and* geographically from scenes and memories in *The Waste Land*'s first lines that take place amid European high culture (sledding in the mountains; visiting Munich's Hofgarten) to an ancient Biblical time and setting, allowing each terrain and time to resonate and echo. In the desert, an Other lyric "I" invites his interlocutor to share the cooler shadows of the shelter of what seems like the welcome solidity of "rock" – "(Come in under the shadow of this red rock)" (26) – but the possibility of solace is only momentary. Instead of any lasting comfort he will be shown "fear in a handful of dust" (30); he will be confronted with the terrifying reality of mortality, which Eliot figures as akin to the dust of the desert. Ashes to ashes, dust to dust.

At both the literal and figurative levels, the environments *of The Waste Land* desperately need water: after the pleasant "shower of rain" (9) from "over the Starnbergersee" (8) near its opening, most of the remainder of the poem is dominated by physical and spiritual dryness. In part V, "What the Thunder Said," one speaker falls into a repetitive and almost mad-sounding lament about this most basic lack and need, framing the desire for water with a series of anaphoric, subjunctive "If[s]," bound by rock and desert:

> If there were water we should stop and drink ...
> If there were only water amongst the rock ...
>
>   If there were water
> And no rock ...
> If there were the sound of water only (335–52)

Just as various speakers long for what seems to be unattainable intimacy and connection, the inhabitants of the waste land desperately crave the fundamentals of survival from a natural world that repeatedly fails them. Here, as elsewhere, Eliot may have been anticipating one of the great symptoms of the environmental crisis of our time where the current and projected scarcity of fresh water is heralded by many as *the* single most important global environmental threat. He writes, after all, of "voices singing out of empty cisterns and exhausted wells" (384).

IV

One of today's leading ecocritics, Greg Garrard, has proposed a rough typology for how we render the natural world through art and literature, structuring his book, *Ecocriticism* (2004), on sections devoted to recurring topoi for how human beings imagine the natural world, ranging through topics such as the wilderness and the sublime, to apocalyptic collapse, animality, and modes of human dwelling. One of the central tropes Garrard outlines is that of "the wilderness," a concept he traces back to "the very earliest documents of Western Eurasian civilization, such as *The Epic of Gilgamesh*," which "depict wilderness as a threat, and by the time the Judaic scriptures were written it is viewed with ambivalence at best. After the ejection from Eden, the wilderness is the place of exile ... associated with Satan."[16] The wilderness is also, he notes, a place to escape persecution and to overcome temptation: the "early Christian hermits went to the deserts" (61). Eliot includes many of Garrard's typologies in *The Waste Land* by foregrounding crises related to the wilderness, apocalypse, and animality. Interestingly, although the poem's settings are primarily ones of topographical and environmental extremes (the polluted cityscape and the desert), we do find relief in a few remaining vestiges of the pastoral: places either sheltered from the city's dysfunctions, haste, and noise, or beyond the barrenness of the desert – in riverscapes, the lusher wildernesses of the "jungle" (398) near "Himavant" (397), or in briefly evoked gardenscapes.[17] Even though idyllic escape is rare in *The Waste Land*, in a few charged moments glimmers of redemptive potential offer respite from the poem's existential bleakness. In each case, the almost epiphanic breakthroughs to another order of things occur within ecosystems at a remove from urban pollution and the trials of the desert. I would like to focus on two of these instances: the "hyacinth garden" (35–42) from the poem's first section, and the forest "Where the hermit-thrush sings in the pine trees," (356) from the final section.

Indeed, in the "hyacinth garden" the speaker comes close to a sexual-romantic nirvana after recounting a memory of a gift of hyacinths to a beloved figure, finding himself in a blinding and silent state that briefly transcends the poem's paralyzing dialectic of "death in life" to reach a place beyond this dualism: "I was neither / Living nor dead" (39–40). But, as elsewhere in Eliot's poetry, this illumination is quickly followed by collapse and bathos: the verse paragraph concludes with Richard Wagner's "*Oed' und leer das Meer*" ("Desolate and empty the sea") from his tragic opera, *Tristan und Isolde*, signifying that Isolde's long-awaited ship is not appearing on the horizon. Meanwhile, the hyacinth is, of course, an early spring flower – one of the first – a flower that lets us know that springtime has definitively arrived. Even though we also hear echoes of Apollo's accidental killing of his beloved Hyacinthus here, the passionate gift of these flowers offers a welcome contrast to the city's walking dead and buried corpses that might "sprout" (72), intimating at least some growth and regeneration. But we see at once that we can register this scene only as a falling or failing bucolic that parallels the already fallen city as well as the "cruel[ty]" of April's "lilacs" that emerge from "the dead land." As Lyndall Gordon writes, "This might-have-been has no place in the waste of the present, where there is no longer a fertile love with the power to transform."[18]

Another moment of temporary respite from the trials of the poem occurs in the remembrance of the hermit-thrush's song. The speaker here, still longing for water, conjures the tranquility of "Where the hermit-thrush sings in the pine trees" (356) as a signifier of refuge. In Eliot's "Notes" he explains that he had heard this bird in "Quebec Province," and he directs the reader to the well-known birdwatcher's companion guide, Chapman's *Handbook of Birds of Eastern North America*, which he quotes at some length. The hermit-thrush, Chapman writes, "'is most at home in secluded woodland and thickety retreats.... Its notes are not remarkable for variety or volume, but in purity and sweetness of tone and exquisite modulation they are unequalled.'" Eliot adds, "'Its water-dripping song' is justly celebrated" (note 357). That Eliot refers to Chapman – one of the pioneers of early twentieth-century ornithology – indicates at least a sophisticated amateur's interest in birdwatching, and his stress on the hermit-thrush's preferred habitats as "retreats" further underscores the interests and desires the poem expresses for places of respite and peace that would both be sheltered from the chaos of modernity and could provide shelter.

Indeed, in the concluding chapter of Eliot's book of criticism, *The Use of Poetry and the Use of Criticism*, published just over ten years after *The Waste Land* appeared, he asks a poignant question that might help to illuminate the recurring longings for places or symbols of natural purity that we find nestled in the poem:

> Why, for all of us, out of all that we have heard, seen, felt, in a lifetime, do certain images recur, charged with emotion, rather than others? The song of one bird, the leap of one fish, at a particular place and time, the scent of one flower, an old woman on a German mountain path, six ruffians seen through an open window playing cards at night at a small French railway junction where there was a water-mill: such memories may have symbolic value, but of what we cannot tell, for they come to represent the depths of feeling into which we cannot peer.[19]

All of the memories Eliot mentions here are from the perspective of an *outside*: either in a landscape, or on its boundary. And the "one bird" about which he writes may just refer to the hermit-thrush. Richard Caddel suggests that in Ezra Pound's poetry, right through *The Cantos*, "we're being made to look at and listen to real birds ... in their surroundings. Throughout these *Cantos* there is observed nature in one form or another: clouds, light, insects, grass, plants, and so on. We can even note the natural climate."[20] By contrast, in *The Waste Land* Eliot gives us animals, birds, and "nature" as always inextricably bound to culture, myth, and meaning-making: his nightingale sings like Ovid's bird; his dry desert is the wasted locus of the modern psyche in echo of the Old Testament desert of temptation which in turn calls up an ecological system that is out of balance; even his crickets are Biblical. An exception to this binding of culture with nature, though, seems to be the "one bird," which feels more like a signifier of pure (and purifying) experience than a metonym, metaphor, or symbol that would lead us somewhere else. With the hermit-thrush Eliot wants us to hear the real thing, even if only spectacularly far away in a remote and northern woodland and remembered as a fragment of nostalgia.

V

Eliot's poetic renditions of ecological awareness are not new, of course, and there have been several excellent books on the concerns that earlier poets of the eighteenth and nineteenth centuries – especially William Wordsworth – expressed about early signs of pollution and the loss of rural lands to urban development and industrialization.[21] Jonathan Bate points to John Ruskin's critique of 1871, where Ruskin borrows from John Stuart Mill to insist that "The first three [principles of political economy] ... are Pure Air, Water, and Earth."[22] Ruskin, Bate shows, "perceived the relationship between deforestation and drought" with a remarkable "prescience," while he railed against the polluted state of English rivers as being akin to the "common sewer." Ruskin even complains that the rain itself "falls dirty."[23] As Raymond Williams argues, literary laments about a lost pastoral age have often wished to identify a precise time period for this disappearance; as he shows, though, pinpointing any dateable loss can take us as far back as Eden.[24] Still, by the early twentieth century the reality of overcrowded cities and persistent urban and industrial pollution had become inescapable facts of life, yet very little attention has been paid so far to modernist engagements with ecological questions. As for the twenty-first century, Richard Caddel observes that we now live in "an age when nature can no longer be seen as infinite and eternal," and "when we can no longer afford to think of nature without thinking of ecology."[25]

I do not think that Eliot would disagree with Wordsworth's claims in his 1798 poem, "Tintern Abbey," that we are always in dialogue with our surroundings, being "Of eye and ear, both what they half-create, / And what perceive" (107–8).[26] The difference is that for Eliot, nature, when it appears, exists already in a kind of postlapsarian *second* fall. Like Wordsworth he may still be able

> to recognise
> In nature and the language of the sense,
> The anchor of my purest thoughts, the nurse,
> The guide, the guardian of my heart, and soul
> Of all my moral being. (108–12)

But moments such as the (pained) reveries in the hyacinth garden, the song of the hermit-thrush, and appeals to "Sweet Thames" are fleeting, scarce, and insufficient to the task of redeeming the wasted land and its suffering. Instead, *The Waste Land* registers an economy of lack where we still desperately need the natural, but where the natural is precariously circumscribed, compromised, and tragically unavailable for more than the briefest of moments.

Near the end of *The Waste Land* Eliot stages a nightmarish vision in which our land and cities have reached the point of apocalyptic collapse:

> Falling towers
> Jerusalem Athens Alexandria
> Vienna London
> Unreal (373–6)

The major centers of culture that Eliot names are as broken and "Falling" as the inhabitants of the waste land (we remember, for instance, "The broken finger nails of dirty hands," 303, and the nursery-rhyme chant, "London Bridge is falling down falling down falling down," 426). Seen "over the mountains" – as if through a panoptic lens that takes into account the surrounding vistas and not just the isolated cities – these cities are, once again, rendered as "Unreal" (376), as if *The Waste Land*'s settings and environments register an all-too-real *unreality* that has exceeded our abilities to make sense of it. Yet the tone of these lines that witness apocalypse sounds almost indifferent and resigned – as does Eliot's own voice when he reads the poem aloud[27] – as if the consciousness that observes such environmental, social, and spiritual calamities has internalized the world-as-chaos and can now only project a commensurate barrenness onto the world.

I begin to wonder if we might consider *The Waste Land* as, at least in part, an eco-poem that is already sounding the warning about environmental disaster that we are facing in the (post)modernity of today. Eliot writes, apocalyptically, of "hooded hordes swarming / Over endless plains, stumbling in cracked earth" (368–9). As we know, poetry can do political work, and although Eliot has been criticized for being too staunchly conservative, it is very possible that in terms of its ecopoetics *The Waste Land* functions both as a memorial for what had already been lost or destroyed, and as a harbinger for the ecological crises we are experiencing today. The environmental devastations of the First World War alone were unprecedented, with 16 million dead, countless mines abandoned and ready to explode, destroyed towns, villages, and whole mini-ecosystems and natural habitats all over Europe scarred with trenches, bombed-out fields, and mass graves. In this way, *The Waste Land* stands as a poetry of crisis, whether we have been able to hear it or not. As Eliot knew, "human kind / Cannot bear very much reality" (*Burnt Norton*, 44–5); though our ears may not yet be attuned to hearing this kind of message from him. Still, we must admit that from our own vantage point Eliot's "Unreal City" and "Falling towers" have become our *unreal world*: the waste land of 1922 is still the waste land of today, and we are far from abolishing the ills that Eliot was anxiously representing. Still, if we can take Eliot's poem as, in part, a warning, we can also see that such warnings inherently contain hope. A hope, perhaps, that we do not have to keep living our lives in the waste lands of our modernities, and that we do not have to keep wrecking our earth and our ecosystems. The poem closes, after all, with the words, "Shantih shantih shantih" (433) – "the Peace which passeth understanding," as Eliot translates it from Sanskrit. This is an incantation that does both retrospective and proactive work, suggesting that beyond these pages there may be ways to discover peace.

NOTES

1 Lawrence Buell, *The Environmental Imagination: Thoreau, Nature Writing, and the Formation of American Culture* (Cambridge, MA: Harvard University Press, 1995), 288.

2 In his note to line 60 Eliot indicates that he is borrowing allusively from Charles Baudelaire's *Les fleurs du mal*. Baudelaire's book is generally considered to be the most important early instance in a post-pastoral literary tradition that renders modern urban life as baneful and ennui-filled. Consider, too, the recurrence of polluted fog in Eliot in relation to some of Charles Dickens's nineteenth-century portrayals of London, including the opening of *Bleak House*: "Fog everywhere. Fog up the river, where it flows among green aits and meadows; fog down the river, where it rolls defiled among the tiers of shipping and the waterside pollutions of a great (and dirty) city." Charles Dickens, *Bleak House* (1853; London: Penguin, 2003), 9. I am grateful to Patrick Moran for reminding me of this important parallel.

3 Michael North observes that this line comes directly from Canto Four of Dante's *Inferno* "in which Dante descends into the first circle of Hell, or Limbo, where those who died without baptism languish, sighing impotently, for there is nothing that can be done about their condition." T. S. Eliot, *The Waste Land*, ed. Michael North (New York: Norton, 2001), 7.

4 John Davy Hayward Bequest, King's College Library, Cambridge University.

5 Edmund Spenser, "Prothalamion," *The Yale Edition of the Shorter Poems of Edmund Spenser*, ed. William A. Oram, Einar Bjorvand, Ronald Bond, Thomas H. Cain, Alexander Dunlop, and Richard Schell (New Haven, CT: Yale University Press, 1989), 761.

6 Richard Lehan, *The City in Literature: An Intellectual and Cultural History* (Berkeley: University of California Press, 1998), 134.

7 Jonathan Bate, "The Economy of Nature," reprinted in *Ecocriticism: The Essential Reader*, ed. Ken Hiltner (New York: Routledge, 2015), 77.

8 Timothy Clark, *The Cambridge Introduction to Literature and the Environment* (Cambridge: Cambridge University Press, 2011), xiii. Italics in the original.

9 For the "First" and "Second" Caprices see Eliot, *Inventions of the March Hare: Poems 1909–1917*, ed. Christopher Ricks (London: Faber and Faber, 1996), 13 and 15.

10 For compelling arguments about the presence of Emily Hale in Eliot's poems about nostalgic and proleptic longing, see Lyndall Gordon's *The Imperfect Life of T. S. Eliot* (London: Virago, 2012).

11 There is not space here to consider the centrality of the sea in Eliot's poetry, though we might at least say that it appears amazingly often, and, like the water of *The Waste Land*, it can be both destructive and restorative.

12 Eliot, "Hamlet and His Problems," *The Sacred Wood: Essays on Poetry and Criticism* (London: Methuen, 1960), 100.

13 Barry Lopez, "Landscape and Narrative," *Vintage Lopez* (New York: Vintage, 2004), 6–7.

14 Terry Gifford, "Pastoral, Anti-Pastoral, and Post-Pastoral," *The Cambridge Companion to Literature and the Environment*, ed. Louise Westling (Cambridge: Cambridge University Press, 2014), 18.

15 Sigmund Freud, "Civilization and Its Discontents," 1930*a* [1929], *The Standard Edition of the Complete Psychological Works of Sigmund Freud*, trans. James Strachey, 24 vols. (London: Hogarth Press, 1978), vol. XXI, 69–70.

16 Greg Garrard, *Ecocriticism* (London: Routledge, 2004), 61.

17 I owe thanks to Jahan Ramazani for suggesting that moments of respite *do* occur in a few instances outside of the pastoral, within the city; for example, in the aesthetic (and religiously inflected) contemplation of the "Inexplicable splendor of Ionian white and gold" in Magnus Martyr Church (265).

18 I quote from Lyndall Gordon's chapter in this volume, "'Mixing/Memory and Desire': What Eliot's Biography Can Tell Us," 45.

19 Eliot, *The Use of Poetry and the Use of Criticism* (1933; London: Faber and Faber, 1968), 148.

20 Richard Caddel, "Secretaries of Nature: Towards a Theory of Modernist Ecology," *Ezra Pound: Nature and Myth*, ed. William Pratt (New York: AMS Press, 2002), 139.

21 For groundbreaking explorations of the relation of Romantic poets to landscape and ecology see especially John Barrell's *The Dark Side of the Landscape: The Rural Poor in English Painting 1730–1840* (Cambridge: Cambridge University Press, 1983).

22 Qtd. in Jonathan Bate, 92.

23 Ibid., 93.

24 Raymond Williams, "The Country and the City," 1975, reprinted in *Ecocriticism: The Essential Reader*, ed. Ken Hiltner (New York: Routledge, 2015), 35–8.

25 Caddel, 139.

26 William Wordsworth, "Lines written a few miles above Tintern Abbey," *William Wordsworth*, ed. Stephen Gill (Oxford: Oxford University Press, 1990), 134.

27 Eliot's way of reading *The Waste Land* aloud is famously controversial for the idiosyncracies of his accent, tone, and emphasis.

ANTHONY CUDA

Coda: *The Waste Land*'s Afterlife: The Poem's Reception in the Twentieth Century and Beyond

"And as for *The Waste Land*," wrote Edmund Wilson less than a decade after the poem first appeared, "it enchanted and devastated a whole generation."[1] Over the course of nearly a century now, generation after generation of scholars has confronted its enchanting and devastating powers, attempting to amplify, channel, or redirect them by emphasizing certain of its elements at the expense of others. As teachers, Eliot suggests, we may choose to "point to good literature and then be silent," presenting readers with "necessary and interesting facts" about the work.[2] But for scholars, the edgy and avant-garde features of *The Waste Land* – its allusiveness, its poignancy, its junctures and disjuncture – compel us beyond those necessary facts into widening circles of interpretation and debate. In this essay, I hope to convey how that interpretation and debate has transformed in the years since the poem's publication, how the contested territories of the poem have been mapped and redrawn by succeeding generations – each time in the attempt to comprehend what Eliot calls the "collision" of encountering the poem afresh (521).

"All critical judgments excite criticism," Eliot proposes.[3] In roughly chronological order, and without addressing contemporary reviews of the poem, this essay will follow the dialectic whereby the judgments of early critics like Edmund Wilson and Cleanth Brooks excited the criticism of succeeding generations (Grover Smith and Hugh Kenner, for instance, or A. Walton Litz and Lyndall Gordon), which was in turn challenged and critiqued by later scholars. I will pay particular attention to the ways in which certain questions and ideas about the poem quickly gain and lose currency, whereas others return or remain to shape our understanding of *The Waste Land*, and of its enchantments and devastations, into the twenty-first century.[4]

Early Commentaries: 1924–43

Four landmark early commentaries on *The Waste Land* – by I. A. Richards, Edmund Wilson, F. R. Leavis, and F. O. Mattheissen – traced the lines of debate that contemporary scholars still follow, including the problem of the poem's organization; the effect of its allusions and quotations; the multiplicity of its voices and the existence of a single protagonist; and the question of its overall trajectory or progress. I. A. Richards, an early supporter of Eliot who became a regular correspondent and interlocutor, included a brief appendix to the second edition of his widely influential study in method, *Principles of Literary Criticism* (1924; 2nd edition 1926) that deals primarily with *The Waste Land*.[5] Richards extols both the poem's evasion of a logical, narrative order as well as its commitment to "a music of ideas," stressing its pattern of motifs and repetition that results in "a coherent whole of feeling and attitude" (293). He argues that the poem is essentially a compressed epic, and he concludes by asserting its universal qualities and suggesting that it embodies "the plight of a whole generation" (295). In addition, in another, later essay, Richards makes the well-known statement (to which Eliot objected in print) that Eliot had effected "a complete severance between his poetry and *all* beliefs."[6]

In *Axel's Castle* (1931), Edmund Wilson expands upon his own earlier reviews (including "The Poetry of Drouth," 1922) to characterize *The Waste Land* as a poem concerned with "emotional starvation" and cultural sterility.[7] Wilson suggests that its desolation reflects the aftermath of World War I, "our post-War world of shattered institutions, strained nerves and bankrupt ideals," and he argues that, to confront these conflicts, Eliot abandons the symbolism of Laforgue and Corbière and embraces the new formal techniques for which the poem had become so renowned (106). Wilson also maintains that we need not understand all of Eliot's allusions for the emotive and imaginative power of *The Waste Land* to communicate itself. The poem conveys a completeness, he argues, that is not contingent upon its erudition (113).

F. R. Leavis also devotes a chapter to Eliot in his seminal *New Bearings in English Poetry* (1932), objecting to the already common view that *The Waste Land* longs nostalgically for a bygone era.[8] He expands upon Richards's musical analogy, arguing that the repetition and alteration of motifs generate a formal order in the absence of a more recognizable organizing principle. The multiplicity of voices, he contends, is intended "to focus an inclusive human consciousness," one that contains elements of all personalities (95). Most significantly, Leavis maintains that *The Waste Land* "exhibits no progression;" "the poem ends," he argues, "where it began" (103). F. O. Matthiessen's *The Achievement of T. S. Eliot* (1935) is among the best early syntheses of Eliot's work. Like Wilson, who discerns in the poem "the sterility of the Puritan Temperament,"[9] Matthiessen finds that *The Waste Land* possesses a sense of detachment and spiritual calling indebted to nineteenth-century American literature. Ultimately, he also agrees with Wilson in regarding the poem as an intense reflection of "the post-War state of mind" with its "intolerable burden" and "lack of purpose and direction."[10] These four foundational interpretations all frame the poem in formalist terms, recognizing an order and organization to *The Waste Land* as well as registering its broad cultural and historical scope. None, though, posits a trajectory toward spiritual or cultural fulfillment.

That task fell to Cleanth Brooks, whose "*The Waste Land*: A Critique of the Myth" first appeared in the *Southern Review* in 1937 but gained its widest readership after it was reprinted in his *Modern Poetry and the Tradition* (1939); it has been reprinted many times since.[11] Brooks undertakes the most exacting and holistic interpretation of the poem yet, particularly regarding the Grail motifs and underlying fertility rituals to which Eliot's notes refer. Earlier, Matthiesen had doubted "whether Miss Weston's valuable study has enabled me to feel the poem more intensely" (50); George Williamson had likewise suggested, "what we need to understand is the emotional structure of *The Waste Land*, not the anthropology."[12] But for Brooks, the proper (that is, not excessive) use of the framework derived from Sir James Frazer's *The Golden Bough* and Jesse Weston's *From Ritual to Romance* is "essential for an understanding of the poem."[13] Rebuking the "misrepresentations" of the poem's nihilistic despair and disillusion by critics like Wilson – a proponent of what he calls "the stock interpretation" (166) – Brooks argues for *The Waste Land*'s unity and narrative progress, which involves a protagonist on an epic journey through a land of spiritual and cultural decay. Brooks discerns a positive spiritual outcome in the poem, one modeled on the regenerative successes of the fertility rituals that Frazer and Weston describe. Brooks's work is also an early example of the enduring critical tendency to rely heavily upon Eliot's post-conversion views in order to understand and alleviate the anxieties of the earlier poems. Thus, he regards the wasted land as the product neither of postwar dread nor of emotional derangement but of "the secular attitude which dominates the modern world" (144).

Getting Used to *The Waste Land*: 1956–68

Several revelations by Eliot himself in the late 1950s must be included in any account of the poem's reception; they have been quoted and excerpted to such an extent that they now appear almost as marginalia to *The Waste Land*. The first is his suggestion, in "The Frontiers of Criticism" (1956), that his notes had "led critics into temptation."[14] He admits that he composed them "with a view to spiking the guns of critics of my earlier poems who had accused me of plagiarism" (121). Referring to the notes as a "remarkable exposition of bogus scholarship," he writes: "I regret having sent so many enquirers off on a wild goose chase after Tarot cards and the Holy Grail" (121–2). Another oft-quoted statement by Eliot appears in his *Paris Review* interview (1959) with Donald Hall, wherein he refers to the poem as "structureless" and discusses Pound's revisions.[15] Then, on the topic of obscurity in his early work, he says: "In *The Waste Land*, I wasn't even bothering whether I understood what I was saying. These things, however, become easier to people with time. You get used to having *The Waste Land*, or *Ulysses*, about" (Ibid., 64).

The two accounts that demonstrate just how "used to having *The Waste Land* about" scholars had become were also the two most influential interpretations of Eliot's work from this time until his death in 1965: Grover Smith's *T. S. Eliot's Poetry and Plays: A Study in Sources and Meaning* (1956) and Hugh Kenner's *The Invisible Poet: T. S. Eliot* (1959). Both works demonstrate a significant shift in critical attitudes and approaches to *The Waste Land*, and both remain relevant to contemporary interpretations. Scholarship had certainly begun to document the poem's dense network of sources before Smith; George Williamson's *A Reader's Guide to T. S. Eliot* (1953) is one such important forerunner. But Smith was the first to undertake an encyclopedic survey of sources throughout Eliot's extant corpus, and his two chapters on *The Waste Land* were the first to integrate systematically the familiar anthropological sources with less familiar ones from religion, literature, music, and mythology. Like Brooks, Smith assumes the existence of a protagonist, whom he calls "the quester," and he argues for a continuous arc of development through the poem. The plot of *The Waste Land*, "as Tiresias recounts it," includes failures at crucial moments of potentially regenerative initiation: thus, he writes, "the quest fails, and the poem ends with a formula for purgatorial suffering."[16]

Hugh Kenner, on the contrary, insists that *The Waste Land* is "graspable without source-hunting, and without even appeal to any but the most elementary knowledge of one or two myths and a few Shakespearean tags."[17] Kenner believes that the poem dramatizes the problems of isolation and anguished solitude that had occupied Eliot since his doctoral study of the philosophy of F. H. Bradley. On the vexed question of the notes, he declares, "we shall do well to discard the notes as much as possible:" "they have bedeviled discussion for decades" (150). Kenner may be remembered by many for his idiosyncrasies and irreverence, but his chapters on *The Waste Land* derive their persuasiveness from his meticulous and sensitive examination of its points of view, its implied narration, and what he calls its "functional obscurity, sibylline fragments so disposed as to yield the utmost in connotative power" (159). His ingenuity sometimes leads him into dubious territory, as when he suggests that the hyacinth girl is the drowned victim of a murder akin to those later described in Eliot's plays (162–4). But overall, his refusal to "tour the Eliot territory in chartered buses" results in valuable insights and correctives (xi). Perhaps most importantly, his rejection of the "official" Eliot provided readers with a new and less staid alternative to the imperious figure that had become the target of critiques such as *The T. S. Eliot Myth* (1951), in which Rossell Hope Robbins calls Eliot "a poet of minor achievement" whom critics had "exalted ... into a great poet and an advanced cultural leader."[18]

It would be difficult to overstate the value of a book like B. C. Southam's *A Guide to the Selected Poems of T. S. Eliot* (1968), which assembles and condenses the available scholarship on Eliot's work into orderly, readable annotations keyed to line numbers and mostly free from the burden of argument. Southam's guide, which reached its sixth edition in 1994, devotes a third of its nearly 300 pages to documenting the sources, allusions, and textual and publication details of *The Waste Land*. Southam offers translations from the editions that Eliot owned; he provides context from periodical publications and correspondence; and, in the introduction, he considers the vexed status of the notes at length. At times, his annotations are brief and purely factual (the Starnbergersee, "a fashionable lake-resort just south of Munich, visited by Eliot in August 1911");[19] at others, they synthesize the work of previous scholars; and at still others, they offer new insights about possible sources, such as Rupert Brooke's "The Old Vicarage, Grantchester" and the "poignant flashes of memory" and desire that it shares with "The Burial of the Dead" (139). Southam also transcribes invaluable notes on the poem by John Hayward, Eliot's longtime friend and flatmate, who jotted them on manuscripts while he was helping to prepare a French translation in 1946–7.

After the Facsimile Edition: 1971–3

Arguably the most important publication in the history of the poem's critical reception was brought forth not by a scholar but by the poet's widow, Valerie Eliot, who edited the facsimile edition of *The Waste Land*'s earliest "reception." *The Waste Land: A Facsimile and Transcript of the Original Drafts Including the Annotations of Ezra Pound* (1971) invigorated and transformed scholarship on the poem for a multitude of reasons, not least that it seemed to grant the author's own posthumous approval to the growing number of critics already beginning to argue against the alleged unity and structural coherence of the poem. The most notable of the many initial responses to this trove of archival materials is Richard Ellmann's review in *The New York Review of Books*, which draws upon Eliot's biography to argue that "the poem may be a covert memorial to Henry Ware Eliot, the unforgiving father of the ill-adventured son."[20] William Empson arrives at a similar conclusion in his extended review-essay on the edition,[21] while Helen Gardner's "*The Waste Land*: Paris 1922" continues the effort to decipher the order of the manuscript's composition and gauge the effects of Pound's excisions.[22] But the most exhaustively researched and persuasively argued account of the new materials was undertaken by Lyndall Gordon, first in "*The Waste Land* Manuscript" (1974) and then, wholly afresh, in her biography *Eliot's Early Years* (1977).[23] Gordon's archival research – and her close examination of watermarks, typefaces, and other material evidence – produces a compelling narrative of the poem's personal origins, dating back to fragments likely composed in 1914. Gordon regards *The Waste Land* as a narrative of spiritual revelation and upheaval, and in the first essay, she concludes that Pound's excisions shifted the "hoard of fragments" away from Eliot's highly personal, spiritual torment and toward a representation of "common cultural experience."[24] In *Eliot's Early Years* (revised and reprinted with its sequel as *T. S. Eliot: An Imperfect Life* in 1998, and then further revised in 2012), Gordon again draws upon unpublished manuscripts and archival materials to describe the poem's origins in Eliot's disintegrating marriage, its continuation of the powerful spiritual sensibility evident in his earliest poetry, and its movement toward "purification and metamorphosis."[25] She also amplifies her earlier reading of Pound's revisions, arguing that he actually "blocked, at several points, Eliot's impulse to exhibit the strength as well as the sickness of the suffering soul."[26]

Of the three essay compilations published in the early 1970s to coincide with the fiftieth anniversary of the poem, A. Walton Litz's *Eliot in His Time* (1973) testifies most forcefully to the proliferation and vitality of new responses after the facsimile edition.[27] The most provocative contributions to this volume emphasize *The Waste Land*'s modes of fragmentation, dislocation, and interruption rather than its structures and coherence. In "*The Waste Land* Fifty Years After," Litz himself urges readers away from the "standard," fixed interpretations of the poem as a narrative of religious experience (referring to the "burden of spiritual significance" that it had been forced to bear) and toward its more chaotic, satiric, and experimental elements.[28] Against critics who detect moral values and judgments in the poem, Litz maintains that Eliot's intention was, rather, "a delicate balance of attitudes" (7). He writes: "much might be gained if readers of *The Waste Land* could, for a few years, adopt the motto which Mark Twain affixed to *Huckleberry Finn*: 'persons attempting to find a moral in [this work] will be banished; persons attempting to find a plot in it will be shot'" (7). In "The Urban Apocalypse" from the same volume, Hugh Kenner suggests that the original poem was much more clearly a satiric portrait of London, an "urban panorama refracted through Augustan styles," and that revision produced the apocalyptic tone that dominates the final text.[29] An equally compelling study in the volume, however, is "New Modes of Characterization in *The Waste Land*" by Robert Langbaum, who argues on behalf of the poem's undetected continuities and thus against Kenner and Litz. The continuity of character, Langbaum concludes, allows for "a more consistent structure on the model of romantic monodrama."[30]

Nearly ten years after the appearance of her edition of *Knowledge and Experience in the Philosophy of F. H. Bradley* (1964), a milestone in Eliot studies, Anne C. Bolgan published *What the Thunder Really Said* (1973), in which she combines her expertise on Eliot's doctoral work with a reassessment of the facsimile edition to gauge the distance between the poem's potential and its achievement. Bolgan contends that *The Waste Land* was "aiming to be" a monologue similar to Eliot's earlier work yet broader in scope, but that Eliot encountered unresolvable conflicts, both philosophical and literary, implicit in the project; "the poem foundered" as a result.[31] She concludes that *The Waste Land* is a failure, though "of such failures, it can only be said that we could certainly use more of them" (163).

Interlude: Jean Verdenal, John Peter, and James Miller

Few contemporary scholars would deny that Eliot enjoyed a rich and formative relationship with Jean Verdenal, the French medical student whom he met in Paris in 1910 and who died in 1915 during the war. To understand, however, the significance of James E. Miller's claims about homoeroticism in *T. S. Eliot's Personal Waste Land: Exorcism of the Demons* (1977), we must follow a circuitous route: first, back to 1969, when John Peter's "A New Interpretation of *The Waste Land*" was revised and republished in *Essays in Criticism*; then, back to the original appearance of Peter's article in the same review in 1952, when it sparked controversy by contending that the poem's speaker had "fallen completely – perhaps the right word is irretrievably – in love" with "a young man who soon afterwards met his death."[32] Throughout the poem, but especially in the figure of the drowned sailor, Peter argues, the speaker makes oblique tributes to an intense experience of homoerotic love and bereavement. Soon after the article appeared, Eliot's solicitors sent a letter insisting that its "further dissemination" be halted and that unsold copies of the journal be destroyed (166). Though Peter later insists that this action made copies of the issue rare and "unprocurable for seventeen years," editor F. H. Bateson reports that only thirty undistributed copies were destroyed.[33] In his "Postscript" to the 1969 version, reprinted with subtle revisions after Eliot's death, Peter abandons his former discretion about identifying the speaker with Eliot, and simply asserts that "anyone reading Eliot with real attentiveness today, I think, can hardly avoid the conclusion that in his youth he had a close romantic attachment to another man" (166).[34] In 1976, George Watson challenged Peter's emboldened speculation with his own biographical research, a well-documented investigation into Verdenal titled "Quest for a Frenchman," in which he demonstrates that Verdenal was not likely a model for Phlebas and that, despite the intensity of Eliot's relationship with him, there is nothing to suggest that either man was homosexual.[35]

In 1977, however, James E. Miller extended Peter's argument in *T. S. Eliot's Personal Waste Land*, in which he argues that *The Waste Land* was shaped primarily by Eliot's memory of this singular relationship and bereavement. Although Miller emphasizes that his argument does not hinge upon Eliot's sexuality, he nonetheless contends that the loss and devastation conveyed throughout *The Waste Land* derive mainly from the author's powerful and sexualized memories of Verdenal, his grief over the man's death, and the anguish resulting from Eliot's precipitous marriage to Vivienne. Scholars criticize Miller for his "detective-fiction" style and the circularity by which he speculates about the poem based upon speculations about Eliot's personal life, speculations that are, themselves, derived from an interpretation of the poem.[36] He elaborates an iconoclastic and influential thesis, however, that has continued to influence portrayals of Eliot's life, including Michael Hastings's play *Tom and Viv* (1984) and especially Carol Seymour-Jones's scurrilous biography, *Painted Shadow: A Life of Vivienne Eliot* (2001). Other critics have tended to recapitulate Miller's conclusions with a critical shorthand of sorts. For instance, with one reference to Miller's book in its entirety, Wayne Koestenbaum simply refers to "Eliot's arguably sexual interest in Verdenal," which is "repressed in the poem" and therefore produces "hysterical discontinuities."[37] Contemporary scholars of other modernist writers have followed suit, referring to "Eliot's possible latent homosexuality" and relying on Miller and Seymour-Jones to support assertions such as "Eliot's expression of his tender love toward Verdenal fills the pages of *The Waste Land*."[38] Miller himself expanded his own thesis to encompass the whole of Eliot's early career in *T. S. Eliot: The Making of an American Poet: 1888–1922* (2005).

A number of studies that address the poem more persuasively in terms of gender and queer studies have emerged in recent years. In *Deviant Modernism* (1998) Colleen Lamos suggests that the poem "depicts in painful and desperate ways the modern dilemma of masculine heterosexuality" and is "symptomatic of modern masculine uneasiness."[39] Cassandra Laity and Nancy Gish coedited *Gender, Desire, and Sexuality in T. S. Eliot* (2004), which has become an indispensable source on these topics throughout Eliot's work.[40] In particular, in his contribution, "T. S. Eliot, famous clairvoyante," Tim Dean offers a compelling alternative reading of *The Waste Land* based on queer theory, one which also deftly critiques biographical speculation about Eliot's sexuality.[41] In "T. S. Eliot: The Performativity of Gender in *The Waste Land*" (2005) and elsewhere, Cyrena Pondrom focuses upon how "textual qualities which foster gender ambiguity" force readers to construct complicated and often implicitly gender-biased discourses about the poem.[42] Ed Madden's *Tiresian Poetics* (2008) and Gabrielle McIntire's *Modernism, Memory, and Desire: T.S. Eliot and Virginia Woolf* (2008) both offer further reflections upon what Madden calls a "troubled relation" to the male body, homoerotic discourses, and male sexuality.[43]

Philosophy, Hermeneutics, and Biography: 1979–late 1980s

A spate of essays and monographs in the late 1970s and 1980s brought the increasingly popular methods of literary theory to bear on *The Waste Land*. Some involve more or less straightforward "applications" of deconstructive approaches to the literary text, like those by William Spanos and Margaret Uroff.[44] In "*The Waste Land*: Ur-Text of Deconstruction," Ruth Nevo proposes an argument that has since become familiar indeed, namely, that Eliot's poem prefigures the strategies of poststructuralist theory, that it can "now be read as a postmodernist poem … as a deconstructionist Ur-text, even as a Deconstructionist Manifesto."[45] In *T. S. Eliot and the Poetics of Literary History* (1983), Gregory S. Jay also argues that deconstructive and psychoanalytic methods were already implicit in Eliot's work. Cyrena Pondrom uses a similar formulation regarding gender performativity.[46] Cultural studies and feminist theory intervened around this time, just as they did in the discipline of literary theory generally, to critique deconstructive readings. For instance, Alison Tate argues that *The Waste Land*, despite its seeming disjunctions and polyvocality, is a text firmly embedded in the hierarchical Western literary tradition, one that "echoes the order of a tradition narrowly based in terms of sex and class" and therefore simply magnifies stereotypes and hierarchies while parading as "the acceptable face of modernism."[47]

Several works from the 1980s, also grounded in theory, exemplify the periodic tendency to downplay the importance of *The Waste Land*'s structures, myths, and allusions and to emphasize instead its absences and omissions. In *T. S. Eliot's Negative Way* (1982), Eloise Knapp Hay adapts existentialist philosophy in an attempt to read *The Waste Land* without the distorting hindsight of Eliot's conversion and later writings. For Hay, it is "a poem of radical doubt and negation, urging that every human desire be stilled except the desire for self-surrender, for restraint, and for peace."[48] Harriet Davidson also owes the *ethos* of her *T. S. Eliot and Hermeneutics* (1985) to the philosophy of existentialism, especially that of Martin Heidegger, arguing that *The Waste Land* "is a poem full of strategic absences."[49] As readers, she reflects, our first and most salient experience of the poem involves, in fact, "the absence of expected connections or sources;" more important still is what she calls the "powerful and disturbing" absence of a central and controlling consciousness (2–3). In *The Poetics of Impersonality: T. S. Eliot and Ezra Pound* (1987), Maud Ellmann offers a psychoanalytic reading that draws from Freud and Kristeva to argue that *The Waste Land* is "a sphinx without a secret:" "to force it to confession may also be a way of killing it."[50] She contends that Eliot's central focus in the poem is waste and detritus, or "the abject;" that the poem dramatizes the fear of infection and anxiety about taboo; and that these anxieties help it to "stage the ritual of its own destruction" (109).

Reading The Waste Land: Modernism and the Limits of Interpretation (1990) by Jewel Spears Brooker and Joseph Bentley resembles the work by Hay, Davidson, and Ellmann in its focus on evidence of interpretation and processes of hermeneutics, but it is framed primarily by Eliot's own philosophical background rather than by post–World War II philosophy and critical theory. That is, Brooker and Bentley discern a variety of interpretative practices at work *in the poem itself*, acts that occur before any interpretations by scholars. They describe their project as "metahermeneutics: interpretation of interpretations and of their denial."[51] Brooker and Bentley show how *The Waste Land* provokes increasingly complicated and bifurcated problems of understanding. The authors argue that the poem's power ultimately emerges, however, from below or "before" these layers of interpretation, a "condition of infancy" (Piaget) or an "immediate experience" (Bradley) that precedes them, or in their words, "a perfect wordless love that existed before all languages and all meaning" (222).

Valuable advances in biographical studies of Eliot in the 1980s – including Peter Ackroyd's *T. S. Eliot: A Life* (1984) and Lyndall Gordon's *Eliot's New Life* (1988) – were accompanied by several wide-ranging attempts to synthesize Eliot's corpus, two of which deserve mention here. In the chapter of *Thomas Stearns Eliot: Poet* (1979) dealing with *The Waste Land*, "Tiresias Transformed," A. David Moody argues on behalf of the poem's powerful focus on the individual, rejecting accounts that emphasize solely its cultural and historical commentary: "to read the poem only as a critique of its culture ... is to be rather simple minded; it is to make out the mind of Europe perhaps, but to miss the poet's mind."[52] Moody finds a profoundly individualized effort toward self-transcendence, a distinctly emotional (as opposed to spiritual) transcendence that carries the poem's focus beyond the limited perspective of Tiresias. Ronald Bush's *T. S. Eliot: A Study in Character and Style* (1984) is equally wide-ranging, drawing from Eliot's life and work to address how the poet gives form and order to psychological pressures. In two chapters, "The Poet's Inner World of Nightmare" and "Unknown Terror and Mystery: *The Waste Land*," Bush argues persuasively that the power of *The Waste Land* arises from the ways that it channels and organizes "the world of unconscious impulse," particularly the way that it resembles the patterns of nightmare and dreamscape rather than those of conventional epic narrative or quest. What connects the segments of the poem "is precisely what connects the disparate segments of our most distressing dreams.... A dramatic situation emerges, intensifies mysteriously ... and then, just before the situation is clarified, disperses; then a new situation arises that seems comfortingly different but is in fact the same anew."[53] Moody and Bush's shared emphasis on the individual, psychological elements of the poem reflect another periodically recurring critical desire, namely, to renew the experience of reading *The Waste Land* by rediscovering its personal, emotive energies rather than tracing its philosophical or hermeneutic complexities.

Returning to Origins: Late 1980s–present

Several influential studies in recent decades have begun to follow a recognizable pattern that we might describe as a return to origins, whether these be anthropological (primitivism and decadence), economic (publishing institutions and periodical networks), scholarly (earlier readings of the poem), or material (typewriters and watermarks). Robert Crawford's *The Savage and the City in the Work of T. S. Eliot* (1987) is one such influential study with particular importance for understanding how *The Waste Land* fits into Eliot's lifelong attempt to calibrate the relationship between primitive and sophisticated societies. Crawford's most valuable contribution to scholarship pertaining to *The Waste Land*, however, is the evidence he assembles to show its indebtedness to the urban visions of decadent poets Francis Thompson, John Davidson, and Rudyard Kipling. Jewel Spears Brooker undertakes a valuable series of returns in *Mastery and Escape* (1994), particularly in the two chapters that offer needful correctives to widespread misunderstandings of the places of Frazer and Bradley in *The Waste Land*.[54] Calvin Bedient returns to earlier readings of the poem and its central poet-quester or romantic hero in *He Do the Police in Different Voices: The Waste Land and Its Protagonist* (1986). Bedient argues for "an all-centering, autobiographical protagonist-narrator" that unifies the poem and clarifies its most powerful elements.[55] In *T. S. Eliot and the Politics of Voice: The Argument of* The Waste Land (1987), John Xiros Cooper advocates another explicit return, this time to the poem's "sociohistoric contexts," particularly its engagement with the cultural and ideological inheritance of Victorian England. Cooper contends that *The Waste Land* "mercilessly dismembers the typical humanist accounts of experience inscribed in the discursive practices of the progressive Victorians."[56]

The most significant publications on the poem in recent years are Lawrence Rainey's *Revisiting* The Waste Land and *The Annotated Waste Land with Eliot's Contemporary Prose*, simultaneously published in 2005. The central element of *Revisiting* The Waste Land is Rainey's meticulous examination of hundreds of letters and typescripts in the attempt to date accurately the bundle of fragments and poems included in the facsimile edition. Rainey follows every lead with forensic attention to detail, from chainlines and watermarks to swapped typewriters with wide vs. crabbed finishing strokes. His argument persuasively demonstrates that, contrary to what some scholars had believed, *The Waste Land* was composed, with few exceptions, in the order in which it ultimately first appeared. Combining his forensic analyses with a scrupulous examination of biographical accounts allows Rainey to reconstruct the most definitive chronology of the poem's composition yet.[57] Rainey's other chapters address the elaborate prepublication maneuvering of Eliot, Pound, and several potential publishers of the poem, as well as the drastic transformation of *The Waste Land*'s reputation in the decades following its appearance. As so many scholars have done, Rainey contends that Cleanth Brooks "profoundly misread" the poem by discerning its unified, Christian theme, and that scholarship still suffers from his misreading.[58] He urges readers to liberate themselves from the "dominance" of New Critical readings like Brooks's and to experience, instead, its "lacerating wildness" by returning to a point of view similar to that of the poem's earliest readers (127–8). Rainey's edition of the poem, *The Annotated Waste Land*, includes copious annotations on the poem and on eleven uncollected pieces of prose, as well as a collation of variants from all versions of the poem through 1936.

Perhaps the most refreshing and influential contemporary research has been the result of a return to underappreciated aspects of the poem's cultural and historical contexts. Matthew Gold, Amanda Harris, and Nancy Gish, for instance, have all written compelling accounts of the long shadows cast across the poem by the psychological theories and practice of Roger

Vittoz, who treated Eliot at Lausanne, and Pierre Janet, whom Eliot studied at Harvard.[59] Another fruitful and influential line of contemporary research involves Eliot's long-underestimated appreciation of popular culture, including music hall and jazz; Sebastian Knowles, Jonna Mackin, Barry Faulk, and especially David Chinitz in his *T. S. Eliot and the Cultural Divide* (2003) have offered valuable new information about this aspect of his career and of *The Waste Land* in particular.[60]

There is little doubt that scholarship is on the cusp of another major shift in the critical history of *The Waste Land*. The first volume of Eliot's letters (1898–1922) was revised and republished in 2009 under the editorship of Valerie Eliot and John Haffenden, whose swift production of subsequent volumes continues to affect the study of *The Waste Land*. For instance, in the fourth volume (1928–1929), Eliot confides to E. M. Forster that "the *Waste Land* might have been just the same without the War."[61] The annotated, definitive edition of Eliot's complete prose is being published, in eight volumes, under the general editorship of Ronald Schuchard. And Faber and Faber will soon issue the first scholarly edition of Eliot's complete poems, edited by Christopher Ricks. Such a remarkable fusion of scholarship, along with the new access to unpublished and archival materials, will lead to a deepening and transforming awareness of the rich, strange, and dangerous magic of what is likely the twentieth century's most discussed poem. On the brink of a new era in Eliot studies, it is hard to disagree with Paul Muldoon when he declares, in the 2013 landmark reissue of the Boni and Liveright first edition of the poem, "It's almost impossible to think of a world in which *The Waste Land* did not exist."[62]

NOTES

1 Edmund Wilson, *Axel's Castle: A Study in the Imaginative Literature of 1870–1930* (New York: Charles Scribner's Sons, 1931), 113–14.

2 T. S. Eliot, "The Education of Taste," *The Athenaeum* 4652 (June 27, 1919): 521 [520–21].

3 Eliot, "John Donne," *The Nation and the Athenaeum* 33 (June 9, 1923), 332 [331–32].

4 There are ample resources available for readers interested in contemporary responses to *The Waste Land*, especially in Jewel Spears Brooker's *T. S. Eliot: The Contemporary Reviews* (Cambridge: Cambridge University Press, 2004). Teachers of the poem will find an accessible selection of excerpts from early reviews in Michael North's *The Waste Land: A Norton Critical Edition* (New York: Norton, 2001), 139–66. See also Michael Grant's *T. S. Eliot: The Critical Heritage* (New York: Routledge & Kegan Paul, 1982), a two-volume compilation of selected reviews by Eliot's contemporaries, and Graham Clarke's expansive *T. S. Eliot: Critical Assessments* (London: C. Helm, 1990), with four volumes of similar excerpts; the second volume includes a selection on *The*

Waste Land through 1987. Other valuable guides to the criticism of the poem include Robert Canary's *T. S. Eliot: The Poet and His Critics* (Chicago: American Library Association, 1982); *T. S. Eliot: Man and Poet*, vol. 2, by Sebastian Knowles and Scott Leonard (Orono, ME: National Poetry Association, 1992); Mildred Martin's *A Half-Century of Eliot Criticism: An Annotated Bibliography of Books and Articles in English, 1916–1965* (Lewisburg: Bucknell University Press, 1972); Beatrice Ricks's *T. S. Eliot: A Bibliography of Secondary Works* (Metuchen, NJ: Scarecrow Press, 1980); and especially the chapter-length surveys of scholarship in the two volumes of *Sixteen Modern American Authors* (Durham, NC: Duke University Press, 1974; 1990) by Richard Ludwig and Stuart McDougal, respectively. Readers interested in a more inclusive and narrative account of the poem's reception should consult the excellent introduction by Lois A. Cuddy and David Hirsch in *Critical Essays on T. S. Eliot's The Waste Land* (Boston: G.K. Hall, 1991), 1–24.

5 I. A. Richards, *Principles of Literary Criticism* (New York: Harcourt, 1926), 289.

6 Richards, *Science and Poetry* (New York: Norton, 1926), 76.

7 Wilson, *Axel's Castle*, 104. In "The Poetry of Drouth," Wilson writes that the poem captures "the starvation of a whole civilization." Qtd. in *T. S. Eliot: The Contemporary Reviews*, ed. Jewel Spears Brooker (Cambridge: Cambridge University Press, 2004), 86 [83–87].

8 F. R. Leavis, *New Bearings in English Poetry* (1932; rpt. London: Chatto & Windus, 1942). Cf. Malcolm Cowley's slightly later remark: "The idea was a simple one. Beneath the rich symbolism of *The Waste Land*, the wide learning expressed in seven languages ... the poet is saying that the present is inferior to the past." *Exile's Return* (New York: Norton, 1934; rpt. Penguin, 1994), 112–13.

9 Wilson, *Axel's Castle*, 105.

10 F. O. Matthiessen, *The Achievement of T. S. Eliot: An Essay on the Nature of Poetry*, 3rd edition (1935; New York: Oxford University Press, 1959), 21.

11 See, for example, Leonard Unger's *T. S. Eliot: A Selected Critique* (New York: Rinehart, 1948), 319–48; Michael North also reprints it in the Norton Critical Edition. Contemporary scholars frequently suggest that Brooks's reading had an overpowering effect on later scholarship. Lawrence Rainey writes that this essay "profoundly shaped the course of criticism on the poem for the next forty years." *Revisiting* The Waste Land (New Haven: Yale University Press, 2005), 117. See, however, Armour H. Nelson's early critical survey, "The Critics and *The Waste Land*, 1922–1949," in which Brooks is merely one among the many contending critical voices. *English Studies* 36 (1955): 1–15.

12 George Williamson, *The Talent of T. S. Eliot* (Seattle: University of Washington Book Store, 1929), 33.

13 Cleanth Brooks, *Modern Poetry and the Tradition* (Chapel Hill: University of North Carolina Press, 1939), 137.

14 Eliot, *On Poetry and Poets* (New York: Farrar, Straus and Cudahy, 1957), 121 [113–31].

15 Donald Hall, "The Art of Poetry, I: T. S. Eliot," *Paris Review* 21 (Spring/Summer 1959): 53 [47–70].

16 Grover Smith, *T. S. Eliot's Poetry and Plays* (1956; rpt. Chicago: University of Chicago Press, 1965), 71.

17 Hugh Kenner, *The Invisible Poet* (1959; rpt. New York: Harcourt, 1969), 151.

18 Rossell Hope Robbins, *The T. S. Eliot Myth* (New York: Schuman, 1951), 169.

19 B. C. Southam, *A Guide to the Selected Poems of T. S. Eliot*, 6th edition (1968; New York: Harcourt, 1994), 139.

20 Richard Ellmann, "The First *Waste Land*," *Eliot in His Time: Essays on the Occasion of the Fiftieth Anniversary of The Waste Land*, ed. A. Walton Litz (Princeton: Princeton University Press, 1973), 61 [51–66]; originally in *The New York Review of Books* 17 (November 18, 1971): 10–16.

21 William Empson, "My God Man There's Bears On It," *Essays in Criticism* 22 (October 1972): 417–29.

22 Helen Gardner, "*The Waste Land*: Paris 1922," *Eliot in His Time*, 67–94.

23 Lyndall Gordon, "*The Waste Land* Manuscript," *American Literature* 45 (January 1974): 557–70.

24 Ibid., 557, 565.

25 Gordon, *T. S. Eliot: An Imperfect Life* (New York: Norton, 1998), 182.

26 Ibid., 187.

27 See also *Ulysses and The Waste Land, Fifty Years After*, ed. R. G. Collins and Kenneth McRobbie (Winnipeg: University of Manitoba Press, 1972) and *The Waste Land in Different Voices*, ed. A. C. Charity and A. D. Moody (New York: St. Martin's, 1974).

28 A. Walton Litz, "*The Waste Land* Fifty Years After," *Eliot in His Time*, 8 [3–22].

29 Kenner, *Eliot in His Time*, 46 [23–49].

30 Langbaum, *Eliot in His Time*, 109 [95–128].

31 Anne C. Bolgan, *What the Thunder Really Said: A Retrospective Essay on the Making of The Waste Land* (Montreal: McGill-Queens University Press, 1973), 15.

32 John Peter, "A New Interpretation of *The Waste Land*," *Essays in Criticism* 19 (April 1969): 142 [140–75].

33 Ibid., 165; F. H. Bateson, "Preface to the Reprint Edition," *Essays in Criticism* (Amsterdam, 1975), vol. I, no pagination.

34 See Timothy Materer's meticulous examination of the revisions in "T. S. Eliot and His Biographical Critics," *Essays in Criticism* 62 (January 2012): 41–57.

35 George Watson, "Quest for a Frenchman," *The Sewanee Review* 84 (Summer 1976): 465–75.

36 For instance, J. E. Dearlove's review in *American Literature* 50 (November 1978): 499–501.

37 Wayne Koestenbaum, "*The Waste Land*: T. S. Eliot's and Ezra Pound's Collaboration on Hysteria," *Twentieth-Century Literature* 34 (1988): 124 [113–39].

38 Monika Faltejskova, *Djuna Barnes, T. S. Eliot, and the Gender Dynamics of Modernism: Tracing Nightwood* (New York: Routledge, 2010), 81. For a series of articles on the biography of Verdenal, see Claudio Perinot's "Jean Verdenal: T. S. Eliot's French Friend," *Annali di Cà Foscari-Università di Venezia* 35 (1996): 265–75; "Further Notes on the Friendship of Jean Verdenal and T. S. Eliot," *ANQ* 21 (Summer 2008): 44–54; and "Jean Verdenal, An Extraordinary Young Man: T. S. Eliot's *mort aux Dardanelles*," *South Atlantic Review* 76 (Summer 2011): 33–50.

39 Colleen Lamos, *Deviant Modernism: Sexual and Textual Errancy in T. S. Eliot, James Joyce, and Marcel Proust* (Cambridge: Cambridge University Press, 1998), 110–11.

40 Cassandra Laity and Nancy Gish, eds., *Gender, Desire, and Sexuality in T. S. Eliot* (New York: Cambridge University Press, 2004).

41 "T. S. Eliot, famous clairvoyante," *Gender, Desire, and Sexuality in T. S. Eliot*, 43–65.

42 Cyrena Pondrom, "T. S. Eliot: The Performativity of Gender in *The Waste Land*," *Modernism/modernity* 12 (September 2005): 426 [425–41]; see also Pondrom's "Conflict and Concealment: Eliot's Approach to Women and Gender," *A Companion to T. S. Eliot*, ed. David Chinitz (Malden, MA: Blackwell, 2009), 323–34, as well as Patrick Query's "'The pleasures of higher vices': Sexuality in Eliot's Work," in the same volume (350–62).

43 Ed Madden, *Tiresian Poetics: Modernism, Sexuality, Voice, 1888–2001* (Madison, NJ: Fairleigh Dickinson University Press, 2008), 108 [108–75]; Gabrielle McIntire, *Modernism, Memory, and Desire: T. S. Eliot and Virginia Woolf* (Cambridge: Cambridge University Press, 2008).

44 William Spanos, "Repetition in *The Waste Land*: A Phenomenological De-Struction, *boundary* 2 (Spring 1979): 225–85; Margaret Dickie Uroff, "*The Waste Land*: Metatext," *Centennial Review* 24 (1980): 148–66.

45 Ruth Nevo, "*The Waste Land*: Ur-Text of Deconstruction," *New Literary History* 13 (Spring 1982): 454 [453–61].

46 "T. S. Eliot profoundly anticipates a fundamental cluster of concepts taken … to be post-modern," she writes (Pondrom, "T. S. Eliot: The Performativity of Gender in *The Waste Land*," 425).

47 Alison Tate, "The Master-Narrative of Modernism: Discourses of Gender and Class in *The Waste Land*," *Literature and History* 14 (Fall 1988): 169 [160–71].

48 Eloise Knapp Hay, *T. S. Eliot's Negative Way* (Cambridge, MA: Harvard University Press, 1982), 48.

49 Harriet Davidson, *T. S. Eliot and Hermeneutics: Absence and Interpretation in The Waste Land* (Baton Rouge: Louisiana State University Press, 1985), 2.

50 Maud Ellmann, *The Poetics of Impersonality: T. S. Eliot and Ezra Pound* (Cambridge: Harvard University Press, 1987), 91 [91–109].

51 Jewel Spears Brooker and Joseph Bentley, *Reading The Waste Land: Modernism and the Limits of Interpretation* (Amherst: University of Massachusetts Press, 1990), 63.

52 A. David Moody, *Thomas Stearns Eliot: Poet* (Cambridge: Cambridge University Press, 1994), 79 [79–111].

53 Ronald Bush, *T. S. Eliot: A Study in Character and Style* (New York: Oxford University Press, 1984), 61.

54 Jewel Spears Brooker, *Mastery and Escape: T. S. Eliot and the Dialectic of Modernism* (Amherst: University of Massachusetts Press, 1994); see especially "The Case of the Missing Abstraction: Eliot, Frazer, and Modernism" (110–22) and "F. H. Bradley's Doctrine of Experience in T. S. Eliot's *The Waste Land* and *Four Quartets*" (191–206).

55 Calvin Bedient, *He Do the Police in Different Voices: The Waste Land and Its Protagonist* (Chicago: University of Chicago Press, 1986), ix.

56 John Xiros Cooper, *T. S. Eliot and the Politics of Voice: The Argument of* The Waste Land (Ann Arbor, MI: UMI Research Press, 1987), 3.

57 See however Jim McCue's objections to Rainey's chronology in "Editing Eliot," *Essays in Criticism* 56 (January 2006): 1–27.

58 Lawrence Rainey, *Revisiting The Waste Land* (New Haven, CT: Yale University Press, 2005), 124.
59 Matthew K. Gold, "The Expert Hand and the Obedient Heart: Dr. Vittoz, T. S. Eliot, and the Therapeutic Possibilities of *The Waste Land*," *Journal of Modern Literature* 23 (Summer 2000): 519–33; Amanda Jeremin Harris, "T. S. Eliot's Mental Hygiene," *Journal of Modern Literature* 29 (Summer 2006): 44–56; Nancy K. Gish, "'Gerontion' and *The Waste Land*: Prelude to Altered Consciousness," *T. S. Eliot, Dante, and the Idea of Europe*, ed. Paul Douglass (Newcastle upon Tyne: Cambridge Scholars, 2011), 29–37.
60 Sebastian Knowles, "'Then You Wink the Other Eye': T. S. Eliot and the Music Hall," *ANQ* 11 (Fall 1998): 20–32; Jonna Mackin, "Raising Life to Kind of Art: Eliot and Music Hall," *T. S. Eliot's Orchestra: Critical Essays on Poetry and Music*, ed. John Xiros Cooper (New York: Garland, 2000); Barry Faulk, "Modernism and the Popular: Eliot's Music Halls," *Modernism/modernity* 8 (November 2001): 603–21; 49–63; David Chinitz, *T. S. Eliot and the Cultural Divide* (Chicago: University of Chicago Press, 2003).
61 T. S. Eliot to E. M. Forster, August 10, 1929, in *The Letters of T.S. Eliot, Volume 4: 1928–1929*, ed. Valerie Eliot and John Haffenden (New Haven, CT: Yale University Press, 2013), 573.
62 Paul Muldoon, "Introduction," *The Waste Land* (New York: Liveright, 2013), 5 [5–24].

A SHORT GUIDE TO FURTHER READING

Peter Ackroyd, *T. S. Eliot: A Life* (New York: Simon and Schuster, 1984).

G. Douglas Atkins, *T. S. Eliot, Lancelot Andrews, and the Word: Intersections of Literature and Christianity* (New York: Palgrave Macmillan, 2011).

David Ayers, *Modernism: A Short Introduction* (Malden, MA: Blackwell, 2004).

Richard Badenhausen, *T. S. Eliot and the Art of Collaboration* (Cambridge: Cambridge University Press, 2004).

Calvin Bedient, *He Do the Police in Different Voices: The Waste Land and Its Protagonist* (Chicago, University of Chicago Press, 1986).

Harold Bloom, ed., *T. S. Eliot* (Broomall, PA: Chelsea House, 1999).

ed., *T. S. Eliot's The Waste Land*, updated edition (1986; New York: Chelsea House, 2007).

Neville Braybrooke, ed., *T. S. Eliot: A Symposium for His Seventieth Birthday* (New York: Farrar, Straus, and Cudahy, 1958).

Jewel Spears Brooker, *Mastery and Escape: T. S. Eliot and the Dialectic of Modernism* (Amherst: University of Massachusetts Press, 1994).

Jewel Spears Brooker and Joseph Bentley, *Reading The Waste Land: Modernism and the Limits of Interpretation* (Amherst: University of Massachusetts Press, 1990).

Jewel Spears Brooker, ed., *T. S. Eliot and Our Turning World* (Houndmills, Basingstoke: Macmillan Press, 2001).

ed., *T. S. Eliot: The Contemporary Reviews* (London: Cambridge University Press, 2004).

Cleanth Brooks, *Modern Poetry and the Tradition* (Chapel Hill: University of North Carolina Press, 1939).

Ronald Bush, *T. S. Eliot: A Study in Character and Style* (New York: Oxford University Press, 1983).

ed., *T. S. Eliot: The Modernist in History* (Cambridge: Cambridge University Press, 1991).

David E. Chinitz, *T. S. Eliot and the Cultural Divide* (Chicago: University of Chicago Press, 1993).

ed., *A Companion to T. S. Eliot*, (Oxford: Wiley-Blackwell, 2009).

Graham Clarke, *T. S. Eliot: Critical Assessments* (London: C. Helm, 1990).

Sarah Cole, *At the Violet Hour: Modernism and Violence in England and Ireland* (Oxford: Oxford University Press, 2012).

John Xiros Cooper, *The Cambridge Introduction to T. S. Eliot* (Cambridge: Cambridge University Press, 2006).

ed., *T. S. Eliot's Orchestra* (New York: Garland, 2000).

Michael Coyle, Debra Rae Cohen, and Jane Lewty, eds., *Broadcasting Modernism* (Gainesville: University of Florida Press, 2009).

Robert Crawford, *The Savage and the City in the Work of T. S. Eliot* (Oxford: Clarendon Press, 1987).

Anthony Cuda, *The Passions of Modernism: Eliot, Yeats, Woolf, and Mann* (New York: Columbia University Press, 2010).

Elizabeth Däumer and Shyamal Bagchee, eds., *The International Reception of T. S. Eliot* (London: Continuum, 2007).

Harriet Davidson, ed., *T. S. Eliot* (New York: Longman, 1999).

J. L. Dawson, P. D. Holland, and D. J. McKitterick, eds., *A Concordance to the Complete Poems and Plays of T. S. Eliot* (Ithaca, New York: Cornell University Press, 1995).

Denis Donaghue, *Words Alone: The Poet T. S. Eliot* (New Haven, CT: Yale University Press, 2000).

Paul Douglass, *T. S. Eliot, Dante, and the Idea of Europe* (Newcastle upon Tyne: Cambridge Scholars, 2011).

T. S. Eliot, *The Complete Poems and Plays* (London: Faber and Faber, 1969).

The Complete Prose of T. S. Eliot: The Critical Edition: Apprentice Years, 1905–1918, ed. Jewel Spears Brooker and Ronald Schuchard (Baltimore: Johns Hopkins University Press, 2014). Project MUSE. <http://muse.jhu.edu/>.

The Complete Prose of T. S. Eliot: The Critical Edition: The Perfect Critic, 1919–1926, ed. Anthony Cuda and Ronald Schuchard (Baltimore: Johns Hopkins University Press, 2014). Project MUSE. <http://muse.jhu.edu/>.

Inventions of the March Hare: Poems 1909–1917, ed. Christopher Ricks (London: Faber and Faber, 1996).

The Letters of T. S. Eliot, Volume 1: 1898–1922, revised edition, ed. Valerie Eliot and Hugh Haughton (London: Faber and Faber, 2009).

The Letters of T. S. Eliot, Volume 2: 1923–1925, ed. Valerie Eliot and Hugh Haughton (London: Faber and Faber, 2009).

The Letters of T. S. Eliot, Volume 3: 1926–1927, ed. Valerie Eliot and John Haffenden (London: Faber and Faber, 2012).

The Letters of T. S. Eliot, Volume 4: 1928–1929, ed. Valerie Eliot and John Haffenden (London: Faber and Faber, 2013).

The Letters of T. S. Eliot, Volume 5: 1930–1931 (London: Faber and Faber, 2014).

Selected Essays (1932; London: Faber and Faber, 1999).

Selected Prose of T. S. Eliot, ed. Frank Kermode (New York: Harvest, 1975).

The Waste Land: A Facsimile and Transcript of the Original Drafts Including the Annotations of Ezra Pound, ed. Valerie Eliot (New York: Harcourt, 1971).

Maud Ellmann, *The Poetics of Impersonality: T. S. Eliot and Ezra Pound* (Brighton: Harvester, 1987).

Sir James Frazer, *The Golden Bough; A History of Myth and Religion* (1890; Oxford: Oxford World's Classics, 2009).

Nancy Gish and Cassandra Laity, eds., *Gender, Desire, and Sexuality in T. S. Eliot*, (Cambridge: Cambridge University Press, 2004).

Lyndall Gordon, *The Imperfect Life of T. S. Eliot*, revised edition (New York: Norton, 2015).

Michael Grant, *T. S. Eliot: The Critical Heritage* (London: Routledge, 1982).

M. A. R. Habib, *The Early T. S. Eliot and Western Philosophy* (Cambridge: Cambridge University Press, 1999).

Jason Harding, ed., *T. S. Eliot in Context* (Cambridge: Cambridge University Press, 2011).

Jason Harding, and Giovanni Cianci, eds., *T. S. Eliot and the Concept of Tradition* (Cambridge: Cambridge University Press, 2007).

Nancy Duvall Hargrove, *T. S. Eliot's Parisian Year* (Gainesville: University Press of Florida, 2009).

Peter Howarth, *The Cambridge Introduction to Modernist Poetry* (Cambridge: Cambridge University Press, 2012).

Andreas Huyssen, *After the Great Divide: Modernism, Mass Culture, Postmodernism* (Bloomington: Indiana University Press, 1986).

Gregory Jay, *T. S. Eliot and the Poetics of Literary History* (Baton Rouge: Louisiana State University Press, 1983).

Hugh Kenner, *The Invisible Poet* (New York: Harcourt, 1969).

ed., *T. S. Eliot: A Collection of Critical Essays* (1932; Englewood Cliffs, NJ: Prentice-Hall, 1962).

Colleen Lamos, *Deviant Modernism: Sexual and Textual Errancy in T. S. Eliot, James Joyce, and Marcel Proust* (Cambridge: Cambridge University Press, 1998).

Michael Levenson, *Modernism* (New Haven: Yale University Press, 2011).

ed., *The Cambridge Companion to Modernism*, 2nd edition (1999; Cambridge: Cambridge University Press, 2011).

ed., *A Genealogy of Modernism: A Study of English Literary Doctrine, 1908–1922* (Cambridge: Cambridge University Press, 1984).

A. Walton Litz, ed., *Eliot in His Time: Essays on the Occasion of the Fiftieth Anniversary of The Waste Land* (Princeton: Princeton University Press, 1973).

Ed Madden, *Tiresian Poetics: Modernism, Sexuality, Voice, 1888–2001* (Madison, NJ: Fairleigh Dickinson University Press, 2008).

F. O. Matthiessen, *The Achievement of T. S. Eliot: An Essay on the Nature of Poetry*, 3rd edition (1958; New York: Oxford University Press, 1959).

Gabrielle McIntire, *Modernism, Memory, and Desire: T. S. Eliot and Virginia Woolf* (Cambridge: Cambridge University Press, 2008).

Cleo McNelly Kearns, *T. S. Eliot and Indic Traditions: A Study in Poetry and Belief* (Cambridge: Cambridge University Press, 1987).

Louis Menand, *Discovering Modernism: T. S. Eliot and His Context*, 2nd edition (Oxford: Oxford University Press, 2007).

James E. Miller, Jr. *T. S. Eliot: The Making of an American Poet, 1888–1922* (University Park: Pennsylvania State University Press, 2005).

Joe Moffett, ed., *The Waste Land at 90: A Retrospective* (New York: Rodopi, 2011).

A. David Moody, *Thomas Stearns Eliot: Poet* (Cambridge: Cambridge University Press, 1994).

ed., *The Cambridge Companion to T. S. Eliot* (Cambridge: Cambridge University Press, 1994).

Peter Nicholls, *Modernisms*, 2nd edition (1995; New York: Palgrave Macmillan, 2009).

Michael North, *The Dialect of Modernism: Race, Language, and Twentieth-Century Literature* (New York: Oxford University Press, 1994).

Reading 1922: A Return to the Scene of the Modern (New York: Oxford University Press, 1999).

ed., *The Waste Land: A Norton Critical Edition* (New York: Norton, 2001).

Marja Palmer, *Men and Women in T. S. Eliot's Early Poetry* (Lund: Lund University Press, 1996).

Rachel Potter, *Modernism and Democracy: Literary Culture, 1900–1930* (Oxford: Oxford University Press, 2006).

Modernist Literature (Edinburgh: Edinburgh University Press, 2012).

Obscene Modernism: Literary Censorship and Experiment, 1900–1940 (Oxford: Oxford University Press, 2013).

Jean-Michel Rabaté, *1913: The Cradle of Modernism* (Oxford: Blackwell, 2007).

ed., *A Handbook of Modernism Studies* (Chichester, West Sussex: Wiley-Blackwell, 2013).

Craig Raine, *T. S. Eliot* (Oxford: Oxford University Press, 2006).

Lawrence Rainey, *Revisiting The Waste Land* (New Haven: Yale University Press, 2005).

ed., *The Annotated Waste Land with Eliot's Contemporary Prose*, 2nd edition (2005; New Haven: Yale University Press, 2006).

Gareth Reeves, *T. S. Eliot's The Waste Land* (New York: Harvester Wheatsheaf, 1994).

John Paul Riquelme, ed., *T. S. Eliot* (Pasadena, CA: Salem Press, 2010).

Ronald Schuchard, *Eliot's Dark Angel: Intersections of Life and Art* (New York: Oxford University Press, 1999).

Nick Selby, ed., *T. S. Eliot: The Waste Land* (New York: Columbia University Press, 1999).

Grover Smith, *T. S. Eliot and the Use of Memory* (Lewisburg: Bucknell University Press, 1997).

B. C. Southam, *A Student's Guide to the Selected Poems of T. S. Eliot* (London: Faber and Faber, 1968).

Barry Spurr, *Anglo-Catholic in Religion: T. S. Eliot and Christianity* (Cambridge: Lutterworth, 2010).

Paul Stasi, *Modernism, Imperialism, and the Historical Sense* (Cambridge: Cambridge University Press, 2012).

Leon Surette, *The Modern Dilemma: Wallace Stevens, T. S. Eliot and Humanism* (Montréal: McGill-Queen's University Press, 2008).

Michael Tratner, *Modernism and Mass Politics: Joyce, Woolf, Eliot, Yeats* (Stanford: Stanford University Press, 1995).

Jessie Weston, *From Ritual to Romance* (1920; New York: Doubleday, 1957).

Michael H. Whitworth, ed., *Modernism* (Malden, MA: Blackwell, 2007).

Andrea Zemgulys, *Modernism and the Locations of Literary Heritage* (Cambridge: Cambridge University Press, 2008).

INDEX

Ackroyd, Peter, 203
Adams, Henry, 134
Aiken, Conrad, 46
  TSE's letters to, 12, 13, 14, 18, 19,
    39, 104
  TSE's visit from, 48
Alain-Fournier, 11, 113
Aldington, Richard, 117
Alighieri, Dante, 2, 43, 55, 105, 109, 147,
    158, 179
animals, 180–81, 188
  animality, 142, 186, 187
Apollinaire, Guillaume, 93–94
architectural preservation, 34–35
Arendt, Hannah, 34
asceticism, 63
Ash-Wednesday, 178
Auden, W. H., 1
Augustine, Saint, 63, 91, 99
Austen, Jane, 19, 44
avant-garde, the, 3, 87
  Blast, 12, 13, 46
  Dadaism, 97–100
  Imagism, 92, 117
  Maeterlinck, 95–97, 100
  and The Waste Land, 194

Babbitt, Irving, 134
Badenhausen, Richard, 103
Baedeker, 24
Bakhtin, Mikhail, 91
Ball, Hugo, 97
Barbusse, Henri, 157
Barnes, Djuna, 136
Bate, Jonathan, 181, 189
Bateson, F. H., 201
Baudelaire, Charles, 98
  the crowd, 32

Eliot's poetry as post-Baudelairean, 123
  "The Lesson of Baudelaire," 97, 99
  the post-Baudelairean city, 179
  quoted in The Waste Land, 32, 94
  bawdiness, 138
Bedient, Calvin, 204
Benjamin, Walter, 22, 32, 93
Bentley, Joseph, 203
Benveniste, Émile, 90
Berman, Marshall, 29
Betjeman, John, 58
Bhagavad Gita, 56, 61
the Bible, 2, 181
  allusions to, 42, 57, 59, 64–66, 90, 179,
    183, 185, 188
Björk, 118
Blast, 12, 13, 46
Bloomsbury, 39
the body, 36, 44, 46, 79, 137–43, 153, 155,
    167–68, 169, 202
Bolgan, Anne C., 200
Boni and Liveright, 105, 206
Bonikowski, Wyatt, 158
Booth, Allyson, 155, 159
Bosch, Hieronymus, 61, 66
Boston, 11, 44
Bradley, F. H., 169, 197, 203, 204
  TSE's studies of, xviii, 14, 142, 163–64,
    165, 172, 200
  in The Waste Land Notes, 173, 174
Brittain, Vera, 39, 154
Brooke, Rupert, 198
Brooker, Jewel Spears, 203, 204
Brooks, Cleanth, 162, 194, 196, 197, 205
Browning, Robert, 92, 123
Brunner, Edward, 72, 73
Buck, Gene, 72, 121
Buckle, Charles, 40

Cambridge Companions to...

Harriet Beecher Stowe edited by Cindy Weinstein
August Strindberg edited by Michael Robinson
Jonathan Swift edited by Christopher Fox
J. M. Synge edited by P. J. Mathews
Tacitus edited by A. J. Woodman
Henry David Thoreau edited by Joel Myerson
Tolstoy edited by Donna Tussing Orwin
Anthony Trollope edited by Carolyn Dever and Lisa Niles
Mark Twain edited by Forrest G. Robinson
John Updike edited by Stacey Olster
Mario Vargas Llosa edited by Efrain Kristal and John King

Virgil edited by Charles Martindale
Voltaire edited by Nicholas Cronk
Edith Wharton edited by Millicent Bell
Walt Whitman edited by Ezra Greenspan
Oscar Wilde edited by Peter Raby
Tennessee Williams edited by Matthew C. Roudané
August Wilson edited by Christopher Bigsby
Mary Wollstonecraft edited by Claudia L. Johnson
Virginia Woolf edited by Susan Sellers (second edition)
Wordsworth edited by Stephen Gill
W. B. Yeats edited by Marjorie Howes and John Kelly
Zola edited by Brian Nelson

Topics

The Actress edited by Maggie B. Gale and John Stokes
The African American Novel edited by Maryemma Graham
The African American Slave Narrative edited by Audrey A. Fisch
African American Theatre by Harvey Young
Allegory edited by Rita Copeland and Peter Struck
American Crime Fiction edited by Catherine Ross Nickerson
American Modernism edited by Walter Kalaidjian
American Poetry Since 1945 edited by Jennifer Ashton
American Realism and Naturalism edited by Donald Pizer
American Travel Writing edited by Alfred Bendixen and Judith Hamera
American Women Playwrights edited by Brenda Murphy
Ancient Rhetoric edited by Erik Gunderson
Arthurian Legend edited by Elizabeth Archibald and Ad Putter
Australian Literature edited by Elizabeth Webby

British Literature of the French Revolution edited by Pamela Clemit
British Romanticism edited by Stuart Curran (second edition)
British Romantic Poetry edited by James Chandler and Maureen N. McLane
British Theatre, 1730–1830, edited by Jane Moody and Daniel O'Quinn
Canadian Literature edited by Eva-Marie Kröller
Children's Literature edited by M. O. Grenby and Andrea Immel
The Classic Russian Novel edited by Malcolm V. Jones and Robin Feuer Miller
Contemporary Irish Poetry edited by Matthew Campbell
Creative Writing edited by David Morley and Philip Neilsen
Crime Fiction edited by Martin Priestman
Early Modern Women's Writing edited by Laura Lunger Knoppers
The Eighteenth-Century Novel edited by John Richetti
Eighteenth-Century Poetry edited by John Sitter